Canceled

Canceled

Twelve Catholic Heroes That History Turned Into Villains

Steve Weidenkopf

Catholic Answers Press

Published by Catholic Answers, Inc.
2020 Gillespie Way
El Cajon, California 92020
1-888-291-8000 orders
619-387-0042 fax
catholic.com

Printed in the United States of America

Cover design by eBookLaunch.com

Text layout by Nora Malone

978-1-68357-374-6
978-1-68357-375-3 Kindle
978-1-68357-376-0 ePub

To Anna Thérèse Diederich (1999-2023)

I dedicate this book to my beloved goddaughter Anna, who exhibited a joy for life, a deep love for Christ and his Church, and an admirable desire to serve others.

Thank you, Anna, for your love for my family (especially your friendship to my Thérèse), and for your enthusiastic Christian witness, summarized in your Rule of Life:

"I am happiest when I am taking care of other people."

You are dearly loved and greatly missed.

Micah 6:8

Requiescat in pace.

There is a permanent general need for an apologetic drawn from history; but there is a particular need, urgent at the present moment, for a counterattack upon the false history which has been used to undermine the Catholic faith in the minds of men, to shake the confidence of Catholics in themselves, or to confirm in error those who are brought up in error.

—Hilaire Belloc, *Essays of a Catholic*, 1931

Contents

Acknowledgments

Every author is supported by family and friends throughout the task of completing a manuscript, and I am certainly no exception. Accompanying me on the journey of this book was my beautiful wife, Kasey, whose love and patience made this effort possible. Gratitude is also extended to my sons, Jeb and Martin, who, as the remaining children at home, supported the task with understanding and patience. Many thanks are owed to Mark Nalevanko, who read the manuscript and provided comments that made this book better. Once again, I thank the staff at Catholic Answers Press, especially the editor, Todd Aglialoro, who has challenged and supported me through four books now!

Lastly, I give thanks for St. Bruno (1030–1101), founder of the Carthusians, who, despite the desire to remain in monastic solitude, worked tirelessly behind the scenes for the good of the Church in the eleventh century, and whose monks later produced the special spirit Chartreuse, the "elixir of life." His intercession enabled the completion of this project.

Introduction

A historical myth is a widely held interpretation of historical events that is believed, not for its veracity, but because it explains the past in a way that somehow satisfies the worldview of those who believe it. Myth is not simply the result of ignorance or misunderstanding; it is believed because people wish, in spite of all countervailing evidence, to believe it.[1]

—Thomas S. Freeman and Susan Doran

It is not shocking that Catholics have been vilified and scapegoated throughout history. Catholics are called to imitate Christ and should expect the same treatment as their Lord, who said, "A servant is not greater than his master. If they persecuted me, they will persecute you" (John 15:20). In ancient Israel, the Jewish people, in accordance with the dictates of Leviticus, annually chose a goat, which was burdened symbolically with the sins of the people and released into the wilderness. This scapegoat was an innocent beast that united the community through its sacrifice.

Whereas the Jewish practice was rooted in religious tradition and involved the concepts of sin and redemption, the human form of scapegoating consists of an innocent victim, shunned or besmirched by a group in a desire to rid the community of a perceived evil or to deflect blame.[2] In modernity, the tactic of "canceling" has become the weapon of choice (along with scapegoating) to disparage, dismiss, or ruin the reputation of an individual or group. Modern-day critics embrace a posture of superiority and judge the actions of persons in the past without understanding or acknowledging the historical context in which they lived. Modern society is consumed with the immediate and rejects the past by either ignoring it, at best, or crafting a new narrative that undermines the actions and memory of previously important historical actors. The rejection of historical memory produces a lack of historical context, which culminates in a lack of perspective of human events. Therefore, modern man is unable to properly comprehend contemporary happenings with a frame of historical reference and is enslaved in the tyranny of the present.

The loss of the historical past results in the vices of quick judgments, false attribution of motives, and a general hermeneutic of suspicion. These attributes contribute to a negative discourse in modern society, in which every word or action is interpreted in the most extreme manner, producing shrill, sensational commentary that seeks to compel attention.

Cancelation, scapegoating, and persecution constitute core themes in the 2,000-year history of the Church. The honor, reputation, and memory of individual Catholics have been attacked by enemies of the Faith seeking to discredit the actions of the Church. Indeed, the Church was less than a century old when the first instance of Catholic scapegoating occurred.

On the night of July 18, A.D. 64, a great fire erupted in an area of the city of Rome. Ultimately, several districts of the city were devastated, with major damage and loss of life. The fire raged for several days. Once it had abated, the populace was angry and demanded answers about its origin. Rumors surfaced that the emperor was to blame for the fire. In an effort to repel criticism, the emperor invented a scapegoat: he blamed the fire on a small group in the city that refused to honor the pagan gods, the Christians.

This is how the infamous Nero (r. A.D. 54-68) tried to cancel Catholics and initiated the first of many persecutions against the Church. He outlawed the Faith and ordered the arrest and imprisonment of the faithful in Rome. Catholics were horribly tortured and killed under Nero to deflect Roman anger against the emperor.

But the emperor's actions backfired. Tacitus, a Roman senator and historian, recorded that Nero's punishments, instead, engendered "a sentiment of pity [among the Roman people], due to the impression that they [Christians] were being sacrificed not for the welfare of the state but to the ferocity of a single man."[3]

Although Nero's scapegoating proved ineffective, there are numerous examples in Church history where the technique worked quite well. Once Roman persecution ended in the fourth century, the Church experienced relative peace for centuries, and instead of canceling Catholics, secular rulers sought to control the Church. After the collapse of central governing authority from imperial Rome in the fifth century, Western society changed greatly. Politically, tension developed between local secular rulers and the Church, as chieftains, kings, and noble families fought to control bishops, including the bishop of Rome, for their own agendas. A comprehensive papal reform movement in the eleventh century freed the Church from most secular interference, but Church-State conflict continued. The Protestant Revolution in the sixteenth century produced new forms of criticism and attacks against the Church, with vilification and scapegoating reappearing. Enlightened intellectuals, who sought to eradicate the

Church's influence in society, became ardent opponents of the Church and contributed to the modern negative mentality toward many historical Catholics.

The nineteenth century in particular was a time of heightened anti-Catholic activity, especially in the United States. Nineteenth-century European society witnessed great social, economic, and political upheaval, which led to a mass exodus of Catholics seeking safety and greater opportunities in the newly formed nation across the Atlantic.

Traveling in the nineteenth century, especially across the Atlantic Ocean, was an arduous task, fraught with danger. Arriving in the new land of opportunity was, assuredly, viewed by the Catholic immigrants of Europe with great relief and expectation. The United States, less than a century old, was a land ripe with opportunity, where, seemingly, a new life could be forged from hard work and luck. This idyllic situation was not always realized, however, especially for the millions of Irish, German, Italian, and other European Catholics who escaped famine and political turmoil in the Old World only to experience vicious bigotry and hatred in the new one.

The 1900s were a dangerous time to be a Catholic in the United States. The burning of an Ursuline convent in Charlestown, Massachusetts by a Protestant mob in August 1834 was an especially destructive and vindictive act that went unpunished. Anti-Catholic fervor was stoked by propaganda from Protestant newspapers including the weekly *Downfall of Babylon*, edited by Samuel B. Smith (who bragged that he was a former "Popish priest"), and the semi-monthly *American Protestant Vindicator*, edited by Rev. W.C. Brownlee, which was the official newspaper of the anti-Catholic organization The American Society for Promoting the Principles of the Protestant Reformation (also known as The Protestant

Reformation Society).[4] Anti-Catholic rhetoric was a boon to publishers, as evidenced by the printing of more than 400,000 works of fiction and non-fiction before the Civil War.[5]

One work of fiction, although treated by anti-Catholics as truth, contained the salacious tales of Maria Monk, a supposed former nun. Maria's book, the *Awful Disclosures of Maria Monk: As Exhibited in a Narrative of Her Sufferings During Residence of Five Years as a Novice, and Two Years as a Black Nun, in the Hotel Dieu Nunnery at Montreal*, was published in 1836 and achieved spectacular success, with 300,000 copies sold. In her book, Maria told of her upbringing as a Protestant who was sent to the Hotel Dieu convent for education, where she, eventually, converted to the Catholic faith and entered the religious life. However, her joy from a religious vocation turned into a nightmare when, after vows, she was instructed by the mother superior to "obey the priests in all things," including engaging in sexual sins.

Maria, to her horror, discovered that any children born from these unlawful unions between priests and nuns were baptized and then strangled so that they would immediately enjoy the beatific vision.[6] Even more shocking was the alleged execution of nuns who refused the sexual advances of these predatory priests. Maria also alleged that nuns were forbidden to read the Bible in the convent, which confirmed in the minds of many Protestants the anti-Christian nature of the Church.

Maria escaped the terror in Montreal and fled to the United States with the aid of the Rev. William K. Hoyt, who helped her disclose the horrid happenings in the Hotel Dieu. The anti-Catholic press gravitated to Maria's story and used it to attack Catholics and the Church. Many Protestants believed that it provided proof of the growing danger from Catholics in the United States, who wanted to rule the country and enslave it to the foreign pope. Indeed, the book pandered to

Protestants "because it praised their goodness and benevolence while emphasizing the depravity and duplicity of Catholics."[7]

Critics of Maria's sordid tale included her mother, who claimed that Maria had never been to the Montreal convent. She maintained that Maria suffered delusions from a traumatic brain injury as a child, which also led to a wild life of debauchery and constant trouble with the authorities. Maria's only connection to Catholics in Montreal, according to her mother, was as a patient in the Magdalen asylum.[8] The Catholic press highlighted Maria's troubled life, denouncing her as a "liar, a prostitute, a thief, and a murderer" while describing her "Protestant supporters" as "greedy, conniving panderers who would do anything to make a quick buck and undermine the good priests and nuns of the Catholic Church."[9]

Thankfully, several Protestants doubted the veracity of Maria's story and traveled to Montreal to investigate. Two preachers inspected the Hotel Dieu convent and declared the accusations false. They stated that the religious house did "not even remotely resemble the one which she had described."[10]

After several years of notoriety, Maria vanished from New York City in 1837 but reappeared later in Philadelphia. Asked about her disappearance, Maria blamed Catholic priests, who allegedly kidnapped her to stop her "truth"-telling about convents. Eventually, Maria was arrested for pickpocketing in 1849 and died the same year at the age of thirty-three.

The sad tale of Maria Monk illustrates the heightened tension in the new United States between a majority-Protestant and a minority-Catholic population. The arrival of millions of Catholics to the predominantly Protestant United States spawned the creation of the first major third political party, known officially as the Native American Party (after 1855, it was known as the American Party) and unofficially as the "Know-Nothing" Party. This nativist, anti-immigrant, anti-Catholic organization sponsored platform planks such as the deportation of foreign beggars and criminals, a twenty-one year naturalization period, mandatory Bible reading in public schools, and the removal and restriction of Catholics from public office.[11] The Native American Party promised voters a return to true democracy by the election of party candidates at the local level by a majority vote of party members rather than the delegate method at national conventions. The party swept local, state, and congressional elections in the mid-1850s resulting in a hundred congressmen, eight governors, and a majority-share in six states.[12]

There was also a secret wing of the Native American Party, called the Order of the Star Spangled Banner (OSSB). Membership was restricted to Protestants of Anglo-Saxon ethnicity. OSSB members were initiated in a secret ceremony that included the memorization of passwords and special handshakes, rejection of the Catholic faith, and a solemn oath never to betray the order. If asked about the party, members were to report, "I know nothing," which spawned the unofficial moniker.

The success of the Know-Nothings demonstrated the anxiety of Protestant Americans over Catholic immigration, a fear that aroused more energy and attention than the question of slavery, although that topic would soon take center stage in the succeeding decade. When Catholic clergy worked with Democratic Party legislators to pass laws allowing taxes from Catholics to support parochial rather than public schools in some states, it "provided concrete evidence of the long-warned-of-papal plot to control the United States."[13]

The hysteria produced by Catholic immigration was sustained by anti-Catholic propaganda that attacked not only the Church's doctrine, but also its history. It was this historical attack that drew the attention of the Roman pontiff, who recognized a dire threat to the Church.

On August 18, 1883, Pope Leo XIII (r. 1878–1903) issued *Saepenumero considerantes*, a letter on historical sciences. Pope Leo was concerned that Church history in the late nineteenth century was being written with an anti-Catholic perspective. He was particularly irked that the enemies of the papacy performed "a task at once of injustice and of danger in paying more attention to their personal rancor than to truth, with the evident object of straining history by means of falsification." In an effort to combat the myths and false narratives, the pope made the archives of the Vatican Library accessible to academics so they could use primary sources and other documents in the task of writing authentic Church history. Pope Leo also opined on the various reasons for the historical attack against the Church, which included the desire to discredit and lessen the Church's influence in the world, the agenda of ex-Catholics who agitate against the Faith, the hatred of religion in general, and the necessity for Protestants to demonstrate that the Catholic Church is a man-made organization. Finally, the pope asked why people believe the historical myths about the Church and answered by acknowledging that sometimes the attacks are unintentional, because people are simply repeating what they have heard or been taught. The pope was deeply concerned about the education of children, who were taught these falsehoods of Catholic history in school, which proved challenging to eradicate later in life because effort is rarely made to study and learn the truth.

Leo's letter came at a fortuitous moment in Church history, as the century that witnessed increased attacks against the Church also spawned a change in the study of history in academic institutions. The Catholic understanding of history was most influenced by St. Augustine (354–430), who viewed human history as linear events punctuated by climaxes, with a distinct beginning (creation by God *ex nihilo*) and a definitive end (the Second Coming). Augustine also emphasized that God oversees and is involved in human history, most evidently in the Incarnation, which is the central event in human history. All history radiates outward (both forward and backward) from the coming of the God-man. History, then, is the unfolding of God's salvific action in the world, whereby men endowed with free will participate either virtuously or with vice.

The historian tells the story of these men and women in the context of God's plan of salvation. History is about reality and the discovery of truth, but it is also the preservation of human memory. History was not taught as a separate subject in medieval grammar school or universities and did not become an independent academic subject until the late eighteenth century. Prior to then, history was taught as a form of literature, where the story of men and women, groups, and nations were told and handed on to subsequent generations.

The nineteenth century produced a substantial change in the studying, teaching, and understanding of history, which moved from literature to science. It was Leopold von Ranke (1795-1886), a German nationalist and Lutheran scholar at the University of Berlin, who helped usher in the "scientific historian," whose job was to "examine critically as many sources as possible with an eye to conflicting and contradictory accounts of a single event." The historian "would adjudicate these conflicting accounts based on the evidence alone, free from the biases of received traditions."[14]

One of the goals associated with this new approach to history was the creation of the "objective historian," or one who could investigate the events of the past free from all biases. Although this approach can produce positive benefits, such as textual criticism (appropriately applied) and the questioning of previous interpretations of historical documents, people, and events, it is nearly unattainable because "historical memory, like all memory is selective" and "is not objective but personal and participatory."[15] A historian should never suppress evidence that impacts his conclusions, but the selection and interpretation of the historical material is very much a product of the historian's worldview.[16] Even the modern focus on historical texts, although generally considered more accurate than reliance on oral tradition, is fraught with subjectivity. Historical documents are rarely complete, as their preservation is highly dependent on individual actions to maintain collections and individual judgments on what documents to keep.[17]

In the twentieth century, history was enveloped within the social sciences and embraced a perspective that it is nearly impossible to discover the truth about historical events and persons.[18] Although this vision of history may not contribute directly to the canceling of Catholics of the past, it perpetuates the false narrative about these men and women by advocating that the truth can never be known about them, because "it is naïve to think that historians can accurately re-create what has happened in the world."[19] The concerns of Pope Leo about historical attacks against the Church and the memory of its members proved providential, as centuries of vitriol continued and even found new expression in the modern world.

The modern pantheon of villainous Catholic personages of the past is vast and includes specific individuals, such as Popes Innocent III and Pius XII, Mary Tudor, Christopher Columbus, and Marie Antoinette, as well as groups of people, such as crusaders, inquisitors, and conquistadors. These individuals and groups have been canceled by Enlightenment thinkers, Protestant apologists, secularists, and even so-called "Catholics" who take the name but not the belief of the Church.

Enlightened critics of the Church attacked the glorious medieval period of Christendom by creating false narratives about crusaders and inquisitors, along with the most important pope of the age, Innocent III. Protestant opponents attacked the Church's origins and relationship with the Roman Empire by crafting the myth of the Great Apostasy and the role of the emperor Constantine in creating the "Roman Catholic" Church. English Protestants painted a picture of bloody persecution under the Catholic queen Mary Tudor and established the axiom that Catholics were traitors to the realm through the vilification of Guy Fawkes. Modern-day secular critics of the Church seek to overthrow the Christian traditions of the Western world by creating false historical narratives about the discovery and colonization of the New World by Christopher Columbus and the conquistadors, most notably Hernán Cortés. Secular opponents also seek to destroy the political influence of the Church through a false presentation of important Catholic rulers such as Marie Antoinette and Bl. Pope Pius IX. Some individuals who identify as Catholic but do not practice the Faith or embrace the Church's teachings (especially in matters of morality) use well-known Catholic leaders as examples of an authoritarian Church, which is, at best, out of touch with modern Catholics or, at worst, in league with the vilest dictators in human history. These opponents use Pope Pius XII and his alleged antisemitism and alliance with Hitler as proof of a nefarious papacy. Others use Pope Benedict XVI (as pope and as Joseph Cardinal Ratzinger) as the example of an overbearing and out-of-touch papacy.

The reasons critics of the Church cancel Catholics of the past vary, but one explanation for the tactic in modern times is the acceptance of the fallacious concept of *presentism*, a bias in historical interpretation that judges the past based on modern sensibilities. This criticism often produces efforts to rewrite history and ignore the positive contributions of people in the past, or to cancel their memory and tear down any recognition of them.

This book seeks to identify the forms of historical attacks against Catholic history using selected historical Catholics as examples. Each individual is placed in the proper historical context, which is essential for any authentic interpretation of their actions. This book is not an apologia for all the actions and choices of the selected historical Catholics, nor is it a whitewash or a triumphalist panegyric. Rather, it seeks an honest, factual, and Catholic assessment of the men and women of history who have been vilified and canceled to serve the agenda of the enemies of the Church.

Chapter 1

Enlightened History

The Enlightenment was opposed to what Europe had become as a result of evangelization. . . . The entire drama of salvation history had disappeared as far as the Enlightenment was concerned. Man remained alone: alone as creator of his own history and his own civilization; alone as one who decides what is good and what is bad, as one who would exist and operate even if there were no God.[20]

—Pope St. John Paul II

In the seventeenth and eighteenth centuries, an intellectual movement, which included elements hostile to religion, came to the forefront in European life. These intellectuals, motivated by hatred for the Catholic Church and prompted by arrogance, opined that society was happier without the influence of the Church, which they argued was "worn out, immature, inherently hypocritical, hostile to progress, and above all, unreasonable."[21] Anti-Catholic thinkers wanted society to move from an age of faith to an *Age of Reason*, a term coined by the American revolutionary propagandist Thomas Paine while imprisoned in Paris.[22] They viewed faith as a darkness enveloping the mind, which religion in general and the Catholic Church in particular held captive. Only reason could "enlighten" the intellect and free it from the darkness of faith.

Enlightened thinkers divided into two camps concerning religion. A "moderate" group discounted faith generally, although they allowed for personal belief in God and argued that the Church should have no role in the public sphere (especially in politics). Another more radical group exhibited materialistic, democratic, anti-religious, and anti-traditionalist characteristics, best exemplified by the famous quote from one of this wing's most notorious advocates, the Frenchman Denis Diderot (1713–1784): "Man will never be free until the last king is strangled with the entrails of the last priest."[23]

Proponents of the Enlightenment sought changes in the fundamental meaning of philosophy by focusing its object on the mind and its thoughts rather than reasoning based on the observation of reality. Intellectuals consumed themselves with thought exercises concerning knowledge by asking questions such as "How do we know we know?" One of the major questions of knowledge at the time was "How do we know we exist?", which René Descartes (1596–1650), a Catholic educated by the Jesuits and a veteran of the ruthless Thirty Years War, tried to answer through the method of *rationalism*. Descartes posited that if nothing is known with certainty, which many Enlightened thinkers believed, then the only certain thing is doubt. He then "reasoned" that the only certain, clear, and distinct idea that cannot be doubted is that a person thinks, and if a person is thinking, he must exist—which Descartes succinctly described with the Latin phrase *cogito ergo sum*, "I think; therefore, I am."

These "rational" discussions delved into other topics as Enlightened thinkers questioned nearly every aspect of society, including humanity in general. Many intellectuals viewed humans in different groups and advocated that some ethnic groups were different species and less human than others.

This line of "reasoning" led to arguments justifying slavery and other moral injustices.[24]

Enlightenment intellectuals were not content only to discuss their ideas; they also desired a radically altered society, where "reason" reigned supreme and political, economic, and moral actions were unencumbered by Christian influence. The achievement of that goal depended on controlling the institutions of higher learning in Europe, which required weakening the Catholic Church's role in society in general and the eradication of the Society of Jesus (the Jesuits) in particular.

At the end of the eighteenth century, the Jesuits controlled hundreds of universities and seminaries in Europe. Enlightened thinkers embarked on a campaign to expel the Jesuits from European countries so that royal or secular control of their institutions of higher learning could occur, which would allow the cult of reason to become dominant.

François-Marie Arouet (1694–1778), known by the moniker Voltaire, made it his life's mission to destroy the Jesuits and the Catholic Church. Voltaire wrote several critical and satirical pamphlets and tracts against the Church and was one of the main authors of the *Encyclopédie*, a collection of articles on various subjects from an "enlightened" perspective. His writings caused trouble for the Frenchman, who was arrested, incarcerated in the Bastille, and eventually exiled to England.

Despite receiving an education from the Jesuits, Voltaire actively campaigned for their suppression. He recognized that if secular rulers could be convinced to expel the Society and confiscate their colleges and universities, it would be an easier task to convince those same rulers to suppress the Church and its influence. In 1773 he wrote, "Once we have destroyed the Jesuits, we shall have our own way with the infamous thing. . . . In twenty years there will be nothing left of the Church."[25] Voltaire's dream was realized twenty years later in his homeland, when the French revolutionary government persecuted Catholics, confiscated the property of the Church, and then suppressed it.

Voltaire was not the only secularist to set his sights on the Society of Jesus. The Enlightenment attack against the Jesuits began in Portugal, when King Joseph I (r. 1750–1777) the king signed a decree ordering their expulsion from Portugal and Brazil in 1755. A few years later, in 1761, the French *Parlement* issued a decree banning French subjects from entering the Society, forbade Jesuits from teaching theology, and barred attendance at Jesuit schools. Three years later, King Louis XV (r. 1715–1774) expelled the Jesuits from France and all its dominions. The Spanish king Charles III (r. 1759–1788) followed suit in 1767.

Pope Clement XIV (r. 1769–1774) was under intense political pressure from the leading monarchs of Europe to enact ecclesiastical penalties against the Jesuits. The pontiff acquiesced to these pressures on July 21, 1773 with the bull *Dominus ac Redemptor*, which suppressed the Society of Jesus after 239 years of faithful service to the Church. Although the pope did not pass judgment on the Society in terms of the charges brought against it by secular rulers, his shameful surrendering to political pressure caused the Jesuits to cease to exist for a generation, until their society was re-established in the bull *Sollicitudo Omnium Ecclesiarum* by Pope Pius VII (r. 1800–1823) after Napoleon's abdication in 1814.

Freed from the "clutches" of the Jesuits, the colleges and universities of Europe were primed for the influence and control of Enlightenment thinkers to take root. The age of faith had succumbed to the "age of reason," which produced skepticism, moral relativism, and secular humanism. The ideals of the Enlightenment remain dominant in the modern world—a world that exalts empiricism, materialism, and individualism and ridicules faith; persecutes the Church; and rejects authority, objective morality, and holiness.

Although many Enlightenment thinkers mainly focused their attack on the Church, they also sought the re-interpretation of academic subjects, including history. History, for these philosophers, provided an example of the barbarity and cruelty of humanity influenced by religion. This negative and cynical view of past human activity spawned a particular focus on the Middle Ages, an age of faith, where society was united in a worldview provided by the great enemy of reason and progress, the Catholic Church. Although medieval Europe was far from a Christian utopia, society was organized around the Church's liturgical calendar, and its teachings were known, and a general (albeit often unmet) expectation of obedience to those teachings prevailed.

The so-called age of the "Glory of Christendom" produced magnificent cathedrals, exquisite artwork, and a flourishing of scholarly and scientific pursuits. However, this reality was targeted by Enlightenment thinkers, who crafted a false narrative of the Church's history to discredit the Church and weaken its influence in their own time period. Indeed,

> the Enlightenment worshiped reason and the idea of human progress, and this relegated the Middle Ages to an inferior position in its historical vision. The Middle Ages were seen as a period in which mankind was prevented by barbarism and superstition from realizing its full potential. Religion had been the tool of an over-mighty Church that protected its power by keeping people in ignorance.[26]

The events of the Crusades and the Spanish Inquisition (to name a few) and the medieval papacy, especially the pontificate of Innocent III, were so maligned by Enlightenment intellectuals that, despite the recent diligent work of honest academics, their version of "Enlightened History" remains entrenched in the modern mind.

The Enlightenment historical attack "tended to use the crusade not as a historical study in its own right but as a tool in conceptual arguments about religion and the progress of civilization."[27] A vicious critic of the crusading movement was Diderot, editor-in-chief of the *Encyclopédie*, who believed that the Crusades were "horrible wars" during "a time of the deepest darkness and of the greatest folly . . . [where] a significant part of the world [was dragged] into an unhappy little country in order to cut the inhabitants' throats and seize a rocky peak which was not worth one drop of blood."[28] Voltaire heightened the rhetoric with the stinging opinion that the Crusades were "marked by every cruelty, every perfidy, every debauchery, and every folly of which human nature is capable."[29]

In the nineteenth century, Enlightenment propaganda and false narratives about the Crusades found expression in popular novels, especially the works of the Scotsman Sir Walter Scott (1771–1832). Scott embraced the Enlightenment historical attack and portrayed crusaders as individually brave but prideful and motivated by greed and ambition. He also portrayed Islamic civilization as tolerant and superior to the morally bankrupt Christian civilization of Europe. In this 1825 novel *The Talisman*, set during the Third Crusade in the twelfth century, the Muslim general Saladin (1138–1193) features prominently and is portrayed by Scott as chivalrous, courteous, tolerant, wise, and merciful, in opposition to King Richard I the Lionhearted of England, who is depicted as wild, brutal, passionate, and zealous in pursuit of the Crusade.

Enlightenment myths about the Crusades utilize Saladin to illustrate the superiority and tolerance of Islamic culture. Saladin became the symbol in Enlightened European minds of the perfect knight, who was perhaps a secret Christian (though certainly not a Catholic!) and a champion of Enlightenment ideals.

Saladin the noble heathen became a popular figure in Enlightened European consciousness, but only ironically. The actual Saladin was a Sunni Kurdish adventurer who used the power of his office in a Shi'ite caliphate to overthrow it because of his own ambition.[30] Saladin was all but forgotten in the Muslim world until the European myth of the man became the dominant narrative in the nineteenth century.

Though many Catholics earned the vigorous criticism of Enlightenment authors and their supporters in their pursuit of the destruction of the Church, three bear special mention here: the Templars, Pope Innocent III, and Tomás de Torquemada and the inquisitors of Spain. The real story of these individuals reveals flawed yet heroic and charitable figures, who loved Christ and the Church.

The Templars

> *Some, for Christ's sake . . . set out for Jerusalem and there, undertaking a new kind of warfare, so conducted themselves against the enemies of the cross of Christ that, continually bearing about their bodies the death of the cross, they appeared by their life and conversation to be not soldiers, but monks.*[31]

The warriors of what was later called the First Crusade had completed the task set out for them by Bl. Pope Urban II (r. 1088-1099) nearly four years earlier: the liberation of the Holy City of Jerusalem. Their pilgrim vow filled, those known as *crucesignati* ("signed with the cross") longed to return to Europe to their family and friends.

The vast majority of those who survived the grueling campaign of the First Crusade left for home by the end of the year 1099. Their departure was problematic for those crusaders who stayed in the newly liberated Holy Land.

The First Crusade had achieved the unthinkable. Armies of pilgrims from Europe had liberated a significant amount of ancient Christian territory, including the cities of Edessa, Antioch, Jerusalem, and Ascalon, stretching nearly six hundred miles along the coast. This coastal Christian enclave was in a precarious military position, surrounded by hostile enemies on the borders and comprising a majority-Muslim population. Crusading by nature was an episodic endeavor, and the nobles who stayed in the territory of the Latin East, known to historians as the Crusader States, were keenly aware of their perilous tactical situation. In a wholly unexpected way, this worrisome military situation was partially alleviated with the rise of the military religious orders in the early twelfth century.

Crusading was a temporary action, undertaken for a specified goal. But during the reign of King Baldwin II of Jerusalem (r. 1118–1131), there arose groups of warriors who combined the religious life with the military life in a permanent manner. These "warrior monks" lived the evangelical counsels of poverty, chastity, and obedience with the added responsibilities of the defense of Christian territory and the protection of Christians traveling to and living in the Latin East.

The creation of the military religious orders, like many religious orders throughout Church history, was not a planned event, but rather a spontaneous reaction to the unique situation of the small group of Christians in *Outremer* (the Holy Land). In fact, the concept of professed religious living outside a monastery and engaging in the combat arms as a form of charity on behalf of others was revolutionary and unprecedented.

Four main groups of warrior monks developed in the Latin East: the Hospitallers, the Templars, the Teutonic Knights, and the Knights of the Holy Sepulchre. The Hospitallers and Templars were the most prominent and influential because they controlled large castle fortifications in strategic areas, commanded mercenaries and royal armies in the field, and provided economic and financial services to pilgrims and Christian residents alike. The military religious orders were answerable to the pope alone, which caused friction with local bishops and secular rulers. Despite the combination of military prowess with religious vows, the orders were known more for their combat activities than holiness, as "both orders were credited with remarkably few saints in an age when in the eyes of the faithful heaven was filling up with men and women belonging to the new religious orders."[32]

Although the Hospitallers and Templars shared the evangelical counsels and adherence to martial skills, the orders were very different in foundation and orientation.

The Hospitallers traced their origins to the establishment of a hospital in Jerusalem in the mid-eleventh century. The Order of the Hospital of St. John of Jerusalem was officially founded in 1113 by Bl. Gerard Tenque as an independent religious order with a charism focused on devotion to the poor and staffing the hospital to care for sick pilgrims. They followed the Rule of St. Augustine and wore a black cloak with a white pointed cross. The military arm of the order was founded a little more than a decade later, with the creation of brother knights and sergeants.

The Templars were founded a few years after the Hospitallers, in 1120, by Hugh of Payns, a minor nobleman from Champagne, and eight companions, including Andrew of Montbard, the uncle of St. Bernard of Clairvaux. Hugh and his companions desired to form a new brotherhood dedicated to securing the pilgrim road to and from the holy places in the Latin East. A local ecclesiastical council at Nablus in 1120 approved the order, and in 1129, Pope Honorius II (r. 1124-1130) granted his papal endorsement. The Templars followed the Rule of the Cistercians, and knight-brothers wore a white cloak to which a red cross was added in 1139.

Originally known as the Poor Knights of Christ, Hugh's band of warrior monks was favored by King Baldwin II, who granted them part of the royal palace on the Temple Mount in Jerusalem for their barracks, which produced their new moniker: the Knights of the Temple, or the Templars.

Both the Hospitallers and the Templars centered their mission in serving the poor and envisioned themselves as servants to the poor. Indeed, the admission rites of both orders utilized the terms "serf and slave" to highlight this understanding, but with significantly different focus. The Hospitallers asked a man if he was prepared to live as a "serf and slave" of his lords, the poor, whereas the Templars inquired if the man was ready to live as a "serf and slave" of his order.[33] The last Master of the Templars, Jacques de Molay, summarized the distinction between the orders: "The Hospitallers were founded to care for the sick, and beyond that they bear arms . . . whereas the Templars were founded specifically for military service."[34]

The Templars, more than any other military religious order, have been victims of abuse, myths, and false narratives. They have been described as "heroes, martyrs, thugs, bullies, victims, criminals, perverts, heretics, depraved subversives, guardians of the Holy Grail, protectors of Christ's secret bloodline and time-traveling agents of global conspiracy."[35] The Templars have been linked to the Shroud of Turin, the Ark of the Covenant, and secret hoards of treasure.

The Templars are better known in modernity than the Hospitallers, who still exist in non-military form as the Knights of Malta. Myths about the Templars exist in part because of their dramatic downfall and suppression in the fifteenth century at the hands of a greedy and envious French king, but also because of the Enlightenment historical attack, which rejected the medieval Catholic-centric worldview and struggled to reconcile the ideals of a military religious order. In fact, the Templars make the perfect Catholic scapegoat, because the ideals girding their creation and activities are scorned by Enlightenment intellectuals and their modern-day progeny. The historical record illustrates the real story of these warrior monks, who dedicated their lives to service to the poor, to Christian pilgrims, to one another, and to Christ and his Church.

The Templars gained papal acceptance and public recognition through the actions of St. Bernard of Clairvaux (1090–1153), whose treatise *On the Praise of the New Knighthood* provided theological justification for the establishment of military religious orders and their use of weapons in pursuit of their goals. Reflecting on these revolutionary groups in the Church, Bernard remarked, "I do not know if it would be more appropriate to refer to them as monks or soldiers, unless perhaps it would be better to recognize them as both. These are the picked troops of God, whom he has recruited from the ends of the earth."[36] Bernard emphasized the distinction between fighting for temporal and selfish reasons and engaging in combat for spiritual and selfless reasons by indicating that the former may result in the death of the soul, whereas the latter can be eternally meritorious.

Bernard recognized the concern (and criticism) that killing is wrong, regardless of if it is for temporal or spiritual reasons. He opined that killing an evildoer makes one not a "mankiller," but rather "a killer of evil" and an "avenger of Christ" who "is rightly considered a defender of Christians."[37]

Despite the overwhelming support of the famous holy abbot of Clairvaux, there were those who criticized the creation of the military religious orders (although they were always in the minority among medieval contemporaries), and especially the Templars, with their singular focus on military activity. The English philosopher John of Salisbury (1115–1180) criticized the papal privileges given to the Templars and viewed the mixing of clerical and warrior functions with disgust. Isaac de l'Etoile (1100–1169), abbot of a Cistercian monastery near Poitou, France, called the military religious orders "a new monstrosity"[38] and disparaged the warrior monks in a sermon: "They lawfully despoil and religiously kill those who do not know the name of Christ and they proclaim their own men, who perish in these massacres, to be martyrs of Christ."[39] Later in the thirteenth century, Matthew Paris (1200–1259) and others viewed the military religious orders with skepticism, arguing that they benefited from a state of constant warfare in Outremer, and accused them of failure in maintaining control of Christian territory in the Latin East.[40] Toward the end of the thirteenth century, Bl. Raymond Lull (1232–1315) opined that the Hospitallers and Templars should be combined into one for efficiency of purpose and resources and argued that separately, the orders required large monetary investments to support their significant expenses but failed to achieve long-term success.[41]

Despite the contemporary critics, the Templars gained in membership and resources thanks to papal approval; the writing and preaching of Bernard; and a European recruitment drive by the founder, Hugh of Payns. By the halfway mark of the twelfth century, the Templars held extensive and wealthy landholdings in England, Italy, Portugal, Spain, and France. Membership came mostly from knightly but non-noble families.[42] The order allowed for non-traditional associate members, including married couples and elderly or retired individuals, who held administrative positions and shared the spiritual benefits of the Templars, including burial in the order's consecrated ground.

Men joined the Templars for a variety of reasons, but paramount was concern for their salvation and a desire to serve Christ, the Church, and fellow Christians, as Raymond of Luzençon stated in 1140 upon his entrance:

> I [Raymond], renouncing secular life and its pomp, relinquishing everything, give myself to the Lord God and to the knighthood of the Temple of Solomon of Jerusalem, that, as long as I shall live, in accordance with my strength, I shall serve there a complete pauper for God.[43]

The Templars were organized into chapters and provinces, with various military and administrative positions within each structure. Overseeing the order was the Master, who was elected by thirteen members of the order, comprising eight knights, four sergeants, and one priest.[44] The Master was entitled to the use of four horses and a company of associates, including a chaplain, two knights, a clerk, a sergeant, a servant to carry his shield and lance, a farrier, an interpreter, a cook, and in times of war a personal bodyguard of knights.[45]

Notwithstanding the seeming benefits of holding the office, the position of Master was an arduous and deadly duty. All but two Masters died in office, either in battle or in captivity.

Life as a Templar was not for the faint of heart. A detailed set of the order's regulations was compiled in the mid-thirteenth century and consisted of six hundred and eighty-six rules![46] Every recruit was read the rules, which consisted of, among other items, complete obedience to the Master, profession of the evangelical counsels, and daily recitation of the Divine Office. Additionally, Templars were forbidden to retreat during battle without orders, to kill Christians, to kiss a woman (not even a relative), to hunt (except lions), or to wear furs. Members were expected to limit conversations, refrain from laughter, and avoid outbursts of anger, complaining, and talking of past relationships with females. Discipline was enforced by a system of graduated penances, including "loss of habit," for displays of anger and violence, sexual intercourse with women, lying (especially about fellow brothers), misuse or loss of order property, disobedience of a command, and staying a night outside the house without permission. All of these were punished by the return of armor and horses, fasting for three days a week, and other penances for a period of one year and a day.[47] Expulsion from the order resulted from engaging in simony, killing a Christian, stealing, desertion, heresy, sodomy, or abandonment of the banner during battle.

The Templars were far from the intolerant, greedy, and bloodthirsty zealots depicted in the Enlightenment historical attack. They had great devotion to the cross of Christ (they possessed many relics of the True Cross) and fought in defense of Christians. They were friendly with the Muslim and Jewish inhabitants of the territory under their control in the Latin East. Templars allowed Jews and Muslims to practice their faith, approved the construction of synagogues, and even set an area aside in the Cathedral of Acre for Muslim prayer. In the early twelfth century, when Jerusalem was under Christian control, Muslims were not allowed to live in the Holy City but could visit and pray in certain areas. The Muslim traveler Usamah ibn Munqidh recorded not only how he was allowed to pray at a mosque near the former al-Aqsa mosque on the Temple Mount, which had been turned into a church, but also that Templars even expelled a newly arrived crusader who was annoyed at how Munqidh prayed:

> Whenever I visited Jerusalem I always entered the Aqsa mosque, beside which stood a small mosque which the

> Franks had converted into a church. . . . The Templars, who were my friends, would evacuate the little adjoining mosque so that I might pray in it. One day I entered this mosque . . . and stood up in the act of praying, upon which one of the Franks rushed on me, got hold of me, and turned my face eastward, saying, "This is the way thou shouldst pray."
>
> A group of Templars hastened to him, seized him, and repelled him from me. . . . They apologized to me, saying, "This is a stranger who has only recently arrived from the land of the Franks and he has never before seen anyone praying except eastward."[48]

In addition to their military and religious functions, the Templars engaged in economic and financial activity, which, eventually, raised the ire of secular and ecclesiastical authorities. Their houses throughout Europe and the Latin East became "involved in lending cash, storing valuables, and transferring money from one country to another."[49] Travelers to the Latin East could visit a Templar house in Europe and deposit cash and valuables while receiving a "deposit slip," which could be presented at a Templar house at the destination for a withdrawal request minus a service charge. Although this practice greatly benefited pilgrims who feared traveling with large amounts of money and valuables, the fees collected by the Templars enriched the order and allowed it to engage in economic and commercial enterprises outside the foundational scope and purpose of the brotherhood. The Templars managed loans and protected money, jewels, documents, livestock, and other valuables for the humblest pilgrims and the greatest kings of Europe. King Louis VII of France (r. 1137-1180) received financial aid from the Templars during the Second Crusade (1147-1149), and the Templars acted as royal treasurers (via their house in Paris) until the late thirteenth century, when King Philip IV moved the treasury to the Louvre.

Templars participated in most of the major combat operations in the Holy Land throughout the twelfth and thirteenth centuries. When King Louis VII left Paris on the Second Crusade to re-capture the city of Edessa, which had fallen to the Muslim ruler Zengi in 1144, 130 Templars accompanied him. Louis's campaign was fraught with disaster, but a tipping point occurred at Mount Cadmus (in modern-day southwest Turkey), when the army's vanguard climbed the mountain and did not wait for the baggage train (which stretched for six miles) and the rearguard that was still in camp. In this precarious situation, the Turks attacked the French army. When news of the assault reached camp, the king led the rearguard to the mountain but was ambushed, and in the heavy hand-to-hand combat that ensued, the king nearly died. The army suffered heavy casualties, and continuing the crusade seemed in doubt. Louis turned to the Templars and requested their assistance.

Master Everard of Barres assumed command of the army and divided it into groups of fifty, with a Templar in control. The remaining French nobles swore obedience to Templar officers, and, despite continuing attacks from the Turks, the army held together. Eventually, Louis and his nobles reached Antioch and then Jerusalem, where they linked up with the forces of Conrad III, king of the Germans, and local Christian nobles for a failed siege of Damascus.

The Second Crusade was an utter and abject disaster. The failure of this crusade shocked the faithful in Europe, who expected the same type of spectacular success that occurred on the First Crusade fifty years prior. Although blame was assigned to various persons, one chronicler accused the Templars: "King Baldwin would have fulfilled his desire at Damascus had not the greed, trickery, and envy of the Templars got in his way."[50]

Forty years later, when Saladin threatened the Kingdom of Jerusalem, the Hospitallers and Templars fought an engagement against a Muslim reconnaissance force at the Battle of Cresson in May 1187. The Masters of both orders led the small combined military religious order force of several hundred against the larger Muslim army of several thousand, with predictable results. The Christians were annihilated. Only Gerard of Ridefort, the Templar Master, and three other knights escaped the massacre. The battle occurred a month before Saladin's main invasion of the kingdom, and when the Latin East needed the Templars and Hospitallers the most, they were nearly combat-ineffective due to the loss of manpower at Cresson. The remaining Templars fought at the Battle of the Horns of Hattin against Saladin's main force, but that engagement also resulted in heavy Christian losses and paved the way for Saladin to conquer Jerusalem, which fell in October 1187.

Saladin's victories led to the Third Crusade of King Richard the Lionhearted of England; Philip II Augustus of France; and Frederick Barbarossa, King of the Germans and Holy Roman Emperor. After the liberation of Acre by the forces of Richard, Philip, and the local Christians under the command of King Guy of Jerusalem, Richard began his march to Jerusalem. The Templars constituted the vanguard of the crusade army on the march and fought valiantly in the ensuing Battle of Arsuf, where Saladin's forces were routed.

Eventually, the Third Crusade resulted in a peace treaty between Richard and Saladin that provided Christian access to but not control of Jerusalem. Fifty years later, Christians in the Holy Land suffered attacks from the Khwarazmians, Sunni Muslims from Persia and central Asia, who were pushed into the Latin East by the invading Mongols. The Khwarazmians massacred the Christians in Jerusalem and desecrated the holy places.

Several months later, at the Battle of La Forbie, the victorious Khwarazmians killed several hundred Templars and captured the Master. News of these events reached Europe and prompted King St. Louis IX of France (r. 1226-1270) to take the cross. French Templars accompanied the saintly king on his expedition to Egypt, which ended in disaster when Robert of Artois, the king's brother, foolishly advanced without the main army into a Muslim city after fording a river. Hospitallers and Templars attached to Robert's unit followed his lead and were slaughtered by the defenders.

The Christians of the Latin East suffered greatly when Baybars became sultan of Egypt and ruler of Syria in the mid-thirteenth century. Baybars was a Kipchak (or Russian Turk) with a vision to re-establish a unified Muslim empire in the Holy Land akin to Saladin's empire in the previous century. Baybars desired the eradication of the Christian presence in the Holy Land and launched raids into Christian-held territory in the 1260s.

In 1266, he attacked the Templar fortress of Safed in Galilee. The Templars negotiated a safe conduct from Baybars in exchange for surrendering the fortress, but when they opened the gates, Baybars reneged and gave them a choice of conversion to Islam or death. When the Templars refused conversion, Baybars ordered their decapitation.

By the end of the thirteenth century, only a narrow coastal strip of land remained in Christian control. The economically important city of Acre was the prominent Christian enclave. In the spring of 1291, a large Muslim army besieged the city, demanding its surrender, which the Christian defenders refused. The Masters of the Hospitallers, Templars, and Teutonic Knights were in the city and helped muster its defenders. The Christians were vastly outnumbered and suffered through a horrific artillery bombardment for more than a month until a breach in the walls led to the final assault. William of Beaujeu, the Templar Master, was mortally wounded in the ensuing combat. The city fell, and most of the surviving defenders either escaped or were captured.

The citadel and fortified compounds of the military religious orders held out for a time until the Hospitallers and Teutonic Knights surrendered. The Templars remained defiant for another ten days until they also agreed to surrender in exchange for safe conduct out of the city. When a Muslim force came to their compound and harassed Christian women who had taken shelter in the Templar tower, the Templars attacked them and closed the compound. When the sultan Al-Ashraf Khalil arrived at the tower and reaffirmed the safe conduct despite the Templars' behavior, the Templar commander and non-wounded brothers left the enclosure. They were captured and beheaded. Eventually, the Muslims mined the Templar tower, killing those within.

The fall of Acre marked the end of nearly two hundred years of Christian control of the Holy Land and the last major combat operation involving the Templars, who ran afoul of the king of France only sixteen years later.

On October 13, 1307, French royal officials arrested the Templars by order of King Philip IV, "the Fair" (r. 1285-1314). Technically, the arrest was illegal, since the Templars were a religious order and subject only to ecclesiastical, not secular law. Interestingly, there is no record of violence during the arrest, which is odd, considering the military purpose of the Templars but understandable when the brothers arrested comprised mostly administrators, craftsmen, agricultural workers, and those temporarily in France.[51]

Historians debate the reason for the arrest of the Templars in France, but a financial motive seems likely. The Templars possessed considerable wealth and properties in every region in France (and throughout Europe). Philip had devalued the currency in 1295, which led to rapid inflation, the doubling of the cost of living, and riots in Paris. It is possible that financial pressures prompted the king to believe the wild rumors and accusations about the Templars then circulating in France. It is also possible that Philip IV believed that it was his royal duty to investigate the alleged immoral and heretical practices of the order.

William of Nogaret, a royal lackey described by a contemporary as "a body without a soul" and the child of Albigensian heretics, developed the charges against the Templars, which included sodomy, idol worship, and invalid Masses, along with requiring novices to deny Christ three times, spit on a crucifix, and stand naked in front of a member of the order who would then kiss them as a symbol of their acceptance.[52]

Pope Clement V (r. 1305-1314) opened a papal investigation into the order, which eventually consisted of diocesan hearings and a papal commission. The papal investigation indicated that most of the royal charges against the Templars were unproven, and in the areas outside France and England, the secular inquiries against the Templars came to nothing. However, under intense political pressure from Philip IV, Clement agreed to discuss the Templars at the ecumenical Council of Vienne (1311-1312). The assembled bishops voted to subdue the order, so the pope promulgated the bull *Ad Providam* on May 2, 1312, which suppressed the Templars but passed no judgment on their guilt or innocence as to the accusations of immorality and heresy.

Although King Philip may have initiated the attack against the order to obtain their wealth and property, he was disappointed when the pope gave Templar lands and wealth to the Hospitallers. Templar brothers who were innocent of the charges and those who confessed and reconciled were provided with pensions and allowed to live either in Templar houses (now controlled by the Hospitallers) or with the Cistercians or Augustinians. Impenitent and relapsed Templars were imprisoned or executed.[53] Master Jacques de Molay was burned at the stake by royal edict in Paris in March 1314 and was soon followed in death by Pope Clement in April and King Philip IV in November.

After their suppression in the early fourteenth century, the Templars ceased to occupy the minds of Europeans until Enlightened intellectuals used the order to criticize the crusading movement and further their propaganda campaign against the Church. Ironically, the rise of Freemasonry in the eighteenth and nineteenth century resurrected the memory of the Templars, as some Freemasons claimed ancient lineage to the Templars, who, in their interpretation, were suppressed by a "repressive religious and political establishment."[54] The Templars, with their secrecy, military prowess, financial dealings, and suppression, were easy targets for Enlightened authors seeking to hijack Catholic history and vilify medieval Christians to lessen the influence of the Church in their own time period.

Sadly, the canceling of the Templars continues in the modern world, with false narratives posing as pseudo-history such as *Holy Blood, Holy Grail* (1983) and *The Da Vinci Code* (2003), where the Templars are linked to the so-called Priory of Sidon, the guardians of the secret bloodline of kings descended from Jesus and Mary Magdalene. Moreover, some "conservative" extremists such as the Norwegian terrorist and mass murderer Anders Behring Breivik claim membership in a reincarnated Templar order. These modern-day fanatics and the Enlightened intellectuals before them sully the sacrifices of these warrior monks of the twelfth and thirteenth centuries, who offered their lives in service to Christ, his Church, and their fellow Christians.

Pope Innocent III

> *Innocent, like other great historical figures, has suffered from being judged in the light of later events and on different terms from his own.*[55]

Enlightened intellectuals and their later adherents attacked the papacy, especially the pope's secular authority, because the secular state was paramount in their worldview. Politics and statecraft should be free from the influence of the Church, they believed. Kings and secular rulers should reign supreme and rely on the obedience of their subjects without the interference of a foreign prince like the pope.

The Enlightened historical attack against the Church focused on the medieval period, especially the crusading movement, and the papacy. These critics found the perfect pope to cancel in Innocent III (r. 1198-1216), a medieval pontiff who stressed the supreme authority of the Roman pontiff and devoted significant energy to the Crusades in the hope of liberating Jerusalem.

Pope Innocent III has been portrayed as a dictatorial ruler bent on world domination who focused too much energy on temporal affairs. He advocated a "theocratic doctrine" that attributed "supreme temporal and spiritual power to the papacy," which some critics have used as evidence of his megalomania and desire to be "lord of the world."[56]

Notwithstanding his detractors, Innocent was a deeply devoted man of the Church, who "was sometimes mistaken, but he acted in all things for God's glory."[57]

Born into a noble Roman family, Lotario dei Conti of Segni was the nephew of Pope Clement III (r. 1187-1191), who later created Lotario a cardinal. The bright young Lotario began his formal education in Rome, where he developed an appreciation for Greek literature and culture. In his early teens, Lotario was sent to Paris to study at the university. Further studies took him to the University of Bologna, where he studied civil and canon law. He was the first university-educated Roman pontiff in Church history, and his pontificate marked the end of the "monk popes" of the eleventh century and the advent of the "lawyer popes."[58]

When the ninety-two-year-old Pope Celestine III (r. 1191-1198) died, the cardinals assembled and debated his successor. A clear favorite emerged when three doves flew into the hall, and the whitest of them rested on the head of Cardinal dei Conti of Segni, who was elected and chose the name Innocent. The new pope was thirty-seven years old, the youngest successor of St. Peter in a century and a half.

Innocent's eighteen-year pontificate was the longest of any papal reign in the thirteenth century. Innocent was a deacon and cardinal, but not a priest, when elected pope (this was not uncommon in the medieval period), so he was ordained priest and then bishop. Papal consecration at that time occurred usually on the Sunday following election, but Innocent decided to postpone his consecration until February 22, the Feast of the Chair of St. Peter.[59] Innocent chose as his papal motto the phrase *Fac mecum Domine Signum in Bonum*, taken from Psalm 86:17, "Show me a sign of thy favor, that those who hate me may see and be put to shame because thou, Lord, hast helped me and comforted me," which illustrated his deep love of the Lord and a recognition that his pontificate would focus on spiritual and not temporal glory.[60]

Innocent exuded self-confidence, and he was impatient but not arrogant or overbearing. He loved puns and wordplay and had a good sense of humor. A contemporary described him as "of medium stature and handsome appearance." He did not tolerate rebels and troublemakers, but he was "strong and consistent, magnanimous and astute, a defender of the Faith and a foe of heresy. In matters of justice he was unbending but in mercy he was compassionate. He was humble in prosperity and patient in adversity."[61]

Before his pontificate, Innocent authored the popular devotional treatise "On Contempt for the World" as well as several theological treatises that illustrated his profound knowledge of Sacred Scripture. He also wrote "The Misery of the Human Condition," which elucidated the turmoil and troubles of everyday life. The later Italian poet and scholar Petrarch (1304–1374) greatly admired this work, which was extremely popular and remained in circulation for centuries, and annotated an edition.[62] Innocent also produced a theological reflection on the sacrament of marriage ("The Four Kinds of Marriage") and a commentary on the liturgy ("The Sacred Mysteries of the Altar").

As pope, Innocent inherited a Rome controlled by competing and warring families, who built defensive towers and other fortifications to rule sections of the city. A prosperous and peaceful city required strong papal leadership to arrest the family clashes and constant food shortages and provide greater economic opportunities for the city besides the ever-present tourism and pilgrimages.

Innocent viewed his temporal role as leader of the city of Rome and the Papal States in light of his relationship with the German kings and emperors. The greatest political concern of popes at this time was the German king or emperor merging his northern Italian lands with the imperial claim to the Kingdom of Sicily in the south, since such a union would place papal territory in central Italy in an unpleasant vise-like situation and threaten its independence.

Although the Italian situation remained a constant concern, Innocent is most known (and criticized) for his assertion of papal authority and power *vis-à-vis* secular authority and power. Innocent III firmly believed in the universal jurisdiction and authority of the Roman pontiff, derived from Jesus, who gave the keys to the kingdom of heaven and earth to St. Peter. Innocent expressed this abiding belief in papal authority and power in his frequent use of the scriptural passage from Jeremiah 1:10—"I have set you this day over the nations, and over the kingdoms, to root up and to pull down, to waste and to destroy, and to build and to plant"—and in his systematic use of the title "Vicar of Christ."[63] Innocent did not view the papal office as providing unrestrained power, as his critics assume; rather, he recognized the twin aspects of papal power as service and dominion rooted in imitation of Christ. Papal power did not replace secular power, nor did he see his role as dictator of the world. He respected the rights of secular rulers and saw limits to papal power. He tried to live in accordance with his contention that rulers should "be truthful in speech, gentle in heart, and just in deed."[64]

Innocent III's first papal address was a substantial statement on the relationship between spiritual power and temporal power. Previous popes, most especially St. Gelasius I (r. 492-496) and St. Gregory VII (r. 1073-1085), had commented on the role between the spiritual power and secular power while asserting the supremacy of the former. Innocent maintained and expanded that view by insisting that secular rulers assist the pope in the work of extending the Faith throughout the world and maintaining a justly ordered society.

Innocent recognized that temporal power was autonomous within its own realm and that kings represented Christ the king in their territory and to their people, but the pope, as vicar of Christ, could intervene in secular affairs when warranted as mediator and moral judge. He wrote, "Whereas princes have only individual provinces, kings only individual kingdoms, Peter surpasses them in fullness as well as in breadth, for he is the vicar of the one to whom the earth and its fullness belong, the world and its inhabitants."[65]

Innocent's direct supreme temporal power was limited to the Papal States. He recognized the temporal power of kings and emperors, and he even desired strong secular rulers—provided that they did not interfere in ecclesiastical affairs and "could be controlled."[66] Innocent's vision of the papacy included the pope as a shepherd, but that vision did not mean that the pope was passive in the exercise of his office, especially in spiritual and moral matters.

One example of Innocent's exercise of temporal and spiritual power concerned the kingdom of England. In the spring of 1208, Innocent placed England under interdict, an ecclesiastical penalty that forbids the administration of the sacraments, among other penalties, and he excommunicated King John (r. 1199-1216) in 1209. The king refused to accept the pope's candidate, Stephen Langton, for the office of archbishop of Canterbury, desiring instead another man. The tense situation and stalemate continued for several years, until Innocent formally deposed John, which prompted the now sufficiently chastened king to save his position by accepting Langton as archbishop and, on his own initiative, making England a papal fief, which Innocent then restored to John to administer. As one chronicler noted, commenting on this episode, "everyone stood in greater awe of Pope Innocent than his predecessors for many years past."[67]

A few years later, when John was forced by the English nobility to sign the Magna Carta, Pope Innocent declared that treatise null and void—not because of its contents, as is sometimes alleged in criticism of the pope, but because of the manner of its creation. Innocent was lord of England, and any obligations imposed on John without the pope's consent were invalid.

Innocent's vision of papal power and authority and his political policies were consistent with his predecessors, especially the reforming popes of the eleventh century. He demanded an educated, celibate, and virtuous clergy who set an example for the laity of authentic Christian living. He embraced the eleventh-century papal reform mantra that "the Church shall be Catholic, chaste, and free: Catholic in the faith and fellowship of the saints, chaste from all contagion of evil, and free from secular power."[68] Secular powers, Innocent insisted, should not select clerics, try them in secular courts, or abuse the clergy or confiscate their property.

Innocent's reform program was focused not solely on the Church's external relationship with secular rulers, but also on internal ecclesial affairs. Innocent commissioned, under the supervision of Peter Beneventano, an official collection of his papal decretals, which was known as the *Complatio Tertia* and, along with other canonical compilations, especially that of Gratian, formed the foundation of canon law. Innocent also established the process for canonization, which was previously highly subjective, with various procedures and processes throughout the Church. Under Innocent's process, reports of miracles were no longer sufficient of their own accord, but the life of the candidate had to be thoroughly examined as well. He also mandated that only the pope could canonize.

Innocent pursued a two-pronged reform program centered on the Roman Curia and the universal episcopate. He organized the Roman Curia into the departments of the chapel, which handled liturgical and ceremonial functions; the chancery, which produced papal bulls and letters; and the chamber, which oversaw papal finances. He was not dictatorial in his measures, but rather made use of local and regional councils to promulgate and implement his reform initiatives.

Innocent concentrated on reforming the episcopacy by appointing virtuous men to dioceses throughout the Church and removing unworthy bishops, especially those in southern France, whose negligence allowed the spread of the heretical Cathari or Albigensian movement. He bemoaned the quality of bishops in southern France, calling them

> blind men, dumb dogs who can no longer bark . . . men who will do anything for money. All of them, from the greatest to the least, are zealous in avarice, lovers of gifts, seekers of rewards. Through such men the name of the Lord is blasphemed. . . . They say the good is bad and the bad is good; they turn light into darkness and darkness into light, sweet to bitter and bitter to sweet. They do not fear God nor respect man.[69]

He also limited the influence and power of local bishops in relationship with secular rulers by appointing papal legates and encouraging appeals to Rome from diocesan courts.

Innocent mandated the *ad limina* ("to the thresholds"—that is, of the apostles Peter and Paul) visits of bishops to Rome every four years. He insisted that bishops make pastoral visits to the parishes in their diocese and reform their clergy by requiring proper education and formation, especially in canon law.

In an age when marriage was a contest in the political arena, Pope Innocent defended the Church's teaching on the sacrament. He confirmed an earlier teaching of Pope Alexander III (r. 1159–1181) that consent of the bride and groom constitutes marriage, not the ceremony or the presence of the priest or families. He spoke out against secular rulers who abused marriage or treated it with contempt.

Innocent's renewal program also included recognition and support of the new mendicant religious groups, the Order of Friars Minor and the Order of Preachers, which launched a great spiritual restoration in the Church. The orders of St. Francis (1181-1226) and St. Dominic (1170-1221) revitalized the Church, as their members focused on holy lives in a community through active works such as preaching, teaching, and serving the poor. The Dominicans were founded during Innocent's reign but were granted approval by his successor, Honorius III. Innocent approved the Franciscans in 1210, after the pontiff experienced a particularly vivid and impressionable dream. In the dream, Innocent saw the Lateran basilica swaying violently and on the verge of collapse when a little poor man ran to its defense, holding the ancient edifice steady with his hands and shoulders. The pope recognized the poor man in the dream as St. Francis, who had traveled to Rome seeking Innocent's approval of his new religious order.[70]

The summit of Innocent's reform initiatives, and his entire pontificate, was the ecumenical Fourth Lateran Council in 1215. Innocent hoped the council would solidify his previous ecclesial reform actions and develop plans for a new crusade to liberate Jerusalem. The council was a momentous and well-attended event, with nearly three thousand clerics and laity involved. The council produced seventy canons on topics such as heretics and the Jewish people, organizational and judicial reforms, marriage law, clerical appointments, and reforms of the clergy and laity.[71] It also instituted the annual *Easter Duty*, which requires Catholics to receive the sacraments of confession and Eucharist at least once a year, preferably during the Easter season. Plans for a crusade were discussed and formulated in Innocent's post-conciliar papal letter *Ad Liberandam*. The council was the crowning achievement of Innocent's pontificate (he died the next year) and solidified his pontifical program of reform.

In concert with his reform initiatives, Innocent III devoted significant energy to the crusading movement. Indeed, "the number, scope, and variety of Innocent's crusades were unprecedented and never replicated."[72] A contemporary account of his life indicates the intense focus the pope placed on the Crusades: "In the midst of all his work, he quite fervently longed for the relief and recovery of the Holy Land and anxiously mulled over how he could achieve this more effectively."[73]

Innocent described the crusading movement as the *negotium crucis*, "the business of the cross," or, more appropriately, the *negotium crucifixi*, "the business of the crucified."[74] His focus on the Crusades is exemplified not only by the number of crusades he initiated, but also by the innovations he brought to the movement. In his 1213 bull *Quia Maior*, Innocent advocated for crusading as a moral imperative. Addressing those military men who failed to go on crusade, the pope said,

> If indeed there be by chance any man so ungrateful to the Lord our God, we firmly state on behalf of the apostle Peter that they . . . will have to answer to us on this matter in the presence of the dreadful Judge on the Last Day of Severe Judgment.[75]

The emphasis on crusading was implemented not only through papal pronouncements, but also through the liturgy, where Innocent encouraged monthly processions to pray for the liberation of Jerusalem. He also decreed the singing of Psalm 79 ("O God, the heathen have come into thy inheritance; they have defiled thy holy temple; they have laid Jerusalem in ruins") at every Mass following the exchange of peace, while the congregation lay prostrate.[76]

After the fiasco of the Fourth Crusade (1201–1205), where Western knights traveled to Constantinople and sacked the city, Innocent sought to control future expeditions. He believed that the Church should manage and administer the armed pilgrimages to the Holy Land through papal legates, but the Fifth

Crusade (1218–1221) failed, in part, because of the poor leadership and decision-making of Cardinal Pelagius, the papal legate.

Innocent was successful in other crusading innovations, including more supervision and coordination of preaching and recruitment efforts, enforcement of crusader vows, expansion of spiritual benefits, and finances. Crusading was expensive, and many warriors found it difficult to raise the necessary cash to undertake the expedition east. To help them, Innocent imposed a tax on the clergy and contributed funds from the papal treasury to finance crusades. Previously, married men needed permission from their wives to take the cross, a stipulation instituted by Bl. Pope Urban II at the beginning of the Crusade movement to ensure the rights and safety of women, but by Innocent's pontificate, men were using that restriction as an excuse not to go on crusade. So he abrogated the requirement.

Innocent expanded the spiritual benefits associated with the crusading movement to increase home-front participation from non-warriors. He granted indulgences not only to those who campaigned, but to those who financed a warrior's participation. Previously, taking the cross meant participation for the duration, but Innocent changed the nature of crusading by granting the same indulgence to men who pledged military days of service (usually forty) during the Albigensian Crusade in southern France.

Some critics place blame on Pope Innocent III for the sack of Constantinople during the Fourth Crusade, but the historical record clearly illustrates that he did not approve of the crusaders' actions. When the crusade army mustered in Venice in the summer of 1202 without enough money to pay the Venetians in accordance with their treaty obligations, Enrico Dandolo, the *doge* (or city leader) of Venice, concocted a plan to attack the city of Zara with the crusaders in order to receive his agreed-upon renumeration. But Zara was a Christian city under the control of King Emeric of Hungary, who had taken the crusader vow, so an attack on the city was forbidden.

Debate raged among the crusaders, but the majority agreed to Dandolo's plan. When news reached Rome, Innocent vehemently disagreed with the diversion and sent letters to the crusade leaders forbidding them to attack Zara under the pain of excommunication. The crusade leaders hid the pope's letter from the rank and file so they would pursue the attack on Zara spiritually unencumbered.

When the army arrived there, Abbot Guy of Les Vaux-de-Cernay confronted Dandolo and the crusade leaders. Holding a copy of Innocent's letter, Guy commanded, "I forbid you, on behalf of the pope of Rome, to attack this city, for those within are Christians, and you are crusaders!"[77]

Innocent's warnings were not heeded, and the crusaders conquered Zara. They decided to spend the winter in the city for rest and re-supply and during that time were visited by representatives of a renegade Byzantine prince, Alexius Angelus, whose father, Isaac II, had been blinded, deposed, and imprisoned by his own brother. Seeking to restore his father to the throne, Alexius Angelus requested the crusaders' assistance. Once again, when Innocent was informed that the crusaders were contemplating another diversion to attack another Christian city, he sent a stinging letter of rebuke to the nobles, warning them "not to return to their previous sins [attacking another Christian city] like dogs returning to their own vomit."[78] Aware that Alexius Angelus had promised the reunion of the Eastern Church with Rome if the crusaders went to Constantinople, the pope in his letter invalidated that justification for an attack: "Let no one among you rashly convince himself that he may seize or plunder Greek lands on the pretext that they show little obedience to the Apostolic

See."[79] He pointedly told the crusaders to "give up these pointless diversions and feigned commitments: cross over to save the Holy Land."[80]

Unfortunately, the nobles did not heed the pope's commands. They sailed with the Venetians to Constantinople, where they eventually installed Alexius Angelus and his father on the throne. But after a palace coup and the murder of Alexius, they sacked the city in a spasm of violence.

The sack of Constantinople marred the crusading movement and continues to impact East-West relations today. Critics of the Church continue to blame Pope Innocent specifically and the papacy in general for the fiasco of the Fourth Crusade, despite Innocent's repeated warnings to the crusade nobles. Indeed, after news of the conquest and sack reached Rome, he wrote a letter to the main crusade leader, Boniface of Montferrat, condemning their actions and chastising them for their choices:

> You rashly violated the purity of your vows, and turning your arms not against the Saracens, but against Christians, you applied yourselves not to the recovery of Jerusalem, but to seize Constantinople, preferring earthly to heavenly riches. . . . These "soldiers of Christ" who should have turned their swords against the infidel have steeped them in Christian blood, sparing neither religion, nor age, nor sex. . . . They stripped the altars of silver, violated the sanctuaries, robbed icons and crosses and relics. . . . The Latins have given example only of perversity and works of darkness. No wonder the Greeks call them dogs![81]

No other pope spent as much time, energy, or focus on the crusading movement as did Innocent III. Despite his best efforts, the crusades of his reign never achieved the goal of liberating Jerusalem. However, his crusading innovations influenced the movement for centuries.

Pope Innocent III died in 1216 at the age of fifty-six, after an eighteen-year pontificate. Viewed by his critics as a megalomaniacal dictator bent on creating an ecclesial superpower, Innocent loved Christ and the Church and pursued his temporal and spiritual goals and policies in accordance with that deep faith. Canceled for the alleged evils of the medieval papacy by proponents of the Enlightenment historical attack because of their anti-religious and anti-Catholic worldview, Pope Innocent III "was less moved by the desire to enhance personal and familial wealth than any secular prince of his day, and he was more humane than most."[82]

Spanish Inquisitors

The fashionable practice, especially since the eighteenth century, of automatic, or dogmatic, damning of the Spanish Inquisition, is mainly founded not upon knowledge but upon prejudice, sanctified propaganda, and the manifestly unjust but popular habit of using post-Enlightenment canons—ritualistic, moralistic, political, religious, humanitarian—as bases for judging pre-Enlightenment phenomena.[83]

The Spanish Inquisition, like the crusading movement, is one of the most maligned and misunderstood events in Church history. Akin to the false portrayals of the Templars, Spanish inquisitors are depicted as sadistic monks gleefully torturing thousands (sometimes millions!) of innocent Spaniards and burning them in the name of Catholic orthodoxy. The false narrative of the Spanish Inquisition has been used to cancel and vilify not only individual inquisitors, but also the entire Catholic nation of Spain, due to the *Black Legend*, which paints "an image of Spain as a nation of fanatical bigots, an image popularized by her foreign (mainly Protestant) enemies in the mid-sixteenth century, and which survived long after the tribunal's final extinction."[84]

As with the crusading movement, false narratives about the Spanish Inquisition were birthed in the age of the Protestant Revolution but grew to maturity in the Enlightenment. Adroit use of the printing press by Protestants spread myths about the Spanish Inquisition rapidly throughout Europe. Protestants wrote that the Spanish Inquisition was a threat to liberty and was the "supreme institution of intolerance."[85] Additionally, Spanish inquisitors were depicted as cruel clerics who "do nothing but seek their private gain and commodity, with craft defrauding and spoiling of other men's goods."[86]

In 1567, Reginaldus Montanus, the pen name of an exiled Spanish monk turned Lutheran heretic, wrote the book *A Discovery and Plaine Declaration of Sundry Subtill Practices of the Holy Spanish Inquisition*, which became the main Protestant narrative for the Spanish tribunal. Montanus focused his work on the impact of the Inquisition on Spanish Protestants, a minority in Spain, and created an inquisitional "martyrology" of the victims.[87] By the end of the sixteenth century, Montanus's propaganda was translated into English, French, Dutch, German, and Hungarian.

The Dutchman Philip van Limborch contributed to the Protestant false narrative of the Spanish Inquisition with his 1692 book *History of the Inquisition*. The Protestant false depiction and scapegoating of the Spanish inquisitors continued in the nineteenth century with John Motley's *The Rise of the Dutch Republic* in 1855. Motley wrote of a "bench of monks" who "condemned thoughts not deeds" and "arrested on suspicion, tortured till confession, and then punished by fire."[88]

Protestant propagandists of the Spanish Inquisition were joined by Catholic voices in the fifteenth and nineteenth centuries. In the late fifteenth century, Spanish troops were operating in Italy against French forces. The Italians viewed the Spaniards as oppressors, and Italian diplomats throughout European courts were vehement critics of Spain and used tales of its inquisition in a campaign of calumny.[89]

Approaching the end of the nineteenth century, during the First Vatican Council, German Catholic opponents of the document *Pastor Aeternus*, concerning papal primacy and the charism of papal infallibility, used the myth of the Spanish Inquisition to attack the conciliar document. Writing under the pseudonym Janus, the German priests Johan Ignaz von Döllinger and Johannes Huber published the book *The Pope and the Council* in 1869, where they argued that papal infallibility was the creation of the Spanish Inquisition: "A wholly new institution and mighty organization had been introduced to make the papal system irresistible, to impede any disclosure of its rotten foundation, and to bring the infallibility theory into full possession: it was the Inquisition."[90]

Anti-Catholic Enlightened intellectuals used the Spanish Inquisition to try to cancel the Church and further their goal of eradicating the Church from the public sphere. They crafted a historical attack that presented the Spanish Inquisition as stifling knowledge and scientific advancement in Spain so that the general populace maintained a level of ignorance and barbarism through the controlling activity of bloodthirsty inquisitors. Voltaire and other Enlightenment "thinkers" not only viewed the Spanish Inquisition as the paradigm of intolerance, but also depicted its inquisitors as fanatical and dangerous agents of the state. The Inquisition was depicted as an out-of-control religious tribunal with supreme powers to arrest, interrogate, torture, and execute unsuspecting and innocent men and women. Charles Louis de Secondat (1689–1755), known as Montesquieu, wrote in *The Spirit of the Laws* that the Spanish Inquisition "confused ideas of Christian charity with a most peculiar barbarism, in its form and foundation, so as to astonish the entire Universe."[91]

Artists and novelists in the eighteenth century also contributed to the Enlightenment historical attack against Spanish inquisitors. The English novelists Matthew Lewis and Ann Radcliffe in their respective works, *The Monk* and *The Italian* (both published in 1796), "produced extended and lurid depictions of grotesquely unfair trails, fanatical clergy, and scenes of torture."[92] In 1797, the Spanish court painter Francisco de Goya y Lucientes (1746–1828) produced a series of eighty satirical sketches known as *Los Caprichos*, which made subtle references indicating that the Inquisition had handicapped the Spanish people under the tyranny of religious superstition. Later, in 1816, he painted *The Tribunal of the Inquisition*, which showed the tribunal as a despotic and domineering organization.[93]

Serious historical research into the Spanish Inquisition began in the nineteenth century, but those historians were influenced by the Enlightenment historical attack against the Church. The first history of the Inquisition using documents from its archives was published in 1817 by Juan Antonio Llorente (1756–1823), a former priest and general secretary of the Inquisition in Madrid turned Freemason and exile in France. His *Critical History of the Spanish Inquisition*, though embraced by later historians, suffered from an anti-clerical bias and was rife with exaggerated statements and statistics of those remanded to the secular arm for execution. Llorente believed the Inquisition was the root cause of Spanish problems, writing,

> The horrid conduct of this *holy office* weakened the power and diminished the population of Spain, by arresting the

> progress of arts, sciences, industry, and commerce, and by compelling multitudes of families to abandon the kingdom; by instigating the expulsion of the Jews and the Moors; and by immolating on its flaming shambles more than *three hundred thousand victims!!*[94]

Twenty years later, the American historian William H. Prescott (1796-1859) published the book *History of the Reign of Ferdinand and Isabella*, which agreed with Llorente's assessment and shaped American opinion on the subject. Prescott believed that the Spanish Inquisition was responsible for "centuries of unspeakable oppression and misery."[95] In the early twentieth century, another American historian, Henry Charles Lea (1825-1909), the son of a Quaker father and Catholic mother, with no formal education, employed researchers to scour European archives for manuscripts of interest. He published a multi-volume work on the Middle Ages and the Spanish Inquisition, which was seen as the first definitive history of the tribunal but was written from a prejudiced perspective and contained inaccuracies.

The Enlightened historical attack on the Spanish Inquisition was rooted in an anti-religious, anti-Catholic, and anti-Spanish worldview, with a singularly focused goal of discrediting the Church and eradicating its influence in society. Spanish inquisitors were depicted as barbaric, sadistic, fanatical monks who tortured and killed thousands, hundreds of thousands, and even millions of innocent Spanish men and women simply for believing differently from their oppressors. The false narratives and myths about the Inquisition in Spain and those who worked for it continue to haunt the Church today. So what is the real story of the infamous tribunal in Spain, and who were these inquisitors, charged with preserving Catholic orthodoxy from the stain of heresy?

Both secular and spiritual rulers were concerned with heresy in Christendom because it threatened the unity of society, produced violence, and endangered the eternal souls of the heretic and those who embraced his error. As a result, heresy was both an ecclesial and a secular crime, but it was punished differently in the ecclesial and secular spheres. On the one hand, the Church desired the repentance, conversion, and readmittance to communion of the heretic. On the other, secular rulers viewed heresy as an active threat to the public good that demanded extreme and swift punishment. Secular authority treated heresy as treason, which resulted in the execution of the heretic, usually by burning at the stake.

Prosecution of heresy, from both the Church and the secular rulers, changed dramatically in the late twelfth century. The revival of Roman imperial law and the formation of universal canon law in the twelfth and thirteenth centuries witnessed the demise of *accusatorial* procedure and the advent of *inquisitorial* procedure.

Before the twelfth century, criminal law was a private matter, where victims or their families came forward and demanded justice from the secular authority. The accuser went to court, made an accusation, swore an oath, and called the other defendant to court to answer the charges. The secular authority then made a judgment concerning guilt or innocence (or an ordeal—that is, a physical activity (e.g. trial by combat) that determined guilt or innocence by appealing to an intervention from God was undertaken).[96] But the legal revolution of the twelfth and thirteenth centuries embraced inquisitorial procedure, where a state (or ecclesial) official initiated the legal action, collected evidence, interviewed witnesses, and sought the confession of the accused.

Under inquisitorial procedure, confessions became the "queen of proofs," and inquisitors diligently sought them.

Pope Lucius III (r. 1181–1185) promulgated *Ad Abolendam* in 1184, which ordered bishops to take an active role in determining the guilt of heretics using imperial Roman rules of evidence. Fifteen years later, Pope Innocent III (r. 1198–1216) in *Vergentis in Senium* described heretics as traitors and applied the imperial Roman punishment for traitors—confiscation of goods and property—to heretics. Innocent also applied the punishment of excommunication to those who harbored heretics. Pope Gregory IX (r. 1227–1241) in the thirteenth century formally instituted the procedures for papal inquisitors in his 1231 bull *Ille Humani Generis*. Pope Gregory appointed "judges delegates" who shared in papal legal authority for a particular case, in a specific region, and for a period of time.[97] These medieval papal inquisitors were the prototypes of the later Spanish inquisitors in the fifteenth century.

Spain in the fifteenth century had a unique history. The country was once a proud province of the mighty Roman Empire, producing more emperors than any other imperial territory. But with the collapse of central governing authority from Rome in the late fifth century, the area was conquered by the Visigoths.

Infighting among the Visigoth nobles in the early eighth century allowed a large Muslim invasion force to enter Spain and pursue a successful military campaign. The Islamic invasion was brutal: many churches were destroyed, books were burned, and Christians suffered persecution and martyrdom from mass crucifixions and beheadings. This newly conquered Islamic territory was known as *Al-Andalus*.

A small enclave of Christian resistance fighters existed in northwest Spain, known as Asturias, and it was from this area that the *Reconquista*, the longest war in human history, was launched. Over the centuries, the Christians in Asturias liberated important cities, including Toledo in 1085, Saragossa in 1118, Cordova in 1236, Valencia in 1238, and Seville in 1248. By the mid-thirteenth century, Islamic-occupied territory in Spain consisted of only the city of Granada in the south. Christian Spain consisted of the two kingdoms of Castile (the larger and more populous) and Aragon, which were united when King Fernando (of Aragon) and Queen Isabel (of Castile) married in 1469. And so the area of modern-day Spain and Portugal had been the site of an intense, nearly eight-hundred-year Christian struggle to reclaim territory conquered by the forces of Islam.

Close contact among Christians, Muslims, and Jews in Spain led to an uneasy coexistence for centuries, but by the late fifteenth century, Spanish Christians felt more secure and powerful, which led to repressive measures against the minority Muslims and Jews.

Spain was home to a large Jewish population since the third century, and most Jewish people lived in separate communities and worked in finance and medicine. In the late fifteenth century, the crown gave an ultimatum to their Jewish subjects—conversion or expulsion—which caused great suffering and societal disruption.

Spanish Muslims (known as *Moors*) were treated favorably by the crown after the surrender of Granada in the winter of 1491. According to the surrender terms (*capitulaciones*) signed by Abu l-Qaim al-Muhli, Muslims were allowed to keep their customs, laws, and property, along with the practice of Islam.[98] But Islamic revolts in the late fifteenth and early sixteenth centuries changed the crown's tolerance of Moors, and more repressive measures were enacted, eventually leading to expulsion in the early seventeenth century.

The religious situation in Spain created a unique environment of conversions by Jewish people and Muslims to the Christian faith for non-spiritual reasons (although authentic spiritual conversions occurred as well) due to societal norms and laws restricting jobs and positions from practicing Jews and Muslims. The result was a distinction in Spanish society between "Old Christians," whose families could trace Christian lineage for centuries, and *conversos*, or more recent Jewish and Muslim converts.

These new converts rarely received formal catechetical instruction, despite the efforts of some clerics, and many continued practicing certain elements of their previous faiths. For example, some Jewish *conversos* maintained a kosher diet (as far as possible), celebrated Jewish holidays and life-cycle events, and even imperfectly observed the Sabbath (e.g., cleaning the house on any day other than Saturday).[99] These practices, known as *Judaizing*, were mostly harmless, but when some *conversos* became well known and connected in Spanish society, jealousy motivated Old Christians to believe sordid tales and conspiracy theories about allegedly nefarious *conversos* who practiced the Christian faith publicly but secretly continued practicing their Jewish (or Muslim) faith. This belief led to fears of a "fifth column" in Spanish society that would lay the groundwork for and participate in a future Muslim invasion. These fears led to repressive measures in Spain that increased in severity throughout the fifteenth century. For example, at Toledo, in 1449, city officials passed laws (known as *Sentencia Estatuto*) barring those of Jewish ancestry from holding public office. These laws were quickly overturned due to opposition from Old and New Christians, but subsequent "purity of blood" (*Limpieza de Sangre*) laws, requiring documentation certifying "pure" Christian blood for generations, were passed throughout Spain for those desiring to hold public office, enter religious life, obtain positions with the Inquisition, or emigrate to New Spain (modern-day Mexico and South and Central America, along with the Caribbean, Florida, and parts of the southwestern United States).[100] The Franciscan friar Alonso de Espina in 1460 published the book *Fortalitium fidei contra Judaeos*, which reported on the transgressions of *conversos* and called for legal action against them.

Conversos, like most Spaniards, lived complex lives. Some were dedicated Catholics, and others masqueraded as Catholics while secretly living as Muslims or Jews, but "many of them existed in an in-between space, not clearly one thing or another, and not necessarily maintaining their attitudes over the course of a lifetime."[101]

When King Fernando and Queen Isabel visited Seville in 1477, they heard the preaching of the Dominican Alonso de Hojeda, who highlighted the *converso* issue and the problem it created in Spanish society. Soon afterward, the monarchs initiated action to solve the *converso* situation and unify the nation. Cardinal Pedro Gonzales de Mendoza was commissioned to petition Pope Sixtus IV (r. 1471–1484) to establish an inquisition in Spain. In the bull *Exigit Sincerae Devotionis Affectus*, promulgated on November 1, 1478, Sixtus granted authority to the Spanish crown to appoint inquisitors to deal with

> many of those who of their own accord were born anew in Christ in the sacred waters of baptism, while continuing to comport themselves externally as Christians, yet have secretly adopted or returned to the religious observances and customs of the Jews, and are living according to the principles and ordinances of Judaical superstition and falsehood, thus falling away from the true orthodox faith, its worship, and belief in its doctrines.[102]

The monarchs appointed the Dominicans Miguel de Morillo and Juan de San Matín as the first inquisitors in Spain.

Power of appointment and dismal of inquisitors rested with the monarchy and not the pope; therefore, the Spanish Inquisition was an organ of the state and used by the crown for its own purposes. It truly was a *Spanish* inquisition and not an *ecclesial* inquisition *in Spain.* Politics, more than religion, drove the creation of the Spanish Inquisition as Fernando and Isabel used the organization to preserve national security and consolidate royal power within their kingdom.

The Spanish Inquisition was created in 1478 and existed in various stages until 1834, so its focus developed and changed through the centuries. The first stage (1480–1525) witnessed the establishment of the organization in several important urban areas (in fact, an individual living in regional areas could possibly never see an inquisitor or have any interaction with the tribunal[103]) and focused on "Judaizing" *conversos.* Most of the cases brought before the Inquisition in its history—and most of the cases that resulted in *relaxation* (or remanding) to the secular authorities and implementation of the death penalty—occurred in this first stage.[104]

The second period (1525–1630) occurred during the rise of Protestantism, and incidents involving "Lutheranism" dominated the case load. During this stage, inquisitors developed a list of errors identifying Protestants, which included denial of purgatory, opposition to the veneration of the Blessed Virgin Mary and the saints, ridicule of the pope, disapproval of clerical celibacy, refusal to confess sins to a priest, lack of fasting during Lent, and denial of the real presence of Christ in the Eucharist.[105] Additionally, this stage witnessed a shift from finding and dealing with *conversos* to focusing on the morality of all Spanish Christians. Deviance from Catholic moral teachings such as bigamy, sodomy, fornication, and solicitation in the confessional, as well as doctrinal errors involving blasphemy and superstitious beliefs and practices, were subject to inquisitorial authority.

Christians accused before the Inquisition were asked to make the sign of the cross and recite four basic prayers (the Creed, Our Father, Hail Mary, and Hail Holy Queen). The inquisitors found that only 40 percent of people before 1555 could recite all four prayers; by 1572, that percentage had increased to 72 percent, and by 1600, it was 82 percent, which provides evidence of the catechetical influence of the Inquisition in Spanish society.[106]

As the Inquisition entered the third (1630–1715) and fourth (1725–1834) periods, the number of cases dropped significantly and mostly concerned Portuguese *conversos* (in the third stage) and those embracing Enlightenment ideals and Freemasonry (fourth stage).

The Spanish Inquisition had authority only over Christians and was not used to persecute practicing Jewish people and Muslims. Inquisitors focused on eliciting an admission of guilt of the sin of heresy through the accused's confession, which, if accompanied by contrition, resulted in the imposition of a penance. As an organ of royal power, the various inquisitorial tribunals were overseen by the Council or *Suprema*, which consisted of six members appointed by the king. In the mid-sixteenth century, a member of the *Suprema* was of Old Christian ancestry, was a member of the minor nobility, was educated in law, and had prior experience as an inquisitor.[107] Located in Madrid, the *Suprema* issued edicts, provided instructions to the tribunals in Castile and Aragon, answered questions from inquisitors, ruled on petitions from the accused, and heard appeals.[108] The inquisitor general, nominated by the monarch and appointed by the pope, presided over the *Suprema* and was usually a member of the episcopacy. The tribunals consisted of three inquisitors, each of whom was at least thirty-five years old, a priest, usually a native of Castile, and university-educated and trained in law rather than theology, and who served an average of five years.[109]

The duties of a typical inquisitor were numerous. He supervised a staff; wrote edicts; reviewed case material; questioned witnesses and the accused; and passed judgment on whether cases had been fully proved, partially proved, or not proved.[110] Assisting the inquisitor were notaries, assessors, constables, wardens, and a quartermaster. Additionally, the prosecutor or *promotor fiscal* interviewed witnesses and prepared and argued the case before the inquisitors. The accused was provided a defense counsel or *procurador* upon request, but the defense worked for the tribunal, not the prisoner, and was technically required to inform the inquisitors if he believed that the accused was guilty, although in practice, that rarely occurred.[111]

A host of local officials assisted the tribunal. Those laymen who acted as messengers and informers for the tribunal were known as *familiares*, and those who initiated investigations, interviewed witnesses, and kept records were known as commissioners (*comisarios*). In the beginning, inquisitors were itinerant, but by 1495, tribunals were established in sixteen locations (twelve in Castile and four in Aragon) and continued as an urban institution for the remainder of the Inquisition's history.

Spanish inquisitors operated under similar procedures as the medieval papal inquisitors in previous centuries. Official instructions and procedures (*ordenanzas*) were created by the inquisitor general. The first set of *ordenanzas* was issued in 1484 by the Dominican Tomás de Torquemada (1420–1498), who has served as the evil poster child of the Spanish Inquisition and been portrayed historically inaccurately, albeit humorously, by the comedian Mel Brooks in his 1981 film *History of the World, Part I.*

Torquemada, a Dominican, came from a distinguished family and was appointed inquisitor general in 1483. His uncle was a famous Dominican who had served as Master of Palace (the papal theologian), attended the Council of Florence, been created a cardinal, and given the title "Defender of the Faith" by Pope Eugenius IV.[112] Torquemada, despite the Enlightened historical depictions as an intolerant zealot, was "energetic and fearless, a strict disciplinarian, but respected by all his subordinates, not only because he was deemed just, but because he was even stricter with himself than with others."[113] He practiced self-mortification and penances, loved solitude and a good book, and was a student of architecture. Known for his piety, Torquemada became confessor to Queen Isabel, against his wishes. He refused all attempts to make him a bishop and a cardinal and never desired the post of inquisitor general, but when chosen, he performed his duties admirably.

As inquisitor general, Torquemada issued a set of procedures that remained in use for seventy years, along with a series of reform measures that included the limited use of torture, improved inquisitorial prisons with better food and conditions, and requirement for the testimony of at least two witnesses before launching an official investigation of a person. Torquemada wanted his inquisitors to be "cautious, circumspect, and charitable" and to "seek nothing but the truth."[114]

Enlightenment intellectuals and historians crafted an image of a bloody tyrant who brought hundreds of thousands of Spaniards before the Inquisition for torture at the hands of sadistic monks who, when finished with their bloodletting, executed the poor free-thinking individuals who dared disobey the Catholic Church. But there is no truth to the depiction of Torquemada as "a priest whose heart was closed to every sentiment of mercy, whose lips breathed only death and destruction, and who united the savagery of the hyena with the venom of the snake."[115] Although imperfect, as all men are, Torquemada was a dutiful son of the Church who desired the conversion of the heretic and his share in the beatific vision.

Inquisitors began their work by presenting their credentials to the secular authorities and announcing their presence at a

Sunday or major feast day Mass. At the end of the homily, an inquisitor would raise aloft a crucifix and ask all present to raise their right hands, make the sign of the cross, and take a solemn oath to support the inquisitors, which required denouncement of known or suspected heretics. After this "Edict of Faith," a period of thirty to forty days of self-recrimination, known as the "Edict of Grace," followed. Those who voluntarily confessed their heresy or deviances with proper contrition during this time were reconciled to the Church and given light penances.

After the "Edict of Grace" began the denunciations, where members of the community were required to report known or suspected heretics to the inquisitorial authorities. The names of the denouncers were kept secret from the accused for their protection and their families'. Contrary to the false depictions of inquisitors as zealous searchers of heretics throughout Spain, heretics had more to fear from neighbors, consumed by petty disputes and jealousy, than from the clergy.

A persistent false depiction of a Spanish inquisitor is the cloaked monk working in the shadows, actively seeking heretics and deviants from Church teaching. Although secrecy was an important element in the Spanish Inquisition, it was not utilized nefariously; rather, it was central to the workings of the Inquisition. Inquisitors were required to judge motive and intent, which are often secret, to determine the guilt or innocence of the accused. Additionally, secrecy was important for everyone's safety. The accused were not given the names of hostile witnesses to prevent revenge. Moreover, the accused were arrested secretly and kept clandestinely in inquisitorial prisons, ostensibly for their own protection, so that if the charges were not proved, the accused's reputation remained intact. This rarely happened in practice, however: when a person went "missing" suddenly, it was easy to deduce the reason and his location.[116]

Denunciations led to investigations and the collection of evidence, usually verbal, from witnesses. The evidence was examined by the Inquisition's theological expert, and if heresy was suspected the prosecutor compiled the charges and issued an arrest warrant. The accused was arrested but not informed of the specific charges at that time. Those arrested were taken to a "secret" ecclesiastical jail until their hearing was completed, which could take months or even years.

Jails were not centers of punishment, but rather holding facilities, and it was widely known that ecclesiastical jails boasted better living conditions than their secular counterparts. Indeed, there are records of those accused of secular crimes in secular jails making heretical statements so they could be transferred to the preferable ecclesiastical jails.[117] Inquisitorial prisons, in some cases, allowed minor children to remain with incarcerated parents, and they provided basic medical care, a priest confessor, and a barber. The accused's goods were confiscated and inventoried and were used by the Inquisition to fund the accused's food and expenses during their incarceration. If the charges were not proved, the goods and property were returned. However, those accused who were reconciled or relaxed to the secular authorities lost their goods and property to the Inquisition, which again used the resources to fund its operations. This practice led to the false charge that the Inquisition targeted affluent individuals.

After the arrest, the accused were interrogated on three separate occasions, where they were asked to provide their family background, a statement of life (*discurso de la vida*), and testimony of any foreign travel and to answer basic questions about the Faith. After the initial interview, the accused were asked to answer the specific charges and provided a defense counsel if requested.

Once the trial commenced, the accused were read the formal accusations and required to answer them. Charges were developed using information obtained from witnesses, oftentimes family members, with no statute of limitations. In 1483, Juan de Chincilla confessed to Jewish practices before the time of the Inquisition. His coworkers' testimony indicated that he seemed a practicing Catholic, but other witnesses provided credible evidence of Judaizing nearly twenty years in the past.[118]

A significant difference between the procedures of the medieval papal inquisitors and those of the Spanish Inquisition was the allowance of a defense counsel to aid the accused. The defense counsel helped the accused answer the charges in writing and develop a list of favorable witnesses who could testify to the good Christian character of the accused. Another defense tactic was to disable hostile witnesses by providing a list of people who had grievances against the accused. Gasper Torralba in 1531 provided the Inquisition a list of 152 enemies. Most of the thirty-five witnesses who had provided testimony against Gasper to the Inquisition were on his list, so he received a light penitential sentence.[119] Another common defense tactic was to claim extenuating circumstances such as drunkenness, insanity, or youthfulness.

If the accused refused repeated opportunities to confess despite a preponderance of evidence of guilt, a torture session might be authorized—but it required a vote by the inquisitors and their consultants. Torture was a common legal technique in Europe for centuries. The use of torture was debated, and some inquisitors did not utilize the technique. Safeguards were enacted to ensure that torture was never used just to punish someone for "thinking differently," but rather as a means to elicit the truth.

When a torture session was approved, the accused was first shown the instruments of torture, in the hope that the mere sight would result in a confession. Torture was supposed to be used only once, although inquisitors developed a work-around to that restriction by "suspending" a session and resuming it later. The *Suprema* partially closed that loophole by limiting the number of suspensions to three, and after 1625, any torture session had to be authorized by the *Suprema*.[120]

Despite the myths associated with the Spanish Inquisition and the portrayal of inquisitors as sadistic torturers, the method was rarely used, limited in duration, and never inflicted by the inquisitors, but rather by a secular official. Multiple individuals attended a torture session, including a physician and a representative of the local bishop. A notary carefully recorded the sessions, annotating the questions asked and answered. Confession under torture was considered under duress, so a free-willed confession was required the day after a completed session—with no threat of resumption—for its use in the inquisitorial proceeding. Torture could not result in the loss of life or limb, and the methods utilized could not break the skin of the accused.

Methods that accommodated the restriction against shedding blood included stretching (*garrucha* or *strappado*), where the accused was hung by the wrists from a pulley on the ceiling with weights attached to the feet, which allowed for raising and suddenly dropping the individual. This jerking motion stretched the body and could result in the dislocation of arms and legs. Another method included water (*toca*), where a person was tied to a rack with the mouth kept open and a linen cloth put down the throat. Water was then slowly poured from a jar into the mouth, which gave the impression of drowning. Binding (*potro*) was another torture method, whereby the accused was bound tightly with ropes, which were slowly tightened.

Overall, torture was not an effective method of achieving the desired result of a usable confession, and over time, Spanish inquisitors abandoned it.

A jury consisting of inquisitors, representatives of the local ordinary, and legal and theological advisers to the tribunal voted on the guilt or innocence of the accused based on the assembled evidence. Once a verdict was reached, the same group voted on a sentence, which was issued either privately or publicly. Public sentencing occurred at an *auto de fe*, which consisted of a procession of the penitents, dressed in specific garments, carrying large wax candles to a large public space in the town. Mass was celebrated, after which the sentences were read aloud. This public spectacle was designed to celebrate the repentance of the contrite, reinforce the Faith publicly, and serve as a warning against obstinate heresy.

Many people associate the *auto de fe* with execution—specifically burning at the stake—but executions were not conducted during the *auto de fe*. Rather, they were usually held outside the city limits upon completion of the ceremony. These affairs were expensive and required significant planning and logistical efforts, so by the eighteenth century, they had become once-in-a-lifetime events.

Various sentences were possible in a case brought before the Inquisition. If the evidence did not prove the case, and the accused confessed to no wrongdoing, a sentence of *acquitted* or *suspended* could result. A suspended sentence released the accused from the Inquisition's jail, but with the prospect of further prosecution if additional future evidence warranted it.

Most individuals (80 percent of all accused) brought before the Spanish Inquisition received penance as a sentence, which involved either *abjuration* or *reconciliation*.[121] Abjuration was used when the accused confessed to the charges and showed contrition or was deemed partly guilty or proven guilty with only circumstantial evidence. Under this sentence, the accused was required to make a public statement of guilt and express contrition and received a penance of religious education, fines, flogging, or exile.[122] Reconciliation was utilized when the guilt of the accused was more fully proved and the crime more serious. Penalties under this sentence involved permanent seizure of possessions, fines, flogging (more lashes than abjuration), banishment and exile, or galley service in the Spanish navy (usually reserved for those convicted of bigamy and sodomy). Additional punishments comprised prison time—which was rarely literally observed and instead involved incarceration in a house, monastery, or hospital—and the wearing of the *sanbenito.* The *sanbenito* was a yellow garment painted with one or two crosses (usually a St. Andrew's or diagonal cross), on the front and back.[123] Obstinate heretics sentenced to reconciliation or relaxation to the secular arm also wore the *coroza*, or a conical paper hat.[124] Penitents were required to wear the *sanbenito* to the *auto de fe* and sometimes for a specified period of time (a few months to life) afterward. When the penitential time was over, the *sanbenito* was hung on the wall of the guilty party's parish church with his name and crime written on it; some garments remained displayed until the mid-1700s![125]

Heresy was viewed as an individual and communal sin in Christendom, so the Inquisition often branded the families of convicted or relapsed heretics as "infamous." This punishment prevented the heretic's family members and descendants from holding public office, carrying weapons, riding horses, possessing various luxury items, and seeking ordination in the Church.[126]

The goal of the Spanish inquisitors was confession and reconciliation of the accused, but since heresy was both an ecclesial and secular crime, and canon law forbade the use of the death penalty by ecclesial courts, obstinate heretics who refused multiple opportunities to recant and confess were relaxed to the secular authorities. Heresy was a capital crime in secular law, so obstinate heretics received the death penalty and were usually executed by burning at the stake.

Enlightened critics of the Church have grossly exaggerated the numbers of those relaxed to the secular arm by Spanish inquisitors. (These exaggerations continue to this day.) It serves the false narrative and myths of these enemies of the Church to inflate the death numbers to genocidal levels. Juan Antonio Llorente provided a number of 300,000 killed in his *Critical History of the Inquisition in Spain*. Other critics, including those in the modern world, cite numbers in the thousands, ten-thousands, and hundred-thousands.[127]

The numbers of those actually relaxed to the secular authorities varied greatly in the various stages of the existence of the Spanish Inquisition, with most cases occurring in the first stage (1480-1520) and averaging around forty per year, for a total of around 2,000 persons.[128] One twentieth-century historical study concluded that less than 2 percent of cases resulted in relaxation to the secular arm—which is to say that nearly 98 percent of cases did *not* result in the death of the accused.[129] The last recorded death sentence for heresy in Spain occurred in 1781, when Dolores of Seville was executed by the secular authorities upon relaxation because she claimed (and refused to recant) belief in a personal apparition of the Blessed Virgin Mary and the ability to release one million souls from purgatory.[130] In summary, "the Spanish Inquisition was not a benign, sympathetic institution; nor was it a vicious bloodbath."[131]

Although the Enlightened historical attack depicts the Spanish Inquisition as an intolerant, bloodthirsty institution, there were more killings of criminals in England during the sixteenth and seventeenth centuries than in Spain. English courts sentenced 750 criminals to death by hanging from 1530 to 1630.[132] Moreover, the number of crimes punishable by the death penalty in England actually increased during the time of the Enlightenment, from fifty in 1688 to 160 in 1765 to 225 in 1815.[133]

The Spanish Inquisition was not a perfect organization, nor were its inquisitors saints, but the historical record does illustrate that the Inquisition strove for justice, followed the legal procedures of the age, and reformed itself when abuses arose. Most inquisitors exercised their duties faithfully and justly. Those who abused their office and its attendant privileges were removed and replaced, and when news of malfeasance reached Rome, numerous popes attempted to intervene but were rebuffed by the Spanish monarchy.

Although most Spaniards supported the repression of heresy, there were some individuals who criticized the Inquisition for its harsh measures, especially the wearing of the *sanbenito*, which was especially despised. Some Spanish clerics thought the Inquisition should focus on catechesis rather than investigation of heresy. However, criticism of the Inquisition's existence and operation was a minority opinion, as most Spaniards supported the institution due to prejudices against *conversos*. Some even used the Inquisition for their own purposes to gain social or religious legitimacy; settle personal quarrels; or challenge political, economic, and social rivals.[134]

Heresy breeds disunity and violence, which is why secular rulers from the earliest centuries of the Church were concerned with erroneous teachings. Christendom was engulfed in a century of violence (1550-1650) as a result of the heretical teachings of the Protestant "reformers," as nearly every area witnessed death and destruction on a grand scale. But the establishment of the Spanish Inquisition preserved Spain from the ravages of these religious wars, which, again, consumed the rest of Europe in the sixteenth and seventeenth centuries.

Despite Enlightened myths and false narratives to the contrary, the Spanish Inquisition was not a despotic institution imposed by the pope or the Church. Nor did it suppress scientific progress or learning or culture. Rather, the Inquisition was created by the Spanish monarchy to deal with a unique social and political situation, and it did not reveal Spain as a backwater, uncivilized, and superstitious nation. Instead, modern historical research has thoroughly discredited the Enlightened historical attack against the Inquisition, its inquisitors, and the Church. Indeed, "the Spanish Inquisition was a far less repressive instrument of ideological control than had hitherto been thought," and "torture and the death penalty were only rarely applied—almost exclusively during the first two decades of its existence. By comparison, other European countries, including England, France, and Germany, continued to burn heretics until well into the seventeenth century."[135]

The diligent work of scholars notwithstanding, popular understanding of the Spanish Inquisition remains influenced by the Enlightenment historical attack—and so the modern world continues to cancel the Catholic inquisitors of Spain.

Chapter 2

Protestant History

[When] the efforts of the Reformers dashed themselves in vain against the strong ramparts of Catholic dogma, they had recourse to a new strategy—namely, encountering the Church in the field of historical questions.[136]

—Pope Leo XIII

The Protestant revolutionaries in the sixteenth century used history as a weapon against the Catholic Church to justify their own erroneous theological positions.

The renegade priest and monk Martin Luther (1480-1546) wrote the first of his three most important treatises in the summer of 1520. In his *Appeal to the Christian Nobility of the German Nation*, Luther made many absurd claims, among them allegations about Church history, especially ecumenical councils. Advocating for the heresy of *conciliarism*—the belief that supreme authority in the Church resides with the bishops assembled in an ecumenical council rather than with the supreme pontiff—Luther argued that "the Council of Nicaea, the most famous of all councils, was neither called nor confirmed by the bishop of Rome, but by the emperor Constantine."[137]

It is true that Constantine issued the invitation for bishops to assemble at Nicaea to discuss the Arian heresy but Pope

St. Sylvester I (r. 314-335) sent two Roman priests, Victor and Vincent, as his legates and appointed Hosius of Cordoba to oversee the proceedings.

Luther was not the only Protestant to attack the people and events of Church history. John Calvin (1509–1564), in his *Institutes of the Christian Religion*, commented on the writings of the early Church Father St. Ignatius of Antioch (d. 115). Arrested by order of the emperor Trajan and transported to Rome for execution, Ignatius wrote seven letters to various Christian communities and individuals. His letters clearly illustrate that the early Church was the Catholic Church, with the same organization, practices, and beliefs. However, Calvin believed that the Catholic Church was a corruption of the early Church and that his rebellion was returning the Christian faith to its early state. When commenting on Ignatius's letters, Calvin quipped that there is nothing "more disgusting than the fairy tales published under the name of Ignatius."[138]

The Protestant Revolt was predicated on falsifying the historical record to justify the actions of those who sought to destroy the unity of Christendom. Understanding the Protestant historical attack against the Catholic Church requires comprehending the movement that spawned one of history's most destructive and destabilizing rebellions.

The Protestant movement was a religious and political revolution that swept through Europe in the sixteenth and seventeenth centuries. Catholic historians have long recognized the revolutionary aspects, but other historians, and even Protestant ones, have also described the sixteenth-century movement this way. Indeed, Martin Luther never called himself a reformer; rather, "he called himself preacher, doctor, or professor and was all of these. Yet he never presumed to be a reformer, nor did he ever claim his movement to be the 'Reformation.'"[139]

The Protestant Revolution focused on a rejection of Church, specifically papal, authority and the destruction of the entire sacerdotal and sacramental system. The movement was marked by two phases: internal and external.[140] Initially, the Protestant movement was an internal event, marked by intense religious discussions within Christendom. However, the religious discussions soon intertwined with political considerations, and what began as an internal movement took on larger implications. Secular rulers saw the movement as an opportunity to strengthen their authority against the Church and as a means to appropriate Church wealth. Externally, the movement developed a new culture, worship, and way of life separate from the Catholic world of Christendom. The unity of the Church was shattered, and the concept of Christendom was cleaved. As with previous heresies, violence followed the religious discussions so that "what began as a sort of spiritual family quarrel and continued as a spiritual civil war was soon accompanied by an actual civil war in arms."[141] Warfare engulfed Europe for a century because of the Protestant Revolution, and the ensuing conflicts radically changed the political, economic, and religious landscape of Christendom.

The Protestant movement did not originate in a vacuum; it was the result of several contributing factors that coalesced in the early sixteenth century. A major factor was the status of the papacy, which suffered from a lack of respect and prestige because of the Avignon Papacy (1309–1378), where the popes lived in southern France, which was followed by the Great Western Schism (1378–1417), when multiple men claimed to be the pope. Resentment against the papacy grew in areas without strong central governing authority, especially German territories. Additionally, secular rulers viewed themselves as independent of the papacy and, in some cases, tried to control the Church in their territory. Secular rulers were envious of

Church lands and wealth, and the flow of funds to the Roman Curia contributed to a growing bitterness against the authority of the papacy.

By the sixteenth century, numerous ecclesiastical abuses had infected the Church. Simony, or the buying and selling of Church offices, was an issue in previous centuries and had been addressed, but the abuse had become prevalent again. Heavy taxes, including annates, or the annual revenue from a diocese provided by a newly ordained or installed bishop to Rome, were a source of angst. Bishops, in order to pay the fees, heavily indebted their dioceses through loans from banking families or participated in another abuse known as pluralism, which is holding more than one diocese. Nepotism was also an issue, especially among the so-called Renaissance popes, who stocked the Roman Curia with relatives in an attempt to maintain family control over the papacy and the Church.[142]

Another ecclesiastical abuse that contributed to a weakening of Church authority was absenteeism, where a bishop did not reside in or was absent for long periods from his diocese. Absenteeism was, in part, an outgrowth of the abuse of pluralism, since a bishop cannot be in two places at once. This abuse wreaked havoc on the sacramental life of the Church, and the Catholic faithful suffered its effects. Some dioceses did not have a resident bishop for nearly a hundred years, and in one case, a bishop entered his diocese for the first time at his funeral![143]

Abuses were not the exclusive domain of bishops. Generally, the Catholic clergy were in difficult straits, although there were exceptions. Many priests flouted their promise of celibacy and lived openly with mistresses. Additionally, training for the priesthood was not uniform throughout the Church, and many clergy were ill formed for the tasks of ministry.

Many people saw the evil of the abuses and the need for Church reform. Vernacular writers such as Dante (1265–1321),

Chaucer (1343–1400), and Erasmus (1466–1536) evoked the spirit of the age by parodying clergy in their writings. The Church attempted a reform movement at the beginning of the sixteenth century, when Pope Julius II (r. 1503–1513) called the ecumenical Fifth Lateran Council (1512–1517). This council produced several reform decrees, but its work was ultimately too little, too late, as it ended only seven months before Martin Luther published his Ninety-five Theses in October.

One factor that contributed to the growth of the Protestant movement, especially the speed of its advance and its ultimate success, was technology. The printing press had been invented previously, but in the fifteenth century, Johannes Gutenberg perfected the instrument by creating printing by metal moveable type, which led to a rapid expansion in publishing houses throughout Europe. By the end of the fifteenth century, sixty of the hundred largest cities in Europe had a press, and publishing was an extremely popular endeavor in German territory.[144]

The Church also utilized this popular machine and was "one of the biggest early customers of printing,"[145] but Protestants, especially Luther and his supporters, did it best. Luther was a prolific writer, and his ideas and thoughts spread rapidly throughout Christendom, achieving far greater success than otherwise possible. The importance of the printing press to the Protestant Revolt cannot be overstated. Towns and cities with printing presses operating before 1530 were fifty-two percent more likely to join the Protestant rebellion than those urban areas without presses.[146]

Other factors also contributed to the success of the Protestant movement, such as the fractured constitution of German territories and the nominal power of the Holy Roman Emperor. German rulers' deep resentment against Rome and papal taxes, and the writings of anti-papal German nationalists like Ulrich von Hutton (1488–1523), provided fertile ground for rebellious teachings. Nobles' greed for Church lands and wealth also fueled the success of the movement. Finally, the military activity of the Ottoman Turks, who threatened the southern borders of the Holy Roman Empire throughout the early stages of the crisis, also contributed. Emperor Charles V focused his efforts and energy on meeting the Turkish threat rather than on dealing swiftly and effectively with Luther's heresy and the revolt of the northern German princes. A large Ottoman army even made its way to the gates of Vienna in 1529, during the height of the Protestant rebellion. The Turkish siege at the gateway to Europe was broken, but the Ottomans' constant provocation was a disturbance that helped the Protestant movement gain ground. In essence, as G.K. Chesterton fittingly opined, the Protestant uprising "was a Christian mutiny during a Muslim invasion."[147]

The Protestant movement impacted Christendom politically, socially, economically, and spiritually. Similar to previous heresies, it also spawned violence, destruction, and death.

Perhaps one of the revolution's most lingering impacts, no less dangerous and insidious than changes in political boundaries and the isolation of the soul from a united Christian community, is the creation of a dominant false historical narrative. History, especially in the English-speaking world, is presented from a Protestant perspective in the written and visual form. Textbooks and movies exhibiting a Protestant and anti-Catholic bias are considered objective, whereas history from a Catholic perspective is labeled prejudicial and false.

Despite the diligent work of serious scholars over the past generation, the Protestant presentation of history remains foremost in the modern Western mind. The Protestant historical attack is especially evident in the canceling of three prominent figures: the Roman emperor Constantine, Queen Mary Tudor of England, and Catholic loyalist Guy Fawkes.

Constantine

> *Constantine has been a whipping boy for a long time, and still is today. In popular culture (Dan Brown, Da Vinci Code), among bestselling historians (James Carroll, Constantine's Sword), and among theologians (Stanley Hauerwas, John Howard Yoder, and their followers), his name is identified with tyranny, antisemitism, hypocrisy, apostasy, and heresy. He was a hardened power-politician who never really became Christian, a hypocrite who harnessed the energy of the Church for his own political ends, a murderer, a usurper, an egotist.*[148]

The Roman Empire experienced an overwhelming political crisis in the third century. From the first to the second centuries, political stability was the order of the imperial day, as the empire was governed by only fourteen emperors. An average imperial reign was thirteen years. However, from the end of the second to the end of the third century, there were seventy emperors—an average imperial reign of eighteen months![149] The result was a shift in imperial origins in the latter centuries of the Roman Empire as "soldier-emperors," mostly from the Balkans, took the purple.

Before the adjustment in the birthplace of emperors came a more significant change—an administrative one that reshaped the ancient and formed the modern world. Diocles, a thirty-eight-year-old soldier-administrator, ascended the imperial throne in A.D. 284. As emperor, Diocles changed his name to Gaius Aurelius Valerius Diocletianus and is known in history as Diocletian.

As the son of slaves (his father rose to be a freeman), Diocletian was man familiar with the necessity of hard work and sacrifice. He joined the army and was known as a great administrator who loved the imperial traditions of Rome and earnestly desired to return the empire to its former strength and glory. Diocletian lived a unique imperial life. He did not consume alcohol, he did not keep mistresses, and he did not spend money extravagantly. He ran the imperial court like his army headquarters, establishing a multi-layered bureaucracy with strict ceremonies and rituals. Very few people were granted audiences, and those who did were required either to prostrate themselves before him or to stand while the emperor remained seated.[150]

Diocletian made a decision in the late third century that made a lasting impact on the empire, the Church, and the world. He recognized that the expanse of the Roman Empire made it virtually ungovernable, especially for one man. So he divided the empire into eastern (Greece, Asia Minor, the Holy Land, and Egypt) and western (Europe and parts of North Africa) halves, with a total of twelve regional jurisdictions, known as "dioceses" after the emperor. Vicars ruled the dioceses with the assistance of a large imperial bureaucracy. Diocletian also established the *tetrarchy*—a political structure designed to provide a smooth transition of power upon the death of the emperor. The tetrarchy was based on four rulers of the empire, with two emperors (*augusti*), one for each half of the empire, and two Caesars, who acted as deputies to the *augusti*. At the death of an emperor, his Caesar automatically became emperor and then appointed a new Caesar. The system was designed to prevent the recurrent civil wars that had plagued the empire during the previous century.

Diocletian ruled the eastern half of the empire and appointed Galerius as his Caesar. In the west, Diocletian's friend Maximian was named emperor, with Constantius his Caesar.

Another aspect of Diocletian's reign was the absence of emperors from Rome. Diocletian chose to live in Nicomedia and visited the Eternal City only once, during the celebration of his twentieth anniversary as emperor. Galerius resided in Sirmium (modern-day Serbia). In the west, Maximian lived in Milan, and his Caesar, Constantius, lived in Trier (modern-day Germany). Rome, the ancient capital, was discarded as an imperial residence but retained influence due to the presence of the Senate and its large population.

For most of his imperial reign, Diocletian focused on administrative and political matters and did not concern himself with the supposedly seditious Christians, who desired imperial indifference. That posture changed early in the fourth century, when the emperor issued a series of oppressive edicts designed to eliminate the Church.

Galerius had influenced Diocletian to initiate what became known as the Great Persecution because of a military readiness problem with the eastern legions. Some Christians in the east refused military service, which caused a manpower shortage in the army. Christians in the army refused to sacrifice to the pagan gods before battle per legion custom and tradition. This angered pagan soldiers and impacted unit morale and cohesiveness.

Diocletian issued the first edict of persecution on February 23, 303, ordering the closing of Christian churches and the surrender of manuscripts of Scripture for destruction. Additionally, Christians, even if Roman citizens, were not allowed the right to answer legal charges against them or to initiate legal action against those who attacked them.[151]

Soon after the edict's promulgation, a fire erupted in the imperial palace at Nicomedia, which was blamed on the Christians and resulted in several martyrdoms.[152] (It was likely caused by a lightning strike.) Later edicts mandated imprisonment for Catholic clergy and then their torture and execution. A final edict in the year 304 required all Romans to sacrifice to the pagan gods. Persecution of the Church was intense and widespread in the eastern empire but infrequent in the west since Constantius, the western emperor, did not enthusiastically implement the edicts.

The Church suffered mightily during the Great Persecution, but it survived and later thrived. Diocletian became the first Roman emperor to voluntarily abdicate when he retired to his cabbage farm in Dalmatia in 305. Galerius became the eastern emperor and reigned for a few years until he died from the effects of venereal disease. The western emperor, Constantius, was near death and requested the presence of his son, Constantine, who was, in effect, an imperial hostage, in Nicomedia. The dutiful son escaped the east and arrived in Britain, where the legions declared him emperor upon the death of his father. That acclamation altered the course of ecclesial and world events and established the reign of one of the most important Roman emperors in history.

Constantine is one of the most enigmatic figures in history. There is no doubt that his influence on secular and ecclesial events was immense, but opinions vary on who he actually was and why he made certain decisions.

Constantine is viewed as the initiator of the Great Apostasy that created the Catholic Church and kept the authentic Christian faith hidden for more than a millennium. He is also seen as an evil tyrant and a lukewarm Christian sympathizer who used the Church for selfish political goals. Perhaps he was an authentic Christian, "gripped with a profound confidence that God had anointed and appointed him to ensure the expansion of the gospel to the Roman world and beyond."[153]

Although there are bountiful interpretations of Constantine and his historical impact, perhaps the one that best illustrates the use of Constantine as a scapegoat in the Protestant historical attack is the belief in *Constantinianism*. Advocated by the Mennonite theologian John Howard Yoder (1927-1997), Constantinianism "refers to a theology and ecclesial practice that took form when the Church assumed a dominant position in Roman society," which is summarized as the "wedding of piety to power."[154] This belief uses Constantine to imagine a pre-Constantine church that was anti-imperial but became pro-imperial with Constantine's conversion.

Protestant adherents of Constantinianism believe that Constantine united politics and the Church, which ended ecclesial independence and produced a subservient Church that composed its teachings at the behest of its secular master. The Church embraced anti-Christian ideas such as justified violence and military service, which it had previously rejected (supposedly).[155]

Constantine's reign marks a shift in ecclesiology, as the Church's new social status within the empire turned it from a church of martyrs ready to suffer violence for the sake of Christ to a church of warriors ready to engage in violence for the glory of Christ.[156] Allegedly, this fundamental change in the Church remains today and infects ordinary Christians who compromise with the secular world.

These various interpretations of Constantine place significant influence on one, albeit very powerful, fourth-century man. So who was Constantine, and how did he view his relationship with the Church?

The odds were not in favor of Constantine winning the struggle for control of the western Roman Empire at the beginning of the fourth century. His chief rival for the throne, Maxentius, was safely entrenched behind the walls of Rome with a large army nearly twice the number of troops Constantine could muster. Against the advice of his generals, Constantine marched the legions from Britain through Gaul (modern-day France) and into Italy to battle Maxentius.

While Constantine marched through Gaul, a miraculous event occurred that changed his life. Constantine and his army witnessed a cross appearing suddenly in the sky with the words *hoc signo victor eris* (by this sign you will be victor) around it.[157] Constantine interpreted this sign as favor from the Christian God and a harbinger of good news in his upcoming battle.

The heavenly sign prompted Constantine to order the painting of the *chi rho*, the Greek monogram formed from the first two letters for the word Christ in Greek, on their shields. Constantine wore the chi rho on his helmet.[158] Additionally, Constantine ordered the creation of the *labarum*, a golden and jeweled cross with a square piece of purple cloth with the chi rho in the center. The chi rho became extremely popular after Constantine's usage, and reproductions of it are found everywhere in the Roman world from the fourth century onward. (Indeed, it is still used in Catholic churches and on liturgical vestments today.)

The adoption of a Christian symbol by a Roman army marked a significant turning point in the history of the Church. Previously, the Roman army was the instrument of state persecution of the Church, of the killing of thousands of Christians. Now Roman troops marched to battle against a rival with the sign of Christ on their shields because of a miraculous sign!

The armies of Constantine and Maxentius clashed in the Battle of the Milvian Bridge on October 28, 312. Maxentius committed a major tactical blunder by leaving his fortified position behind the walls of Rome to engage Constantine's forces across the Tiber River. His troops traveled over a wooden pontoon bridge across the river since the stone bridge in that area, known as the Milvian Bridge, had been partially destroyed to prevent its use by the invading army. The armies engaged in combat, and Constantine proved the better general. Maxentius arrayed his forces too close to the river, which impeded their ability to maneuver on the battlefield. Maxentius ordered a retreat, but the bridge was not strong enough to support the assembled weight of the heavy cavalry and infantry and collapsed. Maxentius was thrown into the Tiber, where he drowned. His body was later recovered and decapitated and taken into the city by Constantine as a sign of his victory.

The Roman populace welcomed Constantine as a deliverer and recognized him as the sole ruler of the western empire. In a move that signaled a new era, Constantine did not go to the Capitol to offer sacrifice to the pagan gods in thanksgiving for his victory. Instead, he attributed his victory over Maxentius to the intercession of the Christian God and showed his gratitude by favoring the Church and receiving instruction in the Faith under the spiritual guidance of Bishop Hosius of Cordoba (257–358).

Constantine became a catechumen but did not receive baptism until he was on his deathbed in 337. His conversion was personal and not imperial: "He approved if his subjects joined him in his faith, but they were far more important to him as subjects."[159] His primary goal was the accumulation and exercise of power, and even his newfound faith and the Church were instruments in accomplishing that goal. Although he was truly grateful for his victory over Maxentius, Constantine viewed the Church as the institution he could use to bring unity and reform to the empire. His ambition was not sated with ruling the western empire; he wanted to rule a united empire. Constantine's vision of the Church and his involvement in its internal affairs became known as *caesaro-papism*—where the emperor reigned supreme in both the temporal and spiritual realms.

Constantine legislated Christian morality as a sign of thanksgiving for his victory, and possibly also because of his new beliefs. Crucifixion was outlawed, gladiatorial games were suspended, temple prostitution was ended, and chastity laws were enacted. Additionally, the ancient pagan *paterfamilias* custom, in which a Roman father was able to reject any child born in the household by refusing to hold the infant after birth, upon which the infant was exposed outside the city walls and left to die, was banned.[160]

Although Constantine favored the Church, paganism remained, and Constantine served in the traditional imperial role of *Pontifex Maximus*, or "bridge-builder," among the various pagan cults. He granted the Lateran palace, property of his wife Fausta, to the bishop of Rome and built a church on the site for the pope, which became (and still is) the pope's cathedral diocesan church (known as St. John Lateran). The emperor made Sunday a legal holiday in which government offices and businesses were closed. Additionally, the Church was exempt from taxation and received funding from the state.

Constantine also reshaped the imperial bureaucracy by appointing Christians to a majority of the important positions of counsels and prefects.[161] He relied on the bishops of the Church to serve as courts of appeal for civil cases, which made the legal process more efficient, as bishops were known to pass judgments after a single hearing, and were more cost-effective and accessible, as bishops did not charge legal fees and heard appeals from all Roman subjects.[162]

Constantine's newfound faith prompted changes to slavery laws as well. Conditions for slaves were improved as legal protections were provided to keep slave families together. Laws enabling the freedom of slaves were enacted, and the Church was given a prominent role in the manumission of slaves. Constantine did not free Roman slaves, which would have been disastrous for the imperial economy, but he encouraged emancipation.[163]

Constantine's impact on the empire was immediate and influenced by the Christian faith but he did not take his measures solely for the glory of God. "His victory needed to be seen as a victory for the god of Constantine . . . not necessarily as a victory for the Christian god."[164] And although Constantine favored the Church, "he remained deeply concerned with the welfare of *all* his subjects and devoted to the notion that he ruled a well-regulated society where people knew their place, Christians included."[165]

Constantine believed that the Church would assist his dream of a united and peaceful empire, but that goal was shattered early in his reign by events in the Church in North Africa. Roman persecution of the Church resulted not only in the bloodshed of Christians, but also severe disagreement among Christians on how to handle those who "lapsed," or gave in to Roman anti-Christian edicts. The *rigorists* believed that lapsed Christians (known as *lapsi*) must suffer prolonged or permanent excommunication for their actions. Lapsed clerics, according to the rigorists, forfeited their ecclesiastical offices and authority, and any sacraments administered by them were invalid. *Laxists*, on the other hand, believed in the possibility of readmission for the *lapsi* with an expression of contrition and a period of penance.

The issue got imperial attention when a group of rigorists in Carthage objected to their new bishop, Caecilian, whose election they contested because one of his episcopal consecrators was allegedly a *lapsi*. Moreover, the Carthaginian rigorists alleged that Caecilian had collaborated with the Roman authorities during the Great Persecution.[166] This group proceeded to elect its own bishop, Donatus, and appealed to the emperor to solve the conundrum of two men claiming to be bishop of Carthage. Constantine was only too happy to oblige the request, because he did

> not feel free to tolerate or to ignore these scandals, which may provoke the Divinity not only against the human race but against myself. For it is an act of the divine good pleasure which has chosen me to rule the world. Should I provoke him, he may choose another.[167]

When Constantine ruled in favor of Caecilian, the Donatists appealed the decision, which prompted the emperor to turn the case over to the bishop of Rome, Pope St. Miltiades (r. 311–314). The pope convened a meeting in Rome, where Donatus pleaded his case but was rejected. Once again, the Donatists refused to abide by the decision, which forced Constantine to convene a meeting of bishops in Arles, who rejected Donatus's claim to the episcopal see. Rigorists would continue to cause trouble for ecclesial and imperial authorities for the next century.

Shortly after the Donatist controversy, Constantine met with the eastern emperor, Licinius, at Milan for the occasion of Licinius's marriage to Constantia (Constantine's sister). The meeting produced an agreement whereby both emperors recognized a legal right for the existence of the Catholic Church. This agreement is commonly referred to as the *Edict of Milan*, although there was never a single edict jointly issued. Instead, in the summer of 313, Licinius promulgated a letter to the governors of the eastern provinces about his agreement with Constantine at Milan.[168] The Faith was legalized, and the Church's property confiscated during Diocletian's persecution was restored.

Licinius honored the agreement reached at Milan for several years, but then he persecuted Christians in the eastern empire. A few years later, Licinius declared war on Constantine in a bid to become sole emperor. At issue was whether the old ways of Diocletian as followed by Licinius or the new ways of Constantine would prove victorious. The Battle of Adrianople in 324 decided the issue in favor of Constantine, whose army routed the eastern forces. Constantine became sole emperor and ruled as such for the next thirteen years.

Constantine's dream as ruler of the world was realized, so he began a large-scale building campaign of secular and ecclesial buildings. He chose the ancient trading city of Byzantium as his new capital and embarked on a four-year construction program that utilized materials from every part of the empire. Known as New Rome, the majestic city was later renamed Constantinople in honor of the emperor and grew in population and prestige.

Constantine financed the building of churches in Rome and elsewhere. His saintly mother, Helena, traveled to the Holy Land, where she built the original Church of the Holy Sepulchre, and discovered the True Cross.

While Constantine focused on building projects, a bellicose North African priest with dramatic flair engaged in destroying the Faith from within, through his heretical teachings about Christ. Arius tried to answer the question posed by many new Roman converts to the Faith, many of whom had entered the Church from a desire of imperial advancement and favoritism, concerning Jesus' relationship with God the Father. The logical Roman mind struggled with the Christian belief in the co-equal and co-eternal Trinity. Arius believed he had found a solution by declaring that God the Father is only God, and Jesus is the most perfect creature of God, so that there was a time when Jesus did not exist. This false teaching spread among the Roman nobility and army, both groups that desired separation from the simple faith of the common people.

Alexander, bishop of Alexandria, quickly condemned Arius's teachings, which prompted accusation of heresy from Arius against Alexander. The situation in Egypt escalated quickly, and, once more, Constantine stepped into the fray for fear of angering God. The emperor wrote a letter of reprimand to the theological combatants:

> Let each of you, sharing an equal spirit of concession, accept the just advice that your fellow servant offers you. And what is that? You ought not to have raised such questions at all, and if they were raised, not to have answered. For such investigations, which no legal necessity imposes, but the frivolity of an idle hour provokes, we should, even if they are made for the sake of a philosophic exercise, lock up within our hearts and not bring forward into public gathering or entrust imprudently to the ears of the people. . . . Give me back peaceful nights and days without care that I too may keep some pleasure in the pure light and joy of a tranquil life.[169]

Imperial involvement in the Church did not stem from a concern for the truth, but rather from political considerations. Constantine was a consummate politician, and like most political authorities, he was concerned with projecting and maintaining power. He could not suffer infighting in the Church because he believed "that a unified Church was essential to the health of the empire."[170] But when Protestants attack the Church by arguing that Constantine's actions changed the early Church into the Catholic Church, their false narrative attributes theological considerations to the emperor that were simply not present.

Desirous of peace, stability, and unity in the Church, Constantine convened the first ecumenical council to settle definitively the Arian controversy. Nicaea was chosen as the location for the council, which was only twenty-five miles from the imperial palace at Nicomedia. The city was well connected to the vast imperial road network, making it accessible to eastern and western bishops. Constantine planned to attend the council, so a location near Nicomedia was important. Additionally, he planned a twentieth-anniversary celebration of his accession and wanted the bishops to attend the gala after the council proceedings.[171] Every bishop was invited to the council, and to ensure maximum participation, Constantine paid all traveling expenses. Pope St. Sylvester I (r. 314-335) did not attend but approved the council and sent several legates.

Constantine attended the opening session and addressed the assembled bishops, noting his concern for unanimity and peace: "To me, internal division in the Church of God is graver than any war or fierce battle, and these things appear to cause more pain than secular affairs."[172]

The conciliar fathers debated Arius's teachings, which only a small number of bishops openly supported, and eventually declared them heretical. A creed was produced documenting the Church's teachings concerning the Trinity and included the word *consubstantial* (*homoousios* in Greek) to describe the relationship between God the Father and God the Son, despite protestation from several eastern bishops that the word had been condemned at the local council of Antioch in 268 (because Paul of Samosata had used it to support his erroneous teaching on the Trinity). Only two bishops refused to sign the creed, and Constantine exiled them as a result. (Exile was a civil punishment, which the emperor did not hesitate to utilize for a spiritual offense.) The council also mandated the Roman tradition for dating Easter (the Sunday after the first full moon after the spring equinox) and passed a series of disciplinary canons with universal enforcement.

The last day of the council was Constantine's anniversary, and the great banquet was held. The emperor was sated and believed that peace and unity in the Church had been achieved. He was sadly mistaken.

The immediate threat of Arianism subsided when the heretic died in 336, but the crisis plagued the Church for the next several centuries. Constantine soon followed Arius into eternity when he died a year later, on Pentecost Sunday. Baptized by Eusebius of Nicomedia on his deathbed, Constantine wore his white baptismal robes and refused to don the imperial purple.

In the dynastic squabbles after his death, Constantine's two brothers, his sister's husband, and three of his five nephews were killed. The youngest nephew, who survived the bloodbath, eventually became emperor in 361, but he rejected his Christian faith and is known to history as Julian the Apostate. Constantine's three sons divided the empire among themselves, but within fifteen years after the emperor's death, two of his sons died, leaving Constantius II as sole emperor. Constantius reigned for nearly a quarter-century. Whereas his father had used the Church to force unity and peace in the empire, the new emperor embraced Arianism and initiated a terrible persecution of the Nicene bishops, including the Roman pontiff.

Constantine's impact on the Church was immense. At the time of his victory over Maxentius at the Battle of Milvian Bridge in 312, Christians constituted fifteen percent of the imperial population; at his death twenty-five years later, nearly a third of the empire worshiped the Triune God.[173]

Constantine was a complex man, and his actions toward the Church involved more than a simple adherence to Christian doctrine. Despite the false narratives from the Protestant historical attack, Constantine did not "Romanize" the Faith, and he should not be scapegoated as the initiator of the Great Apostasy. Constantine did not embrace "Constantinianism," nor did the Church change its teachings to appease the emperor. Instead, Constantine highly favored the Church and gave it the "freedom to be itself, to erect its own legal structures, to organize its own system of conflict resolutions, to carry out its own sanctions."[174] Constantine meddled in ecclesial affairs, but he did so because of who he was—a politician—and not because he desired to remake the Church in his own image.

Mary Tudor, Queen of England

> *Today, despite the fact that much more is known about her reign, she is still the most maligned and misunderstood of English monarchs. For Mary Tudor, the first queen of England, truth has not been the daughter of time.*[175]

Perhaps no greater calumny has been foisted on a dutiful and devoted daughter of the Church in the English-speaking world than the one that weighs on Mary Tudor. The epitome of the Catholic scapegoat, Mary is mostly known by the disparaging moniker "Bloody." Portrayed as "a cruel, obstinate Catholic bigot who burned heretics and married an unpopular Spanish prince," Mary's contribution to her realm and the Church are completely overshadowed by the false narrative and myths perpetuated by the Protestant enemies of the Church.[176] Even the anniversary of her death is subsumed by the recognition that it was her half-sister Elizabeth's "Accession Day." Although popular with her people, Mary was attacked by Protestant rebels, who crafted the false narrative of this brave and faithful woman.

On the eve of Mary's death, the Scottish heretic John Knox (1514–1572), a disciple of John Calvin, published his treatise "The First Blast of the Trumpet Against the Monstrous Regiment of Women," in which he wrote that during Mary's reign, Englishmen were "compelled to bow their necks under the yoke of Satan, and of his proud ministers, pestilent papists and proud Spaniards."[177] Knox argued that political rule by women was forbidden by natural and divine law. He believed that women are by nature "weak, frail, impatient, feeble, and foolish: and experience hath declared them to be inconsistent, variable, cruel, and lacking the spirit of counsel and regiment."[178] The Protestant apologist John Foxe (1516–1587), in his 1563 book *Actes and Monuments of These Latter and Perillous Dayes*, wrote about Mary's reign, "We shall never find any reign of any prince in this land or any other whichever shows in it (for the proportion of time) so many great arguments of God's wrath and displeasure."[179] Foxe's book, which was placed in every church in England during Queen Elizabeth I's reign, described England in the mid-sixteenth century as "the horrible and bloody time of Queen Mary."[180]

Mary is the quintessential canceled Catholic in the Protestant historical attack. The staying power of the Protestant historical attack on Mary Tudor is illustrated by her appearance in a 2002 survey of the most evil men and women in history![181] Her ultimate "sin" was the restoration of true religion to England and the persecution of Protestant heretics and rebels. Additionally, English secular historians attack and blame her for the loss of Calais, the last English territory on the European Continent. Despite overcoming immense odds to claim the throne, solidifying the monarchy for the Tudor dynasty, and establishing the precedent and legitimacy for sole female monarchical rule in England, she forever remains "Bloody Mary." The real story of Mary Tudor shows a strong, brave, and resilient woman who loved Christ and his Church and dedicated her life to her beloved England.

The Tudor family claimed the English monarchy when the Welsh adventurer Henry Tudor defeated King Richard III (r.

1483–1485) at the Battle of Bosworth Field in the summer of 1485, ending the great Plantagenet line of English kings. The Welshman's battlefield victory solidified his specious claim to the throne, and he reigned as Henry VII for nearly a quarter-century. He died in 1509 and was succeeded by his second son, Henry VIII. As young Henry matured, he was known as a passionate, intelligent, and handsome man, but also impulsive, easily dominated, and lacking in self-restraint.

Tudor England was not well respected or liked by other Europeans. Spanish visitors to the island realm referred to the English as "quarrelsome," an image that remained throughout the sixteenth century.[182]

In the year of his accession, Henry VIII married Catherine of Aragon, dowager princess of Wales and widow of his brother, Arthur. Catherine, the daughter of the powerful Spanish couple King Fernando of Aragon and Queen Isabel of Castile, was twenty-three and Henry seventeen when they married. The couple received a dispensation from Pope Julius II (r. 1503–1513) to overrule a contemporary interpretation of Leviticus 20:21 that marriage to a brother's wife was unlawful. Catherine and Arthur Tudor were fifteen when wedded, and Catherine maintained throughout her life that their union was never consummated.

Catherine was an unselfish, pious young woman with a charming disposition who loved to smile. She was extremely popular and beloved by her English subjects. Seven years passed in the marriage before a healthy child was produced. The princess Mary was born on February 18, 1516, after the couple suffered four miscarriages, one stillbirth, and an infant son who died at two months. The young girl was named after her aunt Mary, sister of the king. At young Mary's baptism, a canopy was held over the baby by four knights of the realm, including Sir Thomas Boleyn, father of the famous Anne.[183]

The young girl, known for her beautiful complexion and amiable personality, lived a privileged life as a king's daughter. Educated from a young age, Mary could write in Latin by age nine and learned French and Spanish, which she could read but not speak well. She enjoyed music and dancing, but her health was not always excellent. "She suffered bouts of illness, heart palpitation, and headaches [and] was exceedingly shortsighted, and was prone to melancholy."[184]

As a young woman, Mary spent large amounts from her privy purse on clothes and jewels. She loved playing cards and throwing dice and engaged in gambling to the point that one third of her income was devoted to the vice.[185] However, Mary was not selfish with her money, as she gave to her friends and to charities and provided alms generously.

When Mary was ten years old, her father fixed his eyes on a young woman at court: Anne Boleyn.

Henry was faithful to Catherine of Aragon for the first decade of their marriage, but after that, he pursued the young ladies at court. Most of these dalliances were temporary, but when the king became infatuated with Anne Boleyn, it set into motion events with dire consequences for centuries.

Unlike Henry's other women, Anne was not content with life as a royal mistress. She desired the queenship. Anne's control over the king was complete, so he ordered his lord chancellor, Thomas Cardinal Wolsey (1473–1530), to seek from Rome an annulment of his marriage to Catherine. Wolsey was confident that Pope Clement VII (r. 1523–1534) would grant the king's request and dispatched Bishop Stephen Gardiner to the Continent. However, Clement had more urgent matters at hand, as imperial troops, comprising a large contingent of Lutheran mercenaries, had sacked Rome. The pope did not rule on the king's marriage at that time but allowed Wolsey to conduct a marriage trial in England to gather evidence in the case, with the final decision reserved to Rome.

The "King's Great Matter" opened proceedings in May 1529, with the entire episcopacy of England present. Never before had a reigning king and queen stood before an ecclesiastical court on the state of their marriage, with one asking for a decree of nullity and the other for affirmation of the bond. The following month, Archbishop William Warham of Canterbury read a list of the bishops who supported the king's request. All but one, Bishop John Fisher of Rochester, supported the king. Catherine protested the trial in a letter to Pope Clement, who remanded the case to Rome. Angered at Wolsey's failure to deliver the promised annulment, Henry removed the cardinal as lord chancellor and installed his friend and adviser, Sir Thomas More, in the position. But Henry, frustrated with the outcome of the marriage tribunal, listened to the suggestion of Thomas Cromwell (1485–1540), a royal adviser and sycophant, who argued that the king should threaten Rome with schism and assume control of the Church in England.

Henry began the takeover of the Church in 1531, when he sent a list of demands to a clergy convocation attended by all the bishops and priests in England. The clergy initially protested the king's demands, but eventually they caved under royal threats and pressure. The "submission of the clergy" prompted Thomas More's resignation as lord chancellor.

Emboldened by the surrender of the bishops, Henry openly cavorted with Anne and ordered the separation of Catherine and Mary. Mother and daughter would never physically see each other. The princess was only fifteen years old. The impact of the separation on the young Mary was immense, and she blamed the situation on Anne Boleyn, whose name she refused to utter for the rest of her life, referring to her instead as "that woman."[186]

The king's wish to annul his marriage to Catherine received fresh impetus from the appointment of Thomas Cranmer (1489–1556) in 1532 as archbishop of Canterbury. Cranmer was a secret Lutheran who advocated submitting the king's annulment request to the opinion of Europe's universities. Appointed chaplain to Anne Boleyn in 1531, Cranmer ingratiated himself with the royal mistress and the king. He would prove Mary's nemesis for years and meet a heretic's end during her reign.

In 1533, Cranmer opened his own marriage tribunal, without papal authorization, concerning the "King's Great Matter." Acting illegally, Cranmer pronounced a declaration of nullity between Henry and Catherine and witnessed the king's "marriage" to Anne. Cranmer also baptized and served as godfather to Elizabeth, the king's daughter with his mistress. People in London were quite upset when Anne Boleyn was crowned queen, as they greatly admired Catherine, who loved her adopted homeland. Henry ordered Catherine to surrender the title of queen and use the title "dowager princess of Wales, the widow of Prince Arthur," instead. The king reduced Catherine's household, placed her under house arrest, and forbade all contact and communication with her daughter Mary. Cranmer's decision and the elevation of Anne Boleyn left Mary as "a young woman caught between estranged parents and a new, hostile stepmother."[187] Elizabeth's birth prompted a change in Mary's title: she no longer could use "princess" but was instead referred to as "the Lady Mary, the King's daughter."[188]

The following year, Pope Clement finally issued the long-awaited decision on the "King's Great Matter." The pope defended the bond between Henry and Catherine and declared their union valid. Angered by the pope's decision, Henry brought England into schism when the "Reformation

Parliament" of 1534 passed a series of five acts separating the English from the Catholic Church. The Act of Succession confirmed Cranmer's decision—that the bond between Henry and Catherine was invalid—and declared the "marriage" between Henry and Anne valid. This act also declared Elizabeth the legitimate heir to the English throne and established severe and capital penalties, including loss of property, imprisonment, and death, for slandering the king's union with Anne.

English subjects were liable to take the "Oath of Succession" affirming Parliament's illegitimate stipulations. John Fisher and Thomas More were "asked" to take the oath. Both refused, and both were arrested and imprisoned in the Tower of London and, ultimately, executed. The Act of Supremacy in November 1534 solidified Henry's break with Rome by declaring the English monarch the head of the Church in England.

The next two years were some of the darkest in Mary's life. She could not communicate with her mother, and her father pressured her to accept Anne and Elizabeth. Her world was shattered early in 1536, when Catherine died at fifty-two. The beloved Catherine went to her eternal reward while hearing Mass. Her request to the king to see her daughter one last time as she lay dying was denied. News of the legitimate queen's death produced a jig of joy in Henry and Anne but had the opposite impact on the English people, who blamed the king for her death amid rumors of poisoning.[189]

Later that year, Anne Boleyn fell from grace when she quarreled with Thomas Cromwell concerning the dissolution of England's monasteries. Henry's attack on the Church included the closure of all monasteries in his country, an idea from Cromwell. The seizure of Church property greatly enriched the royal treasury and allowed the king to give substantial sums to his noble supporters and friends. Anne disagreed with the distribution of the Church's wealth and argued with

Cromwell that the funds should be used for the general welfare of the people, including education.

Anne's tiff with Cromwell, combined with and Henry's fickle nature and wandering eye, placed her in a precarious position. Cromwell eventually accused her of adultery, incest, and the poisoning of Catherine and had her imprisoned in the Tower. The toady Cranmer pronounced the king's union with Anne invalid, and the former mistress turned queen was executed on May 19, 1536 by beheading. The day after, Henry was betrothed to Jane Seymour and married by month's end. Mary enjoyed a pleasant relationship with the king's new wife, but Jane died after childbirth in 1537.

The king spent little time with Mary and used her as a pawn in the game of power politics, offering her in marriage to various European nobles. In essence, Mary's life after the death of her mother was akin to being a "well-treated hostage."[190] The king and his cronies, especially Cranmer, pressured Mary to sign statements acknowledging the illegitimacy of her mother's marriage, her status as a bastard, and the king's control of the Church. Mary withstood these pressures for years, suffering psychological abuse, banishment from court, forced separation from her father, and the restriction of household funds. Eventually, she acquiesced and signed a statement of affirmation and support—a decision that she regretted for the remainder of her life.

A few years later, Parliament passed a new Act of Succession (1544) that established Edward, the king's son with Jane Seymour, as legitimate heir, followed by Mary and Elizabeth. It was a significant departure from previous years, when both daughters were held outside the line of succession.

Henry VIII, who brought radical change to the island realm of England, died in 1547. Edward was just a boy of nine, so a regency council ruled the kingdom for several years. It was under Edward's reign that Princess Mary suffered personally for her Faith and grieved over the movement of her beloved England into full-blown Protestantism.

The man who brought so much pain and suffering to Mary became the architect of England's descent into heresy. Seven months after Henry's death, Thomas Cranmer published a *Book of Homilies* in which he embraced the Protestant teachings of *sola fidei* and *sola scriptura* and condemned Catholic sacramentals and pious practices. Cranmer also invited leading Protestant rebels from the Continent to England to assist in his heretical movement. The next year, Cranmer presented his *Book of Common Prayer* to Parliament, which was designed to replace the Mass.

Parliament adopted Cranmer's heretical liturgy and mandated its use throughout England beginning on Pentecost Sunday, 1549. People rioted in Devonshire at the enforcement of the new liturgy, and Mary, in a letter to Emperor Charles V, asserted her noncompliance with Cranmer's liturgy: "In life and death I will not forsake the Catholic religion of the Church our mother."[191] A few years later, when Mary was persecuted for holding fast to the celebration of the Mass, Charles V threatened England with war if the princess was not allowed to practice the true faith.[192]

Cranmer's assault on the Catholic faith continued in 1550 with the revision of the Ordinal, used to ordain priests. With this heretical "ordination" rite, Cranmer broke the chain of apostolic succession in England. In 1552, at the urging of the Protestant rebels Martin Bucer and John Calvin, Cranmer revised his *Book of Common Prayer*, which embraced even more radical Protestant ideas and teachings. Once again, Parliament adopted Cranmer's heretical liturgy and added penalties, including imprisonment, for failure to attend the new services.

Mary continued her resistance to her half-brother's religious laws. The Mass was central to her life, and no legislation or penalties would dislodge her love for Christ and the Church. She frequently repeated the prayer "In thee, O Lord, is my trust, let me never be confounded. If God is for us, who can be against us?"[193] When the Privy Council took her to task for the continual celebration of the Mass in her home, she replied, "You accuse me of breaking the laws and disobeying them by keeping to my own religion; but I reply that my faith and my religion are those held by the whole of Christendom, formerly confessed by this kingdom under the late king, my father, until you altered them with your laws."[194] Despite great pressure and suffering, Mary held fast to her faith and trusted that the Lord would deliver her from her dire situation.

Her deliverance occurred when the young Edward VI died at age sixteen from a bacterial lung infection.[195] Before he died, Edward wrote "My Device for the Succession," which radically changed the order of succession adopted by his father in 1544. Edward disinherited his half-sisters, Mary and Elizabeth, and struck them from the line. Instead, he ordered the throne to pass to Lady Jane Grey and her male heirs. Jane was the eldest daughter of Frances, duchess of Suffolk, who was the daughter of Henry's sister Mary. Jane was declared queen but never crowned or anointed, and she reigned for only nine days before Parliament withdrew its support. Mary had the backing of the nobles and people as the legitimate heir, and so Parliament instead embraced the once shunned Mary Tudor as queen.

The impossible became possible when Mary rode into London on August 3, 1553 at the head of a 10,000-man army. Her arrival in London and acclamation as queen were greeted with widespread celebrations, including bonfires and the ringing of church bells, and was "one of the greatest spontaneous outpourings of joy that had ever greeted the accession of a new monarch."[196] Mary chose as her regal motto *Veritas Temporis Filia* (*Truth Is the Daughter of Time*) and vowed that England "would be a godly, Catholic country with voice and influence and determination to do it."[197]

Mary inherited a realm of nearly three million people, comprising Irish, Welsh, and English subjects. London had a population of sixty thousand (Paris was three times the size), but most of England was an agrarian society. Other Europeans viewed England as a backwater, unhealthy place to live, the general consensus being that unhealthy water drove Englishmen to spend an inordinate amount of time in taverns, with both contributing to widespread disorder and moral depravity.[198] One ill Spaniard living in England believed that his sickness came from the bad water he was forced to drink because he did not drink beer.[199]

English Catholics were grateful for Mary's accession but worried as well because the queen was an older woman (thirty-seven) and not married. Legitimate fear of the throne passing to Mary's Protestant half-sister Elizabeth prompted discussions of marriage and possible suitors for England's first queen. Mary believed that it was in the kingdom's best interest for her to marry a foreigner to raise England's status in the world. She stipulated that the correct suitor must be of royal blood and a faithful Catholic.

Since English law mandated that a woman's titles, property, and income pass to her husband, concern rose about Mary's desire to marry a foreign prince. Emperor Charles V proposed his son, Prince Philip, as the perfect suitor for Mary, and she agreed. Philip was a decade younger than the queen and known as an elegant and fashionable man:

> In appearance he resembled his Portuguese mother more than his Hapsburg father, with his unmistakable Iberian

> bearing. Unfortunately, the overall effect was spoiled by the large jaw and thick lips of his Burgundian ancestors, but if he was not exactly handsome, he certainly had presence and very considerable charm and social skills.[200]

Philip understood French, Italian, and Latin but could speak only Spanish proficiently, which he used in conversation with Mary. (She used French.) It is possible that the couple communicated in Latin as well.

Mary and Philip were married on July 25, 1554, the Feast of St. James the Apostle, patron of Spain. The marriage treaty allayed the fears of the English nobility concerning the role, status, and power of Philip in England: he would not inherit the kingdom if no heir was produced from the union. He was not crowned king and had no regal power, although he was referred to as king. Philip was also not given the customary landed estates of an English royal consort. Finally, the treaty stipulated that England would not join a Hapsburg war, especially any conflict involving the kingdom of France.

When the marriage liturgy was completed, the royal herald announced the new couple: "Philip and Mary, by the grace of God king and queen of England, France, Naples, Jerusalem, and Ireland, defenders of the Faith, princes of Spain and Sicily, archdukes of Austria, dukes of Milan, Burgundy, and Brabant, counts of Hapsburg, Flanders, and Tyrol."[201]

Mary loved Philip, but the prince did not reciprocate the affection. He knew that the marriage was a political union, and he was simply fulfilling his duty. Philip disliked England itself, especially the weather. Unfortunately, no children resulted from the marriage. The Catholic fear of the throne passing to Elizabeth continued unabated throughout Mary's reign.

Eight months before the royal nuptials, Mary faced grave danger to her life and reign when a group of conspirators met in London to foment rebellion. The men were angered at Mary's plan for the restoration of the Catholic faith and disliked her announced marriage to a Spaniard. The conspirators were a motley group that included two members of Parliament, the duke of Suffolk (Jane Gray's father), and the soldier Sir Thomas Wyatt, whose name became affixed to the rebellion. The plotters hatched a plan for simultaneous uprisings throughout England with a subsequent combined and coordinated march on London to overthrow Mary and install Elizabeth on the throne. The rebellion commenced on January 22, 1554, when Wyatt and several thousand men marched on London. They entered the city and met resistance from the royal guard at London Bridge.

The situation was dire, but the woman who had faced fear and death throughout her life rose to the occasion. She rallied the people of London with a stirring public speech, which elicited cries from the crowd of "God save Queen Mary and the prince of Spain!"[202] Wyatt hesitated due to the resistance in London and eventually surrendered, perhaps hoping his voluntary yielding would produce a royal pardon. It was not so: the rebel was executed. Other conspirators, and even those not directly involved in Wyatt's Rebellion, were executed, too, including Jane Gray, who had no knowledge of the plot but whose life was jeopardized by her father's participation. Mary's half-sister Elizabeth was not an active member of the rebellion, but the conspirators' support for her accession, as well as evidence that she may have known about the plot and refrained from informing Mary, led to her arrest and imprisonment in the Tower for a short period of time. The Protestant support and aims of Wyatt's Rebellion solidified in Mary's mind that the greatest threat to her life and the restoration of the Catholic faith came from active heretics, whose eradication became a royal focus.

Mary firmly believed that her accession had occurred so that she could restore the Catholic faith in England. She worked diligently throughout her reign to accomplish that divinely inspired goal, which proved a difficult task. Although Cranmer's heretical movement under Edward VI lasted only five years, the eradication of the Faith was nearly complete. Altars had been stripped, and religious paintings, statuary, and stained-glass windows had been removed or destroyed. The liturgy was altered fundamentally so that Catholic vestments, sacred vessels, and missals disappeared.[203] Physical items were easily replaced, but harder to overcome were the mental and emotional barriers to the Faith instituted during Edward's rule. Re-catechizing the English population, which had been taught to pray, "From the tyranny of the bishop of Rome and all his detestable enormities, good Lord deliver us," was a primary task.[204] The Spanish Dominican Bartolomé de Carranza, who came to England in Prince Philip's entourage, published a catechism in Spanish, which was translated into English, for use by the clergy to educate the faithful. Carranza's catechism was the model for the later *Roman Catechism* promulgated by Pope St. Pius V (r. 1566–1572) at the behest of the Council of Trent.

Overseeing the restoration of the Faith in England was Mary's cousin, Reginald Cardinal Pole (1500–1588). Pole's mother, Bl. Margaret Pole, had been executed by order of Henry VIII (in a very botched beheading) for remaining loyal to the true faith. During Henry's reign, Pole remained on the Continent, nearly became pope after the death of Paul III (despite his status as a layman!), and presided as one of three papal legates at the opening of the Council of Trent. The cardinal urged Parliament to vote for the restoration of the Catholic faith: "I come to reconcile, not to condemn. I come not to compel, but to call again. I am not come to call anything in question already done, but my commission is of grace and clemency to such as will receive it."[205]

Philip also urged Parliament to vote for restoration, which it finally did on November 30, 1544. Pole granted absolution and accepted England's return to the fold.

Pole recognized the vital role of the English clergy in ensuring the permanence of the restoration. He believed that English priests should be educated, paid well, resident in their parish, loyal to the queen and the pope, and focused on authentic preaching. Likewise, the English bishops, according to Pole, should be pastoral, theologically well formed, and loyal to monarch and pope.

Mary did not replace the entire English hierarchy but kept sixteen bishops who had served during the reigns of Henry and Edward. She nominated twenty new men for the episcopacy—men who were university-educated and had suffered for the Faith under her father and half-brother.[206] Thomas Cranmer, an opponent of Mary's throughout her life, opposed the planned restoration publicly with his September 1553 *Declaration of Opposition*, which protested the reintroduction of the celebration of Mass in England. Cranmer was brought before a royal court, and then sent to the Tower for treason.

Although Cranmer's crimes were treasonable offenses, Mary wanted the man, who had encouraged her father to rebel against Rome, who pronounced her mother's "divorce" on his own authority, and who had persecuted her for remaining true to the Faith, tried for heresy. Eventually, Mary's wish was granted, and the heresy trial commenced in September 1555. Cranmer was charged with perjury of his episcopal consecration oath, defiance of the supreme pontiff, and heresy against the real presence of Jesus in the Eucharist. In February 1556, he was laicized in a ceremony that saw him stripped of his episcopal and presbyteral vestments and clothes. Additionally, his head was shaved to remove the tonsure, his fingers were scraped to remove the sacred chrism of his anointing, and he was dressed in secular clothes and remanded to the secular arm of the government.

Faced with the prospect of death for his heresy, Cranmer issued a series of recantations designed to stall his demise, but they were too little and too late. On March 21, 1556, Cranmer was escorted to St. Mary's Church at Oxford for the preliminary proceedings before his execution. He had prepared two speeches (one Catholic and the other Protestant), and when it was his turn to speak, he stated, "As for the pope, I refuse him as Christ's enemy and the Antichrist, with all his false doctrine."[207] The doomed former archbishop, architect of the Protestant movement in England, and persecutor of Mary Tudor, was burned at the stake as an unrepentant and obstinate heretic. The following day, Pole was ordained (finally!) and then consecrated archbishop of Canterbury.

There was widespread support for the Catholic Restoration, but there was also an active Protestant movement with heretical and rebellious intentions. Mary's reign was in jeopardy from these rebels.

In Mary's time, just like in her father's and her half-brother's, religious differences were not viewed as simple matters of opinion. Rather, they were treasonable offenses, because they destroyed the unity and fabric of society. So Mary undertook a concerted effort to address the active presence of Protestant heretics and rebels. This so-called "Marian persecution" is the "best-known, but by no means the best understood, aspect of Mary Tudor's life," and it gave rise to Mary's infamous, and unjust, moniker of "Bloody."[208]

Mary's persecution of Protestant rebels and heretics spawned centuries of myths and false narratives and solidified her role as a Catholic scapegoat. The myth about Mary's actions was initiated during the Elizabethan period but was mostly created in the seventeenth and nineteenth centuries.[209] Elizabethan writers, such as John Foxe, saw Mary's reign as God's punishment for England's sins, but most blamed the Catholic bishops rather than the queen for the persecution.[210] Post-Elizabethan writings shifted the animus to Mary, with historians characterizing England's first queen as "emotionally unstable, neurotic, even hysterical."[211]

Anti-Catholic Enlightenment authors, such as David Hume, contributed also to the false narratives and propaganda about Mary. The term "Bloody Mary" first appeared in print in 1658, a century after Mary's death, in a poem by the Presbyterian minister Nicholas Billingsley, but the moniker was not a common reference for Mary at that point.[212] Eighteenth- and nineteenth-century editions of John Foxe's *Actes and Monuments*, a biased Protestant apologia that became "a powerful tool in the hands of those who wished to attack Catholicism and discredit Mary," contained the term and helped popularize it.[213] The nickname received wide recognition and popularity from Maria Collcott's (1785–1842) *Little Arthur's History of England* in 1835. Collcott wrote, "Mary, the daughter of Henry VIII and Catherine of Aragon, was so cruel that she is always called Bloody Mary."[214]

Unfortunately, the moniker is ever present, and it dampens people's ability to view Mary as anything other than a cruel, bloodthirsty tyrant. Despite the diligent work of historians, Mary is still depicted in English history as the evil Catholic monarch, who almost enslaved England in popery forever.

However, the historical record shows that Mary was initially tolerant of English Protestants. She wrote, "Touching punishment of heretics, we thinketh it ought to be done without rashness," but Wyatt's Rebellion and other Protestant conspiracies changed her view to a more proactive and violent policy.[215] There was no purposeful intention in the beginning of Mary's reign to eradicate English Protestants by burning hundreds at the stake, but there was a desire for unity in religious expression of the ancient faith and a need to defend that faith from heretical teachings that threatened immortal souls.

The "Marian persecution" was a royal operation and not an ecclesial one.[216] Royal commissioners, acting on information from local sources, usually neighbors and relatives, arrested suspected heretics and sent them to the Church for investigation.

Despite belief that "Bloody" Mary's persecution resulted in thousands of deaths, the main historical source (the Protestant John Foxe's book) records that from February 1555 to November 1558, nearly three hundred men and women were burned at the stake by the secular arm as obstinate heretics. An average of seventy-one people were executed annually at multiple execution sites, but mostly in London, and usually in small numbers. (The greatest number of heretics burned on one occasion was thirteen.)[217] Most of the heretics had spent a year in jail before their execution and were afforded repeated opportunities to recant. Many had been arrested previously, treated leniently by the Church, and released, whereupon they continued their anti-Catholic stance and were re-arrested and executed by the secular arm. A number of heretics disrupted Mass or stood outside churches spouting Protestant denials of the Real Presence and papal authority.[218]

Another plot against Mary's life and reign was uncovered in March 1556. This attempted coup, led by Sir Henry Dudley with assistance from Antoine de Noailles, the French ambassador, hoped to overthrow Mary and install Elizabeth on the throne by stealing 50,000 pounds from the royal treasury. Dudley planned to use the sequestered funds to raise an army of exiled Englishmen from the Continent. The plot was discovered by a treasury official, who alerted Cardinal Pole. The fact that the rebels were all Protestant justified to Mary her policy of persecution.

Even with the executions, Mary remained a popular monarch. Most of her subjects never witnessed a burning. Her contemporaries never thought of her as "bloody," and her persecution of Protestants paled in comparison to the viciousness and ferocity against Catholics later during the reign of her half-sister, Elizabeth I.

Mary is also criticized by nationalist English historians angered by the loss of England's last remaining continental territory, Calais, in January 1558. Calais had been in English possession since 1347, when King Edward III captured it during the Hundred Years' War, but had been nothing but token English territory for a number of years before its loss. The town never really Anglicized and was full of French and English Protestants who did not like the queen. Its economic and military importance had waned, but its symbolic value was high, and Mary felt its loss acutely.

Later in the same year that Calais fell, disease ravaged England. People became suddenly ill with unexplained fevers and general malaise. The mystery illness produced the greatest mortality crisis in England since the fourteenth-century Black Death. The death rate was 124 percent higher than average. The illness affected 40 percent of the population and was more prevalent among the ruling class than the peasantry.[219]

In September, the queen became seriously ill, and in November, Mary believed that her end was near. She wrote to Elizabeth, knowing that her half-sister would succeed her, and pleaded with the daughter of Anne Boleyn to maintain the Catholic faith in England. The Spanish ambassador wrote to King Philip II predicting that Elizabeth would do no such thing: "She is a very vain and clever woman. She must have been thoroughly schooled in the manner in which her father conducted his affairs, and I am much afraid that she will not be well disposed in matters of religion."[220]

On November 17, 1588, during the celebration of Mass in her bedroom, Mary Tudor, first queen of England, died. "So peaceful was her passing that those around her did not realize, at first, that she was gone."[221] She was forty-two years old. Later that evening, upon hearing the news of the queen's death, her beloved cousin, Reginald Cardinal Pole, who had implemented her great dream of Catholic restoration, also went to his eternal reward. Elizabeth, the Protestant daughter of Henry VIII and Anne Boleyn, was declared queen a mere six hours after Mary's death.

Mary's legacy as the first queen regnant of England is marred by the Protestant historical attack of her as "Bloody Mary." The woman who was a king's daughter, a king's sister, and a king's wife in life became a tyrant, a "bloody" persecutor of religious dissent, and a Catholic scapegoat in death. This devoted daughter of the Church has been denigrated for centuries by myths and false narratives that use her to highlight the supposed accomplishments of her half-sister. Indeed, not only is Mary's memory overshadowed by Elizabeth, but so is her resting place. When Elizabeth died in 1603, her coffin was placed on top of Mary's, in the same vault, as another insult to the great Catholic queen.

Mary Tudor should be remembered as a woman who may not have been victorious in all things but certainly lived in a manner that illustrated "the triumph of determination over adversity."[222] Traumatized by the acrimonious and public divorce of her parents, isolated from caring relatives and friends, and harassed for her faith, Mary triumphed over these difficulties. Her royal accession was never guaranteed, and the miraculous nature of its accomplishment was never lost on her. She firmly believed that the reason for her queenship was the restoration of the true faith, which she accomplished. Additionally, her reign proved "that a female ruler, whether married or unmarried, would enjoy identical power and authority to male monarchs" and paved the way for the sixteenth- and twentieth-century Elizabeths.[223]

Mary was more than the "bloody" scapegoat presented in the Protestant historical attack. Justice demands her remembrance as a diligent ruler who loved her people, her Lord, and his Church with endless affection.

Guy Fawkes

Remember, remember!
The fifth of November,
The Gunpowder treason and plot;
I know of no reason
Why the Gunpowder treason
Should ever be forgot!
Guy Fawkes and his companions
Did the scheme contrive
To blow the King and Parliament
All up alive.
Threescore barrels, laid below
To prove old England's overthrow.
But, by God's providence, him they catch
With a dark lantern, lighting a match![224]

People are complex creatures, and rarely is one the sum of the worst or best action or decision in life. But some people come to fulfill the role of enemy to satisfy public bloodlust or to justify the continuance of persecution and subjection of a group for centuries.

The man in England who served that role for Protestants was Guy Fawkes, who became a symbol of Catholic traitors and viewed as England's archvillain. Generations of schoolchildren were taught the traditional English poem about Guy and his actions on the fifth of November, which reinforced the view of Catholics as bad subjects desirous of the overthrow of the monarchy.

The failed Gunpowder Plot of 1605, in which Guy was but one of the thirteen conspirators, became a symbol of God's protection over and the rightness of Protestant England. Parliament enshrined this view through the Thanksgiving Act, mandating annual celebrations on November 5 involving fireworks and bonfires where effigies of Guy, and later the pope, were burned in raucous festivities throughout England and later its colonies around the world.

Rare has been the attempt to understand why the Gunpowder Plot was hatched and why Guy Fawkes agreed to be the "trigger" man. Instead, Guy is presented as a Catholic rebel and traitor motivated by hatred for the king and love for a foreign prince, the pope.

Guy Fawkes was far more than a traitor or an "evil terrorist," or the ultimate Catholic scapegoat of the Protestant historical attack. He was a Catholic patriot who suffered for his faith, witnessed his fellow Catholics brutally tortured and executed, and lived under an oppressive regime who made subjecting Catholics the national pastime. He was a frustrated and desperate man, along with others, who believed that his only recourse was a radical act. The plot failed, and it brought not relief, but further sufferings and persecution to the Catholics in England.

The story of Guy Fawkes and why he embarked on the path of regicide begins in Scotland, long before his birth.

Mary Stuart, Queen of Scots, was sixteen years old when Mary Tudor, Queen of England, died in 1558. In Catholic eyes, Mary Stuart was the legitimate heir to the English throne because she was the granddaughter of Margaret Tudor, Henry VIII's sister and a Catholic. However, Mary Tudor recognized her half-sister Elizabeth's claim to the throne despite the latter's heretical beliefs.

Mary Stuart, although a queen, had an extremely difficult childhood and life. Her father, King James V (r. 1513–1542), died when she was only six days old, so she inherited the kingdom with significant political turmoil, exacerbated by the presence of a regency council because of her age. The delicate situation prompted the sending of Mary to France for her safety when she was five years old. During her absence, Protestants, especially from the machinations of John Calvin's disciple John Knox, began a religious and political takeover.

Mary began her education in France and grew to be more like a Frenchwoman than a Scotswoman. She was betrothed to Francis II of France and became queen consort when he ascended the throne in 1559.

Francis's early death the following year prompted Mary's return to Scotland at the age of nineteen. Scotland was a foreign land for the returning queen, and the political climate was inhospitable. Eventually, Mary married her cousin Henry Stewart, earl of Darnley, in 1565, and the couple welcomed a son the following year. Their son, James, was baptized Catholic, but when the hostile religious and political environment forced Mary to abdicate the throne and flee to England, the boy was crowned king (James VI) and raised Protestant.

Mary Stuart spent the next nineteen years under virtual house arrest in England and was eventually executed when implicated, falsely, in a plot to overthrow Elizabeth. The death of the legitimate Catholic heir to the English throne prompted the mobilization of the Spanish Armada in 1588 and the hoped-for restoration of the Faith. The defeat of the Armada dashed English Catholic hopes and solidified Elizabeth's reign.

Elizabeth Tudor (r. 1558–1603) became one of England's longest-reigning monarchs (forty-five years) at the death of her half-sister Mary. Whereas Mary is portrayed in the Protestant historical attack as "Bloody Mary," Elizabeth is viewed as "Good Queen Bess," the great "Virgin Queen" of England, who represented the strong Protestantism of her subjects and who led England into a time of great power and prosperity.

This Elizabethan image represents a "monstrous scaffolding of poisonous nonsense" that has "been foisted on posterity."[225] The myth of Elizabeth was created by nationalist English Protestant historians, who painted a vastly different image of the queen from what contemporaries reported.

The Elizabeth myth, still believed in the modern world, portrays the daughter of Henry VIII and Anne Boleyn as a religiously tolerant (or even indifferent) monarch and the chaste "Virgin Queen" who wedded herself to England rather than to a husband. However, contemporaries understood the queen as a great persecutor of Catholics and a sexually immoral and promiscuous dilettante.[226]

The Protestant historical myth, rather than reality, became embedded in history through the English defeat of the Spanish Armada and the execution of Mary Stuart. The defeat of the Armada, in particular, "associated Elizabeth with English nationalism and English imperialism. Elizabeth became an iconic figure to be invoked in times of national crisis."[227]

Several men operated behind the scenes in Elizabethan England to ensure the queen remained in power. William Cecil (1520–1598) was her most influential and powerful supporter. He served as secretary of state under Elizabeth's half-brother,

King Edward VI, and served the same role under the queen. Cecil established an impressive intelligence network of operatives and spies that kept him abreast of conspiracies and plots against Elizabeth. An ardent Protestant, Cecil used his network to persecute English Catholics and fight Catholic Spain. He played the patriotism card effectively to eradicate the Faith in England by associating treason against the crown and kingdom with adherence to the Church. Catholic priests were viewed as trained assassins in Elizabethan England, and Jesuits were the most hated form of clerics. Cecil, who handed on his intelligence service and anti-Catholic hatred to his son Robert (1563–1612), was one of the "more dedicated, brilliant, indefatigable, and deadly enemies of the Catholic Church" in history.[228]

Queen Elizabeth ushered in the first government-sponsored persecution of the Catholic Church since the Roman Empire. Early in her reign, Parliament passed the Acts of Supremacy and Uniformity, which declared the queen "Chief Governor of all Spiritual and Ecclesiastical Affairs" and restored Cranmer's revised *Book of Common Prayer* as the liturgy of the Church in England. English subjects were required to attend this liturgy every week or face a fine. The law also forbade acknowledging the Roman pontiff as head of the Church. Additional anti-Catholic laws followed, including the "Thirty-nine Articles," a statement of Protestant belief, in 1563, which all clerics were required to affirm. Among the articles was the teaching that the bishop of Rome has no jurisdiction in England and that the eucharistic doctrine of transubstantiation is "repugnant to the plain words of Holy Scripture."[229]

In 1581, conversion to the Catholic faith became illegal and was considered a treasonous and capital offense, subject to the death penalty.[230] A few years later, another piece of legislation specifically targeted Catholic priests and those who helped them. Anyone aiding a Jesuit was guilty of aiding and abetting rebellion, and all Catholic priests ordained after 1559, the year of the Acts of Supremacy and Uniformity, or ordained outside England were banished and, if found, adjudged a traitor to the crown.[231] It was also illegal to leave England without the crown's approval, which was instituted to prevent Catholic men from studying for the priesthood on the Continent at the English College established by William Allen, originally in the town of Douai in French Flanders but later transferred to the French city of Reims.

Allen established his college for English priests in 1568 with the mission of training men to minister to the underground Church in England. Men were prepared for the rigors of a missionary priesthood with a focus on seeing themselves as agents of God and not agents of governmental change in England. There was no discussion of English politics allowed at the college, nor was the queen's name uttered. Debates concerning royal versus papal power and authority were forbidden. These rules were designed to sharpen the men's focus, but also to provide them with a defense if captured by Elizabeth's priest-hunters.

The first priests from the college to return to England arrived in 1574. The first martyr was St. Cuthbert Mayne, who ministered to the persecuted English Catholics for more than a year before his capture in the summer of 1577. He was charged with denying the queen's headship of the Church in England, carrying a brief of indulgences, and possessing a rosary. He was allowed to recant if he swore on Scripture that Elizabeth was the rightful head of the Church. Cuthbert "took the Bible in his hands, made the sign of the cross on it, kissed it and said, 'The queen never was, nor is, nor ever shall be the head of the Church!'"[232] For his insolence, he was hanged, drawn, and quartered.

A few years after Cuthbert Mayne's death, the Society of Jesus began sending priests to England. Elizabeth's persecution, from 1581 to 1590, resulted in the executions of seventy-eight priests and twenty-five Catholic laity.[233] Yet conversions still occurred as people returned to or embraced anew the true faith.

Pope Pius V (r. 1566–1572) attempted to alleviate the suffering of English Catholics with his bull of excommunication of Elizabeth in 1570. Pius wrote in *Regnans in Excelsis* that Elizabeth,

> the pretended queen of England and the servant of crime . . . having seized the crown and monstrously usurped the place of supreme head of the Church in all England... has once again reduced this same kingdom, which had already been restored to the Catholic faith and to good fruits, to a miserable ruin.

The papal hope was that the excommunication, which freed English subjects from their oath of loyalty to the queen, would produce a successful change in the throne, but the action, instead, greatly increased the persecution of Catholics in England. As a result, Pius's successor, Pope Gregory XIII (r. 1572–1585), revised the implementation of the bull so that Catholics were encouraged to obey the crown in civil matters and to refrain from deposing Elizabeth until political and military conditions for such an action improved.[234]

Elizabeth's excommunication provided Willam Cecil with fodder to enshrine an anti-papal and anti-Catholic mentality in England. He utilized the pope's extremely unpopular action to solidify the notion that Catholics were traitors and anti-English because they despised Elizabeth.

Plots against the queen continued throughout the 1580s and 1590s, including the failed plot of the poisoned pommel in

1598, where Edward Squire attempted to kill the queen by smearing poison on the pommel of her saddle. These various plots increased the suffering of English Catholics: fines for *recusancy*, or refusal to attend Church of England services, were significantly raised in 1581 and again in 1587 to make it impossible for commoners to pay and to financially bankrupt Catholic nobility.

Hope was kindled in 1603, when the long-reigning Elizabeth died. England had witnessed debilitating religious turmoil for more than half a century with the embrace of Protestant heresy under King Edward VI, followed by the Catholic Restoration under Queen Mary for five years, followed by active persecution of Catholics under Elizabeth for forty-five years. The strain of the persecution under Elizabeth was intense and immense, and England's Catholics were beyond the breaking point. Elizabeth's successor produced hope within the persecuted faithful initially, but those hopes were soon dashed, which led to the most extreme and violent plot in history against the English crown.

James, the son of Mary Stuart, became king of England at the age of thirty-seven. He had reigned as king of Scotland (as James VI) since 1567, when he was just over a year old. So he came to the throne of England (as James I) as an experienced monarch, wise in politics and aware of the impact of Protestant-Catholic issues on a kingdom. His life in Scotland was consumed with various plots and conspiracies, which prompted great anxiety and distrust.

James was quite interested in sorcery and witchcraft, even writing a book, *Daemonologie*, in 1597 about witches. He encouraged witch hunts in Scotland such that the kingdom, with a smaller population, burned more people accused of witchcraft in the sixteenth century than its more populous neighbor to the south.[235]

In the summer of 1603, James met with the French ambassador and indicated he desired peace between Protestants and Catholics and believed that this could be accomplished by the calling of an ecumenical council. The king even wrote a letter to Pope Clement VIII (r. 1592–1605) requesting papal endorsement of his idea, but he did not receive a reply from Rome.

James, baptized Catholic, was raised Protestant, but his behavior in Scotland seemed to favor a path of reconciliation. English Catholics believed that a period of toleration was possible. In Scotland, James had Catholic courtiers and a Catholic captain of the royal guard and utilized Catholic diplomats.[236] In a religious reversal of the king, his wife, Anne of Denmark, who had been baptized a Protestant, converted to the Catholic faith. Some English Catholics even believed rumors that the king would revert to his baptismal faith. In the spring of 1603, James remarked in a letter to the Earl of Northumberland, "as for the Catholics I will neither persecute any that will be quiet, and give but outward obedience to the law, neither will I spare to advance any of them that will by good service worthily deserve it."[237]

The king's orientation toward Catholics was motivated by more than just religion. He desired an end to the decades-long English war with Spain and knew that King Philip II demanded toleration for English Catholics as part of any peace treaty (although Philip dropped that stipulation in the end for political expediency).

But the early hopes of a tolerant monarch were quashed in December 1603, when James ordered the archbishop of Canterbury to make a list of all "popish recusants" and enforce the laws, especially fines, against them.[238] A few months into the new year, the king publicly stated his "utter detestation" for the papist religion and issued a proclamation expelling every Catholic priest from the realm.[239] In March 1604, Parliament passed the Act for the Due Execution of the Statutes against the Jesuits, Seminary Priests, Recusants, etc., which confirmed all the anti-Catholic Elizabethan laws.[240] This law and James's words proved to English Catholics that life under the new monarch would be the same as under the persecuting queen.

It was into this world of virulent anti-Catholic bigotry, violence, suppression, and oppression that Guy Fawkes was born.

Edward Fawkes, the second son of William Fawkes and Ellen Harrington, married Edith Blake in the late sixteenth century in the northern English city of York. Their union produced one son, born on April 13, 1570, whom the proud parents named Guy, a French name. The boy's surname (pronounced "fox") was also French in origin but a well-established English name at the time of his birth.

Guy's father died when he was eight, and his widowed mother married Denis Bainbridge, a well-known Catholic recusant, nine years later. Guy was sent to St. Peter's school in York, which was staffed with secret Catholics known as "Church Catholics" who outwardly attended Church of England services and appeared faithful to the state religion but were clandestinely adherents of the true faith. Several members of the later Gunpowder Plot attended this school as boys.

Guy was raised Protestant as a young boy but converted to the Catholic faith as a teenager, after his father's death and before his mother's second marriage. His conversion was brought about by the horrid execution of a well-known woman of York, St. Margaret Clitherow (1556–1586). Margaret was the daughter of Thomas Middleton, a former sheriff of the city. She married John Clitherow, a sheep farmer, at the age of fifteen. Margaret converted to the Faith during her marriage, but her husband remained Protestant. She learned about the true faith from Dorothy Vavasour, a midwife, whose house was a clandestine center for Catholics in York.[241] In 1576, Margaret's name appeared on a list of recusants, and the following year, she was arrested by the Elizabethan authorities.

Over the next several years, a similar pattern followed, with Margaret's arrest for refusing to attend Church of England services and then release after a short time. However, royal officials arrested her in 1586 for the crimes of instructing her children in the Catholic faith and maintaining a room in her house for the hiding of Catholic priests. Brought before the court, Margaret refused to enter a plea, and she told the judge, "I know no offense whereof I should confess myself guilty."[242] Asked again to plead the charges, Margaret remained obstinate, saying, "Having made no offense, I need no trial." She placed her trust in God by stating, "I will be tried by none but God and your own consciences."[243]

The indefatigable "Pearl of York" was found guilty and sentenced to death by pressing, a horrific death wherein the prisoner was stripped naked and laid on the ground and had a door or plank placed on him, to which weights were gradually added for three days. If the accused was still alive after the third day, the weights were removed, a sharp stone was placed under the back, the hands and feet were tied to posts, and then the plank and weights were added back, which usually produced death within minutes.

Margaret praised God for her martyrdom. Her execution was accelerated so that the sharp rock was placed under her back and then 896 pounds of weight placed on her body. Her last words were "Jesu! Jesu! Jesu! Have mercy on me!"[244]

The violent death of Margaret Clitherow produced shock and anger in York and even, when news of the event reached London, a letter of outrage from Queen Elizabeth to the people of the city concerning the treatment of a fellow woman.[245]

Along with thirty-nine other English martyrs, Margaret was canonized by Pope St. Paul VI in 1970.

Her death marked a turning point in the life of Guy Fawkes. The blood of the martyr was the seed of a new Christian, as Guy converted to the Faith and devoted his life to Christ and his Church.

Not much is known of Guy's life from his conversion in 1586 to his appearance on the Continent in 1594 as a soldier fighting for Catholic Spain against Protestant rebels in the Eighty Years War. He adopted the Spanish first name Guido during his military time, where he became an accomplished combat veteran and an expert at tunneling and placing gunpowder under enemy fortifications. Even during his military career, Guy was known as a devout Catholic and described by the Jesuit Oswald Tesimond as a man who was "of exemplary and commendable reticence. He went often to the sacraments. He was pleasant of approach and cheerful of manner, opposed to quarrels and strife. . . . In a word, he was a man liked by everyone and loyal to his friends."[246]

Guy was entrusted in 1603 with a special mission to Spain, partly because of his fluency in Spanish but also because of his exemplary military service, to generate support and seek military assistance from King Philip II for an invasion of England to alleviate the sufferings of English Catholics. But the hope of Spanish military assistance evaporated when the Treaty of London between England and Spain was signed in the summer of 1604. English Catholics knew they were on their own.

The same year during which Guy sought Spanish assistance, several plots were undertaken against King James. One involved a plan to kidnap the king and hold him in the Tower of London until he repealed the anti-Catholic legislation. The plan was discovered and two priests arrested and executed for their involvement. The "Main Plot" consisted of an assassination attempt on the king, with the subsequent installation of his Catholic cousin, Lady Arbella Stuart, as queen. This plot was also discovered before implementation and came to naught. The plots strengthened royal resolve against Catholics and continued the propaganda against Catholic priests, especially the Jesuits, as active rebels against the crown.

The actions of the crown against Catholics produced these various plots and drove desperate men to plan desperate measures. Robert Catesby (1572–1605), known as Robin to his friends, was one such desperate man. Although Guy Fawkes is sometimes identified as the leader of the Gunpowder Plot, the plot was the creation of Catesby. In February 1604, Robin met with his friends Thomas Wintour and Jack Wright and told them of his plan to blow up Parliament at its opening session, when the royal family, the lords, and members would be present. Catesby told Wintour, "In that place [Parliament], they have done us all the mischief, and perchance God has designed that place for their punishment."[247] When Wintour hesitated at the design and scope of the plot, Catesby told him that "the nature of the disease required so sharp a remedy."[248]

A few months later, Catesby had recruited two other main conspirators, Thomas Percy and Guy Fawkes. The five men met at a private room at the Duck and Drake pub in London and pledged oaths of fellowship and secrecy concerning their plot. Ultimately, eight additional men joined the conspiracy: Robert Keyes, Thomas Bates, Robert Wintour (Thomas's brother), Christopher Wright, John Grant, Ambrose Rookwood, Sir Everard Digby, and Francis Tresham. Fawkes became the most important member of the plot after Catesby and Wintour, because his military expertise was needed for the gunpowder.

In October 1604, the group began stockpiling gunpowder and wood. Eventually, they acquired thirty-six barrels of gunpowder, which was more than twenty-five times the necessary amount to destroy the Parliament building![249] By the end of the year, the plotters were tunneling from the Lambeth House near the Parliament building, in long shift work conducted in the evenings. By Christmas Eve, they had reached the outer wall of Parliament, which proved too difficult to breach. So they moved to a location across the Thames and rented a cellar in a house next door to Parliament, where they placed the gunpowder barrels. In the meantime, the opening of Parliament had been prorogued from February to October 1605.

The plot involved more than just a huge explosion of gunpowder barrels below the Parliament building. The plan called for Fawkes to light a slow-burning fuse, which would give him fifteen minutes to leave the building for a boat that would take him to the Continent. From there, he was to make his way to Rome to request a papal audience, which would encourage exiled English Catholics in Flanders and Rome to join the cause and invade England. Meanwhile, Catesby and the other conspirators would rally Catholics in England for a march on London in the aftermath of the confusion, death, and destruction from the explosion.

Plague erupted in London in the fall of 1605, so the opening session of Parliament was once more prorogued to early November. In late October, the plot became known outside the small circles of conspirators when a stranger gave an anonymous letter to the servant of Lord Mounteagle, who was Catesby's cousin. The letter warned Mounteagle not to attend the opening session of Parliament, "for God and man have concurred to punish the wickedness of this time. . . . For though there be no appearance of any stir, yet I say they shall receive a terrible blow this Parliament; and yet they shall not see who hurts them."[250] Surprised at the letter and uncertain of its contents and warning, Lord Mounteagle delivered it to Robert Cecil, who showed it to the king.

James believed that the letter indicated the presence of a plot to blow up Parliament, so he ordered a search of all the neighboring houses and buildings. The first search, conducted on November 4, found a suspicious quantity of firewood in one of the cellars of a house adjacent to Parliament. A few hours later, in the early morning of November 5, searchers discovered Guy Fawkes in the house. Guy heard a noise outside the cellar and opened the door to investigate. He was met with a lantern in the face and surprised by the presence of several men. A struggle ensued, and Guy was subdued. The men discovered the thirty-six barrels of gunpowder in the cellar, at which point Guy quipped, "You were lucky to find me outside the cellar; otherwise, none of you would be talking about it now, because you would all have been blown sky-high."[251]

Guy was brought before the king at four in the morning, after having been stripped and beaten. He wore a crucifix and a penitential hair shirt and possessed a rosary. When asked his name, he replied, "John Johnson" and indicated that he planned to blow up Parliament and kill the king, the lords, and the bishops. When the king inquired as to why Guy had planned such a nefarious enterprise, Guy said he was motivated because the king was a heretic.[252]

News of the foiled plot spread rapidly in London on November 5 and spawned celebrations of bonfires and fireworks throughout the city. Parliament passed the Bonfire Observance of 5th November Act, which remained in force until 1850, requiring compulsory celebrations of bonfires annually on November 5 in thanksgiving for the salvation of the king and Parliament. The act, also known as the Thanksgiving Act, placed blame for the plot on Catholic clergy, especially the

Jesuits, despite their lack of involvement in Catesby's caper. The act recorded that

> many malignant and devilish papists, Jesuits, and Seminary priests . . . conspired most horribly, when the King's most excellent Majesty, the Queen, the Prince, and all the Lords Spiritual and Temporal, and Commons, should have been assembled in the Upper House of Parliament upon the Fifth Day of November in the year of our Lord One thousand six hundred and five, suddenly to have blown up the said whole House with Gunpowder: An Invention so inhumane, barbarous and cruel, as the like was never before heard of.[253]

The bonfire celebration was added to the Church of England's liturgical calendar and became one of the most popular English holidays.

The day after his capture, Guy was presented with a list of sixteen questions written by King James. Guy refused to answer. He held fast for a time under intense torture, including the rack, but provided his real name on November 7. A few days later, he gave the royal authorities the names of his fellow conspirators and signed a confession under duress.

Although he may have regretted that act, it did not negatively impact his fellow conspirators, who had been discovered already by the sheriff of Worcester at the Holbeche House in Staffordshire. Catesby and his friends barricaded themselves in the house. When they realized that their gunpowder was damp, they placed it in front of the fire to dry, but someone tripped and dropped hot coals on the exposed powder, causing an explosion that severely injured most of the men in the house. (Ironically, the only explosion from the plot impacted the conspirators![254]) Catesby, Thomas Percy, and Thomas Wintour ran out of the house to confront the sheriff's men. Percy was killed, Wintour and Catesby wounded. Wintour was captured, but Catesby managed to crawl back into the house, where he took a painting of the Blessed Mother off the wall and kissed it before dying.[255] His body was buried but later exhumed by order of Parliament so that his corpse could be hanged, drawn, and quartered. Catesby's head was placed on a pike and posted to the top of a Parliament building as a warning to others.

At the end of January 1606, Guy Fawkes was found guilty of treason and sentenced to die by hanging, drawing, and quartering. He was the "first of the conspirators to be arrested" but "the last to be executed."[256] His body broken from torture and months of deprivation, Guy died instantly from the hanging. His head was stuck on a pike and placed on London Bridge.

Following Guy's death, the king and his henchman Cecil used the plot as an excuse to eradicate the clandestine Jesuits, whom the king referred to as "Puritan-papists" despite the fact that the Gunpowder conspirators had not implicated any Jesuits. In January 1606, a royal notice commanded the arrest of the Jesuit priests Garnet, Gerard, and Tesimond. Garnet, who had known Catesby well, had counseled against the plot but was nonetheless found guilty and executed by hanging, drawing, and quartering on May 3, 1606.

Cecil ensured that Guy Fawkes and his fellow conspirators were seen as evil men bent on destroying England and not as patriotic Catholics fighting to end the suffering and persecution of the faithful. One result of the failed plot was the establishment of an Oath of Allegiance, required of English subjects, that stipulated that

> the Pope, neither himself nor any authority of the Church or See of Rome . . . has any power or authority to depose the King . . . or to authorize any foreign prince to invade or annoy him . . . or to discharge any of his subjects of

> their allegiance and obedience to this Majesty, or to offer any violence or hurt to his Majesty's royal person, state or government.[257]

The pope issued a proclamation forbidding English Catholics to take the oath.

The failed Gunpowder Plot also resulted in additional anti-Catholic laws that furthered the sufferings and humiliations of the faithful in England. Recusants were forbidden from entering a royal palace and could not even come within ten miles of London. English Catholics were not allowed to practice law or medicine, nor to hold a commission in the king's army or navy. Moreover, recusants were not allowed to hold public office or possess weapons or armor, although they were still required (somehow) to answer the county muster, which necessitated a military kit. Crown officers were allowed to enter any house in the realm if in pursuit of Catholics. Recusancy fines were increased substantially, and severe penalties were imposed on Catholics who attended Protestant services but refused communion.[258] A bill in 1613 that required Catholics to wear red hats or multi-colored stockings (the same used by clowns) to identify themselves in public was narrowly defeated in Parliament.[259]

English Catholics suffered under these persecutory laws for more than 250 years. Far from alleviating the sufferings of the faithful in England, the failed Gunpowder Plot greatly increased them.

King James died in 1625 and was succeeded by his second son, Charles I (r. 1625–1649), who was executed by order of Parliament twenty-four years later. Charles I's son, Charles II (r. 1660–1685), converted to the Catholic faith on his deathbed. James II (r. 1685–1688), the brother of Charles II, was Catholic, a fact distasteful to the English nobility, so they supported the so-called "Glorious Revolution" in 1688, when the Protestants William of Orange and his wife Princess Mary assumed the throne.

James II was the last Catholic monarch of England. The Settlement Act of 1701 ensured that only Protestants could ascend the English throne. Moreover, the act stipulated that any person in the line of succession who dared marry a Catholic was automatically excluded from the line of succession.[260]

The memory of Guy Fawkes and the Gunpowder Plot was maintained through the centuries by the annual November 5 commemorations in the English-speaking world, known as "Bonfire Night," "Fireworks Night," or "Gunpowder Treason Night." Effigies of Guy were burned at these celebrations, which soon turned from an anti-treason to an anti-Catholic festival.

The anti-Catholic focus of the November 5 celebrations in England were expressed in an eighteenth-century poem that grew in popularity in the nineteenth century: "A rope, a rope, to hang the pope, a penn'orth of cheese to choke him, a pint of beer to wash it down, and a jolly good fire to burn him. Holloa boys! Holloa boys! God save the King! Hip, hip, hooray!"[261]

November 5 activities in England's North American colonies also turned into anti-Catholic spectacles, as effigies of the pope rather than Guy Fawkes were burned. The American War of Independence was one reason for the shift, as it seemed a bit foolish to the colonists to burn an effigy of Guy Fawkes, who, like the Americans, had tried to loose the bonds of royal tyranny.

Guy Fawkes is unique among canceled Catholics, as his memory has been converted in the modern world from that of an evil traitor and terrorist to a positive figurehead for anarchists and other anti-establishment protesters, who wear caricature masks of Guy and see him as a valiant fighter against the system. This image was partly fostered from the 1988

DC Comics graphic novel V for Vendetta, written by Alan Moore and illustrated by David Lloyd, which was turned into a movie in 2006 with Hugo Weaving and Natalie Portman. Most of the modern-day protesters who use the caricatured likeness of Guy Fawkes, more than likely, have little to no understanding of who the real Guy Fawkes and his fellow Gunpowder conspirators were and why they embarked on such a dramatic and violent plot against the English crown.

If Guy had succeeded in blowing up the Parliament building and killing the royal family, and most of the nobility and clergy of England, he would have fundamentally altered English and Catholic history. Although his actions, which would have killed innocent people, cannot be morally justified, they can be explained and understood from the historical context in which they occurred.

Guy Fawkes, Robin Catesby, and the other Catholics involved in the Gunpowder Plot saw themselves as Catholic soldiers and patriots fighting a war against an oppressive English monarchy that persecuted them for adherence to the true faith. They were desperate men who undertook desperate measures to alleviate their misery. Their failure led their entrenched tormentors to use them to justify continued oppressive measures against English Catholics for centuries.

Chapter 3
Secular History

Today mystery has been banished from man's daily life. If things go wrong, he looks for help to the government or to science rather than to God and religion. No doubt this has freed mankind from the burden of superstition and irrational fear, but it has also left man at the mercy of his own inventions and has substituted the omnipotence of that man-made monster, the bureaucratic, technocratic state—the New Leviathan—for the mystery of nature and the power of God.[262]

—Christopher Dawson

Change was the major theme of the nineteenth century. It occurred in nearly all aspects of society: political systems, family life, occupations, technology, and even academic subjects.

Political revolution swept through nearly every European country in the mid-1800s as these countries embraced democratic, socialist, and nationalist forms of government. The Industrial Revolution brought a radical change to family life as people moved from rural to urban areas and adopted a city-dwelling, factory-working lifestyle. The university, which previously existed to form individuals in knowledge and virtue, became a tool used by governments to train and produce citizens loyal to the state and civil servants to staff the state bureaucracy. History, which previously was viewed as a form of literature where the story of peoples was recounted, became a "scientific endeavor," with an emphasis on *textual criticism*.

The study of history changed so that "the historical profession took shape as a deliberative, self-conscious rejection of anything that might appear to be a traditional approach to history."[263] In the twentieth century, this drastic change in the study of history continued, as historians embraced prevalent theories in the social sciences and other humanities. The fundamental principle of these theories was that it is impossible to know and report the truth about the past.

The rejection of objective knowledge and its application to academic subjects began in France, and from there it quickly migrated to the United States and spread throughout the university system. The ultimate result was a far-reaching change in academic studies, which were focused no longer on the pursuit of truth, but rather on defending and furthering political and social ideologies. The basic principles of the "new humanities" included the rejection of the concepts of objectivity and certainty—truth is relative, not absolute; science is invented, not discovered; and the traditional divisions of academic disciplines were rejected in favor of multi-disciplinary studies.[264]

The rise of *cultural studies* produced a dismissive and hostile attitude to traditional historical sources so that past events were infiltrated with modern notions and political perspective. As an example, any form of Catholic missionary activity is presented as the Church's attempt to turn indigenous peoples into Europeans and is viewed as a form of subjugation rather than a concerted evangelization and catechetical effort rooted in charity.

Viewing history as another science, and rejecting its crucial narrative focus, created an emphasis on historical texts and documents and an effort to criticize their authors. In the end, "written history is reduced to a text that is nothing but the ideological expression of the prevailing cultural system."[265]

Forcing history into the genre of "science" fails to recognize the inherent differences in these academic subjects. History deals with people and events, at specific moments in time, whose decisions and actions cannot be repeated in experimental form. Historians, unlike scientists, produce narratives of individuals and groups of people rather than general, observable and repeatable laws. Historical evidence is multifaceted, and so the emphasis on documents in recent years fails to acknowledge that documentary evidence is always inherently selective and never complete, since preservation is usually a conscious choice by historical actors.[266] Secular humanists embraced the new emphasis in studying history, and they used the changes to craft a new, anti-Western, anti-European, anti-Catholic narrative that specifically sought to malign Catholics in the past to further a post-Christian agenda.

An example of the secular historical attack against the Church is the highly controversial subject of slavery. Secularists use slavery as a weapon against the Church's history by consistently and loudly declaring that the Church encouraged the slave trade and viewed it as morally legitimate. The historical record easily refutes these insidious errors, but secular apologists often meet the truth with rejection and accusations of falsehood.

John Francis Maxwell, author of the 1975 book *Slavery and the Catholic Church: The History of the Catholic Teaching Concerning the Moral Legitimacy of the Institution of Slavery*, argued that until the twentieth century, the Church consistently viewed slavery as morally legitimate. Maxwell's analysis of the failings of the Church to condemn slavery and the slave trade significantly influenced twentieth-century scholarship on the question. Nearly twenty years after Maxwell's book, another commentator echoed his writing: "Only after the cultures of Europe and America changed through the abolitionists' agency and only after the laws of every civilized land eliminated the practice, did Catholic moral doctrine decisively repudiate slavery as immoral."[267]

The secular historical belief that the Church approved or tolerated slavery, especially the enslavement of the Indians of the New World and Africans, became the standard narrative in academia and society in the modern world. The false narrative persists, in part, because historical examples exist of individual Catholics supporting slavery or owning slaves. Secular scholars use these examples as "proof" of the Church's malfeasance without drawing the necessary distinction and clarification that the actions of individual Catholics, contrary to Church teaching, does not constitute authoritative teaching of the Magisterium.

Additionally, scholars have routinely failed to make the necessary distinction concerning the different forms of slavery. The Church has consistently and constantly condemned the practice of *unjust servitude*, which entails the enslavement of a group of people based on race or for the economic gain of others. European nations commonly utilized this immoral form of slavery against African and New World indigenous people despite papal condemnations. Another form of slavery, accepted in Western society since the ancient world, is *just title servitude*, or the involuntary servitude imposed on criminals or prisoners of war. Just title servitude is acknowledged in the modern world through the Geneva Conventions of 1949, according to which nations at war are allowed to utilize prisoners of war for involuntary labor. In the case of just title servitude, the Church has always demanded the humane treatment of the enslaved and encouraged their emancipation. The failure to recognize these distinctions of servitude, especially concerning prisoners of war, has led many scholars, some of whom began their research with a preconceived animus against the Church, to posit the erroneous position that the Church failed to condemn slavery.

Although slavery was common in the ancient world, it disappeared in Europe for centuries mainly due to the Church's efforts. Unfortunately, with the conquest of the Canary Islands in the fifteenth century and the discovery of the New World, slavery returned to European society, which prompted consistent and constant papal condemnations from 1435 to 1890.

The secular historical attack also frequently fails to recognize the lack of temporal authority available to the Church to command secular rulers' adherence to its moral teachings. Indeed, secular rulers regularly ignored Church teachings against slavery, but the popes continued to promulgate bulls about the subject anyway. Eugenius IV (r. 1431-1447) was the first pope to do so with *Sicut Dudum*, issued on January 13, 1435. Eugenius demanded that Christians free all enslaved natives of the Canary Islands within fifteen days. Fifty-seven years before Christopher Columbus's first voyage and the discovery of the New World, the Roman pontiff unequivocally proclaimed the inadmissibility of the enslavement of native peoples.

Secularists usually cite the papal bulls *Dum Diversas* (1452) and *Romanus Pontifex* (1454) of Nicholas V (r. 1447-1455) as "proof" that the Church supported slavery before Columbus's voyage and that these proclamations supported subsequent colonial behavior toward natives. However, understanding these documents requires an appreciation of the historical context of their writing.

They were written the year before and the year after the Ottoman Turks' conquest of Constantinople (1453) and the end of the Roman (Byzantine) Empire. The West was fearful of Ottoman incursions (for good reason), and the Turks controlled a large portion of the vital Mediterranean. Pope Nicholas V wrote *Dum Diversas* to King Alfonso of Portugal to authorize his expedition against the Turks in North Africa and to grant a plenary indulgence for those who went on the expedition. The document allowed Alfonso to confiscate land and "enslave" Muslims as part of the expedition. In terms of slavery, this is not unjust servitude, as secularists contend, but rather just title servitude, or the use prisoners of war for various labors (usually galley service in the fleet). *Romanus Pontifex* granted territorial rights to King Alfonso and confirmed the application of just title servitude over Muslims in North Africa.

After the discovery of the New World, Pope Paul III (r. 1534–1549) issued *Sublimus Dei* on June 2, 1537, which he addressed to all the Christian faithful. Paul here emphasized the teaching that all men are called to receive faith and salvation in Jesus Christ because some argued that the Indians of the New World were eligible for slavery because they did not possess the Faith. But Paul taught, to the contrary, that Indians were rational men endowed with human dignity and capable of possessing the Catholic faith and should not be enslaved.

The need for cheap and abundant labor in the colonies led Europeans to engage in the African slave trade. Papal pronouncements categorically rejected this new form of bondage, too, beginning with Pope Innocent XI (r. 1676–1689) and continuing into the nineteenth century. Gregory XVI (r. 1831–1846) issued *In Supremo* on December 3, 1839, condemning the enslavement of Africans. Pope Leo XIII (r. 1878–1903) promulgated two bulls on the subject: *In Plurimis* (May 5, 1888), which encouraged the bishops of Brazil to support the recent abolition of slavery in that country, and *Catholicae Ecclesiae* (November 20, 1890) was addressed to the bishops of the world to support an end to the African slave trade and to encourage the evangelization of Africa by financially supporting the missions.

Despite the numerous papal pronouncements against slavery, European colonists continued the practice of enslaving the native peoples of the New World and Africans. Papal attacks against slavery were so prominent that the colonial Spanish authorities instituted a law forbidding the publication of papal documents in the colonies without prior royal approval.

Although secularists vigorously denounce the Church on the subject of slavery, it is uncommon to see them condemning the widespread and significant Islamic slave trade in Christians in the sixteenth century. Muslim pirates terrorized and enslaved thousands of Christians living around the Mediterranean for nearly two hundred years. Islamic raiders destroyed churches and even desecrated Christian graveyards by digging up corpses. The raids were designed to destabilize the economies of leading Christian states and to inflict psychological warfare on the Christian population.[268] Secular scholars rarely mention the historical reality of these raids and their impact on Christians. Instead, the secular historical attack cancels certain Catholics to further a false narrative about the Church, to discredit it and limit its moral authority in the modern world.

The secular historical attack focuses primarily on three epochs, and certain individual historical figures incur the bulk of their vitriol. Where slavery is concerned, the storm centers on the actions of European colonists in the New World, particularly Christopher Columbus and the Spanish conquistadors. Next comes eighteenth-century France, where Marie Antoinette garners special and vicious attention. The oft-maligned queen of France is unique in the pantheon of Catholic scapegoats since she was used as one not only after death, but also during her life. Marie's entire life is the story of a scapegoat, who was blamed for the ills in French politics and society and eventually sacrificed on the altar of a vicious anti-Catholic and anti-monarchy revolution. And finally, the secular historical attack tries to cancel the longest-reigning pope in history (besides St. Peter), Bl. Pius IX, to illustrate the "evils" of a Church mired in politics.

The secular historical attack remains dominant in the modern world, illustrated in the books and films of our time. It perpetuates an anti-Catholic bias in academia, the press, and the arts that cancels historical Catholics to dismantle traditional societal structures and re-educate society to embrace secular-humanist principles.

Columbus and the Conquistadors

> *Whatever their flaws or accomplishments, the Europeans and native peoples who first met and began the process in which we are now all living at least deserve to be understood in their own fullness. When we make them over into our own image and likeness, or redefine them in contemporary terms, we use other human beings, now dead, rather than working, as we should, to understand them.*[269]

Although the false historical narrative about Christopher Columbus's motivations and behavior in the New World, along with the subsequent activities of the Spanish conquistadors, was created originally by Protestant propaganda in the sixteenth century, it remains a fixture in the modern world, despite research to the contrary, because of the secular historical attack against the Church specifically and Western civilization generally. The secular historical attack imbibes in a deep-seated, mostly unconscious, but nonetheless nefarious myth about Spain, Mexico, the New World, and the Catholic Church, known as the *Leyenda Negra*, the "Black Legend."

From the fifteenth century through the seventeenth, Spain ruled an empire, greater than Rome and the Mongols, that stretched around the world. Spanish influence, economically, militarily, and politically, was pervasive, which produced jealousy in the other nations of Europe, especially England, the Netherlands, and France.

The Protestant Revolution produced a century (1550–1650) of bitter and brutal violence in Europe, which, among other things, fundamentally changed the Spanish Empire. Spain controlled the area of Northern Europe known as the Low Countries, but after the death of the Holy Roman Emperor, king of Spain, and stalwart defender of the Catholic faith, Charles V, violence erupted in the region. King Philip II struggled to contain the rebellion against Spanish rule, but the conflict outlived him. After a nasty and bloody eighty years, the region was wrested from Spanish control and, eventually, became the two separate nations of Protestant Holland (the Netherlands) and Catholic Belgium.

The struggle against Spanish rule of the Low Countries was politically and religiously motivated and mirrored many of the conflicts in other areas of Europe. Protestants in the Low Countries and later in England skillfully used the printing press to create anti-Spanish and anti-Catholic propaganda that shaped Northern European attitudes and behaviors. This false narrative continued for centuries so that by the late nineteenth century, when Spain declined as a world power and lost its major remaining overseas territories (in the Spanish-American War), the Black Legend was solidified in the minds of most Europeans and their immigrant descendants in North America.

Julián Juderías y Loyot (1877–1918), a Spanish historian, coined the term *Leyenda Negra* in the early twentieth century. The American historian Philip Wayne Powell (1913–1987) provided a definition of the term in his 1971 book *Tree of*

Hate: Propaganda and Prejudices Affecting United States Relations with the Hispanic World:

> The Black Legend professes a belief held by non-Spaniards, particularly northern Europeans . . . that Spaniards and Spanish-speaking Catholics of whatever nationality manifest a personal and national depravity that is uniquely cruel, bigoted, tyrannical, obscurantist, lazy, fanatical, greedy, and treacherous.

The Black Legend takes aim at Spanish historical events and individuals, especially the Inquisition and the conquest of the New World.

Black Legend propagandists developed anti-Spanish and anti-Catholic attitudes about the conquest of the New World by utilizing the works of the Dominican Bartolomé de las Casas (1474–1566). A onetime slave owner who became a Dominican priest and champion of Native Americans, de las Casas intended his books to change Spanish colonial behavior toward the indigenous people of the New World and curb abuses, but their publication had the unintended effect of strengthening negative attitudes toward Spain and her people.

De las Casas's *The Destruction of the Indies* (1542) documented atrocities against indigenous peoples and condemned their enslavement, but the work was hyperbolic and selective. For example, he focused his critique on New Spain, where Franciscans operated, but not in Peru, where the Dominicans worked.

De las Casas tended to the extreme in his views, which manifested in his support for the use of African slaves in the New World instead of Indians. His books, which distorted and over-estimated the numbers of Native Americans killed in the New World, were published in Europe when English and Dutch Protestants challenged Spanish colonial efforts abroad and sought to diminish Spanish power in Europe. De las Casas's work was successful in highlighting actual abuse against indigenous people in the New World, but it focused solely on negative interactions, which created a narrative that those were the only type. The fiery Dominican was not a historian, nor was he writing a historical work. Rather, he wrote an emotional tract for a specific purpose.

Ultimately, de las Casas's work was accepted as historical fact and utilized by other writers in the creation of the Black Legend about Spain and the Church.[270] The Black Legend is particularly rooted in the English-speaking world, which believes the myth that "the English would have treated American Indians in more humane fashion than did the Spaniards. There is not a shred of evidence to uphold this comparative view, and, on the contrary, much to disprove it."[271] Indeed, the Spanish crown created a theological commission to debate Spanish conduct in the New World and specifically discussed the question of whether native peoples could be enslaved. Spain was the only colonial power in the New World to debate officially the ethical questions concerning the treatment of indigenous peoples. Moreover, Spain went to great lengths not to send criminals and the socially unfit to the New World, whereas the English did so as official government policy.[272]

English and Dutch Protestant propaganda criticized the Church and reinforced a negative stereotype that Spain was a land of ignorant people controlled by a zealous, cruel, and bigoted clergy. This determined vilification of certain Spanish individuals, policies, institutions, and history created a false narrative that Spain and the Church represent the antithesis of the modern "enlightened" Western (especially English-speaking) world.

The Black Legend endures today. Its main tenets remain rooted in modern consciousness so that it is nearly impossible to have a rational discussion on the subjects of Spanish colonial behavior, the Spanish Inquisition, and the role of the Catholic Church in Spain and the New World.

In the secular historical attack, Christopher Columbus (1451–1506) is the symbol of European greed and genocidal imperialism. In reality, Columbus was a man of his time—a devout Catholic with an interest in evangelization, motivated by religious and personal goals. During his lifetime, his achievements were criticized and downplayed, and he waned in the public memory until preparations to celebrate the quadricentennial of his first voyage were undertaken in the United States. Irish and Italian Catholic immigrants embraced him and revived his memory, but the man and his motivations became lost in a political, societal, and cultural conflict, anchored by the secular historical attack, which culminated in slandering him as deliberately genocidal—a harbinger of destruction, enslavement, and death upon the happy and prosperous people of the Americas.

Russell Means, a leader of the American Indian Movement, characterized this sentiment with his opinion on the explorer: "Columbus makes Hitler look like a juvenile delinquent."[273] Other critics liken Columbus's voyage to opening a new front in the Crusades as that movement to the east became impossible with the rise of the Ottoman Turks:

> After Columbus, the future for Europe lay to the west, not the east. And gradually, all the energy, excitement and terrible, merciless zealotry that had inspired previous generations to make perilous journeys to the Holy Land flooded back, as Christian adventurers fell over themselves to strike out in the opposite direction. It had taken a long time, but at last the realms of Western Christendom had found their new Jerusalem. They swarmed across the seas there in their thousands, as though God himself had willed it.[274]

In the United States, the vitriol directed against Columbus produces annual protests every October with the observance of Columbus Day. A growing movement wants to abolish Columbus Day as a federal holiday, and several cities already celebrate instead "Indigenous Peoples Day." Columbus has become a Catholic symbol of the modern Western world's obsession with a sanctimonious, victimhood-focused narratives rooted in anti-Catholic bias.

The real story of Christopher Columbus and his voyages to the New World begins in Portugal, with the actions of Prince Henry the Navigator (1394–1460). Henry studied ocean currents and wind movement in order to improve navigation for sailing ships and sent Portuguese vessels and sailors down the West African coast, seeking a trade route to India. He also invented the *caravel*, a light ship that was perfect for long-distance, uncharted exploration.

Henry and his sailors inaugurated the great age of explorers finding new lands and creating shipping lanes for the import and export of goods, including consumables never before seen in Europe. Their efforts also created intense competition among the sailing nations of Europe, each striving to outdo the others in finding new and more efficient trade routes.

It was into this world of innovation, exploration, and economic competition that Columbus was born. A native of the Italian city-state of Genoa, Columbus became a sailor at the age of fourteen. He learned the nautical trade sailing on Genoese merchant vessels and became an accomplished navigator.

On a long-distance voyage past Iceland in February 1477, Columbus learned about the strong east-flowing Atlantic currents and believed that a journey across the ocean could be made because the currents would bring a ship home. So Columbus formulated a plan to seek the east by going west.

He knew that such an ambitious undertaking required royal backing, so he repeatedly pursued royal approval from the king of Portugal.

Finally, in May 1486, he secured a royal audience with King Fernando and Queen Isabel of Spain. The queen was intrigued by Columbus's proposal, but before granting approval, she established a commission to study the request. Members of the royal commission were greatly concerned, primarily because they believed that Columbus's calculation of the width of the ocean was incorrect. They were right: Columbus argued that the distance from the Canary Islands to Japan is only 2,800 miles, but it is actually 14,000!

The royal commissioners submitted a report to the queen in 1490 and argued against approval of Columbus's plan, believing that it would take him three years to reach Asia.[275] Although Queen Isabel initially accepted her commission's recommendation, she changed her mind later and supported Columbus. The explorer requested a patent of nobility, the titles of admiral of the Ocean Sea and viceroy and governor of all discovered lands, and ten percent in dividends of all future trade for his daring trip. Isabel agreed, and queen and sailor signed an agreement in April 1492.

With royal support and his conditions secured, Columbus embarked from Spain on August 3, 1492, with ninety men on three ships: the *Niña*, the *Pinta*, and the *Santa María*. The crew comprised mostly Spanish sailors, with no soldiers, illustrating that the voyage was bent on not conquest, but exploration.

After thirty-three days at sea, Columbus's flotilla spotted land (the Bahamas), which he claimed in the name of the Spanish monarchs. Columbus's modern-day detractors view that as a sign of imperial conquest. It was not; it was simply a sign to other European nations that they could not establish trading posts on the Spanish possession.

On this first voyage, Columbus also reached the islands of Cuba and Hispaniola. He stayed four months in the New World and arrived home on March 15, 1493. The *Santa María* ran aground on Hispaniola, so Columbus was forced to leave forty-two men behind. He ordered the Spaniards to treat the indigenous people well and especially to respect the women, but he discovered on his second voyage that his order had not been heeded.

Columbus made four voyages to the New World, and each brought its own discoveries and adventures. Columbus left on his second voyage in September 1493 with a fleet of seventeen ships and 1,200 crewmen, including five missionaries. The third voyage was the most difficult for Columbus, as he was arrested on charges of mismanagement of the Spanish trading enterprise in the New World and sent back to Spain in chains (though he was later exonerated). Columbus's fourth and final voyage took place in 1502–1504, with his son Fernando among the crew. The crossing of the Atlantic was the fastest ever: sixteen days. The expedition visited Honduras, Nicaragua, and Costa Rica and was marooned for a time on Jamaica.

Most modern accounts of Columbus's voyages mistake his motives by focusing narrowly on the "what"—usually pecuniary or political—rather than on the "why" behind his expeditions. Columbus embraced the Catholic worldview of his age. In a letter to King Fernando and Queen Isabel in December 1492, Columbus encouraged the monarchs to "spend all the profits of this my enterprise on the conquest of Jerusalem."[276] And so his primary motive *was* to find gold . . . but to finance a crusade to retake Jerusalem from the Muslims and fulfill the conditions he believed were necessary for the second coming of Christ![277]

Columbus considered himself a "Christ-bearer" like his namesake, St. Christopher, and believed that the evangelization of all peoples was a condition for Jesus' return. His first words to the people of Hispaniola illustrated his focus on evangelization:

"The monarchs of Castile have sent us not to subjugate you, but to teach you the true religion."[278] The explorer recognized that the native peoples of the New World required catechesis and was angered by the chief missionary who accompanied his second voyage, who believed that baptism with no further instruction was sufficient for the new converts. In a 1502 letter to Pope Alexander VI (r. 1492–1503), Columbus asked the pontiff to send missionaries to the indigenous peoples of the New World so they could accept Christ. Columbus desired the evangelization efforts in the New World to continue after his death, and he established an evangelization fund in his will to finance missionary efforts to the lands he discovered.

Columbus's interactions with the indigenous peoples of the New World generate significant interest among modern people and are the foundation of much myth-making from the secular historical attack. Contrary to the popular myth, Columbus initially treated many of the native peoples with great respect and friendship. He was impressed by their "generosity, intelligence, and ingenuity."[279] He recorded in his diary that "in the world there are no better people or a better land. They love their neighbors as themselves, and they have the sweetest speech in the world and [they are] gentle and always laughing."[280]

Columbus demanded that his men exchange gifts with the natives they encountered and not just take what they wanted. He enforced this policy rigorously: on his third voyage in August 1500, he hanged men who disobeyed him by harming the native people.

The secular historical attack posits that Columbus sailed to the New World intent on the enslavement of the native peoples. That myth is widely believed and difficult to eradicate despite the evidence in the historical record.

Columbus had no plan to enslave native peoples when he began his expeditions, but circumstances during the second and third voyages drove him to implement harsh measures, "including enslavement of Indians captured in military actions when there seemed no other way to restore order. But this was not a policy intended to establish a regime of slavery."[281]

Columbus's views concerning the native peoples changed over the course of his multiple voyages based on his interaction with the various tribes and with unruly Spanish settlers. He was a brilliant sailor, navigator, and fearless explorer, but he was not an able administer, as "his rule of both Indians and Spanish oscillated between being too indecisive and too harsh."[282] Columbus was not a violent man, but he utilized violence at times when his poor leadership led to preventable crises. His intentions were good, as his contemporaries, including de las Casas, who knew him, maintained, but he made critical errors in judgment from which the indigenous peoples suffered.

Like most men, Columbus should not be judged solely on decisions in times of crisis. It is easy to criticize the actions of an individual removed from his circumstances, as the explorer himself noted: "Let us hear what their comments are now—those who are so ready with accusations and quick to find fault, saying from their safe berths in Spain, 'Why didn't you do this or that when you were over there?' I'd like to see their sort on this adventure."[283]

Columbus and his actions in the New World are not immune to legitimate criticism, but the use of this daring explorer, who fundamentally altered world history, as a Catholic target to attack the Church and Western history is a travesty of justice. Whether one believes that Columbus' voyages "inaugurated our globalized world" or "were an accidental geographical byproduct of Portuguese expansion two centuries old, of Portuguese-Castilian competition for Atlantic control a century old, and of Portuguese-Castilian competition for a sea route to India older than Columbus himself," there is no doubt that Columbus was a complex man, and his actions in the New World reflected the complexities of his experiences and the time in which he lived.[284] He is neither the saint nor the genocidal fanatic portrayed by different groups with their own agendas in the modern world.

The secular historical attack also takes aim at the Spanish conquistadors, who followed in Columbus's wake to explore and claim lands in the New World. There are many modern-day myths and false narratives about the Spanish conquistadors, many influenced by the Protestant-created Black Legend, but some are the invention of secularists who view these men with abhorrence.

Conquistadors are generally depicted as soldiers sent by the Spanish crown to subjugate and enslave the indigenous peoples of America. But the men who participated in New World expeditions were not soldiers. They did not view themselves or refer to themselves as soldiers in an army. Rather, they were "armed entrepreneurs" who were already in the New World and joined expeditions—not for pay, but in the hopes of acquiring wealth and status by conquering neighboring territories.[285] Standing royal armies were the creation of the European military revolution in the seventeenth century, so the conquistadors were not soldiers of armies as understood in the modern world. Later historians viewed conquistadors through that lens, rather than from the reality of the sixteenth century. "Thus the conquistadors, long after their deaths, all became soldiers."[286]

The typical conquistador paid for his own weapons and expenses, was trained in a particular trade or profession, and in his mid- to late twenties. These men were semiliterate, mostly from southwestern Spanish families, with some experience of exploration and conquest in the New World. All were willing to risk life and limb to be a member of an expedition that conquered a new, wealthy, and well-populated land.[287]

The false narratives and myths favored by the secular historical attack about conquistadors developed, in part, from the documents produced by these men. Leaders of expeditions sent reports to the Spanish crown to inform it of events and to petition the monarchy for rewards in the form of offices, titles, and pensions. These reports, known as *probanzas de mérito* (proof of merit), were inherently biased and written to downplay negative news and highlight success. Later historians treated these greatly exaggerated reports as factual chronicles and used them as the foundational narrative of conquistador actions, thus creating sensational false narratives.[288]

Another modern-day myth about the Spanish conquistadors concerns the role of the Spanish monarchy. Spanish New World expeditions are usually described as a concerted, planned, ordered, and funded campaign by the Spanish crown, but in reality, the monarchy did not "conceive, organize," or "finance conquest expeditions" or send conquistadors in a royal army to the Americas.[289] The crown did grant licenses and contracts to conquistadors to explore and conquer territory in the New World and bestowed the title of *adelantado* (captain-general) to the leader of an expedition, which could then be changed to *governor* after a successful conquest.

Some conquistador leaders exaggerated their success in the *probanza* reports to ensure the granting of titles by the crown, which was the foundation of accumulating wealth and providing recompense for the expenses incurred during the expedition. Conquistadors were concerned with successfully demonstrating the fulfillment of their contract terms with the crown because their financial solvency rested on such claims. They were not concerned with acquiring land, contrary to popular myths; rather, they wanted to "receive an *encomienda*, or grant of native tribute and labor—not land."[290] The wealth from the land, not the land itself, was what interested them.

This perspective helps to dispel another myth of the conquistadors: that they participated in large-scale enslavement of native peoples. Conquistadors needed native peoples to stay and work on the land to ensure its economic vitality, so they did not generally capture indigenous people to sell as slaves. When the native population substantially declined, due mostly to diseases brought by the conquistadors, the Spanish made recourse to imported African slaves. Conquistadors were not disinterested explorers, but neither were they the bloodthirsty, genocidal monsters typically depicted in the secular historical attack.

Whereas conquistadors *en masse* are derided in the secular historical attack, Hernán Cortés (1485–1547) occupies a pre-eminent place in the modern pantheon of villainous Catholic personages. It is common to find him in lists of the "most brutal" conquistadors.[291] The 500th anniversaries of his landing at Veracruz in 1519 and conquest of Mexico in 1520-1521 produced varied reactions in Spain and Mexico. The modern world calls Cortés's legacy into question, to put it lightly, with active efforts to "cancel" his memory and achievements and to tear down statues erected in his honor (including in his hometown of Medellín, Spain).

While the Church was embattled in the theological revolution, which soon turned political, in German territory in the early sixteenth century, on the other side of the world, an unauthorized expedition of five hundred Spaniards left Cuba for a journey to the interior of modern-day Mexico. Nearly three decades after Columbus's first voyage to the New World, the Spanish conquistador Hernán Cortés landed his ships at Veracruz on Good Friday, April 22, 1519, with multiple objectives, chief among them the conversion of the indigenous peoples to the Catholic faith.

Cortés was a pious man of deep faith, a son of the Church. Bernal Díaz, one of Cortés's companions, who wrote an account of the conquest toward the end of his life, described his leader's faith life: he wore

> just a thin chain of gold of a single pattern and a trinket with the image of Our Lady the Virgin Saint Mary with her precious Son in her arms. . . . He prayed every morning with a [book of] Hours and heard Mass with devotion; he had for his protector the Virgin Mary our Lady . . . as well as the Lord St. Peter and St. James and the Lord St. John the Baptist.[292]

Cortés also launched his expedition for personal advancement and the authority of a governorship. He followed the typical pattern of Spanish colonial efforts in the Americas, wherein conquistadors established a legal basis for the conquest by the public reading of the *Requerimiento* (Requirement) that declared a formal territorial claim and requested the submission of the native peoples.[293] Conquistadors also displayed or made a theatrical use of violence, including public kidnapping of rulers, to subjugate and exploit some native peoples, whom they needed as a compliant labor force. Always outmanned, Spanish conquistadors specifically sought alliances with other native peoples in their attacks against certain tribes. For example, for his conquest of the Aztec Empire, Cortés brought two hundred native Cubans to Mexico in 1519 and gathered other tribes hostile to the Mexica.[294] He was a brilliant leader and motivator of men, but his conquest of the Mexica would not have happened without assistance from other indigenous peoples.

After landing at Veracruz, Cortés marched his troops to the Mexica capital city of Tenochtitlán (on the site of the future Mexico City), a metropolis of 200,000 people in the center of a lake. The Aztec Empire consisted of a warlike people who conquered neighboring tribes to expand their empire and provide the human capital needed to satiate their bloodthirsty gods. The Mexica practiced more human sacrifices than any other New World native peoples.

Every imperial city and large town in Mexico had a central square, from which a temple pyramid rose to the sky. This is where human sacrifices were performed.

The victim was laid on a table, where a priest would cut out his beating heart and hold it aloft for the worshipers to see. The head was severed and thrown with the body down the temple steps. The body was then cut up and given to the family of the warrior who had captured the victim to cook and eat.[295]

The Mexica also practiced child sacrifice to Tláloc, the god of agricultural fertility. Children between the ages of two and seven were killed by having their throats slashed.[296] Imperial law mandated 1,000 human sacrifices a year in every temple, which totaled nearly 20,000 victims annually.[297] Thirty years before the Spanish arrival in the city, an inauguration of the Great Temple took place during which the human sacrificial toll surpassed 80,000 over four days.

Cortés sought the end of the grotesque and barbaric human sacrifices in conversations with the Aztec emperor, Moctezuma II. Eventually, Cortés arrested Moctezuma, an action deemed necessary for Spanish protection, and received permission from the emperor, in January 1520, to allow the placement of an altar, a cross, and an image of the Blessed Virgin Mary in the Great Temple.

Moctezuma was held in captivity for six months before his death. (Accounts differ as to the manner of death, with blame placed on either the Mexica or the Spanish.) When Cortés left the city to deal with the arrival of another Spanish force sent from Cuba to arrest the conquistador for his unauthorized foray, a large group of unarmed Mexica warriors, who had gathered to dance during a temple festival, were massacred by the remaining Spanish. This raised the ire of the indigenous population and forced the Spanish to flee the city. Cortés led his remnant army to Tlaxcala, a neighboring region containing a tribe hostile to the Mexica. Establishing alliances with Tlaxcalans and other indigenous tribes, Cortés and the Spanish captured Tenochtitlán in August 1521, dealing a significant blow to Mexica hegemony.

Cortés was aided throughout the conquest by a former slave known as La Malinche, or Doña Marina, who was stolen or sold into slavery as a child to the Chontal Mayans. La Malinche was among a group of nineteen other female slaves given to the Spanish by the Chontals as part of a peace agreement. La Malinche was baptized and served as Cortés's interpreter: the explorer spoke Spanish to Gerónimo de Aguilar, who spoke Maya to La Malinche, who spoke Nahuatl to the Mexica. La Malinche later became Cortés's mistress and bore the conquistador a son (Martin). In the secular historical attack, La Malinche, like Cortés, has been maligned as a traitor to her people who assisted the conquistadors for selfish material and personal gain.

The conquest of New Spain was a bloody affair. The Spanish suffered significant casualties (more than fifty percent) during the two-year war, but the Mexica suffered substantially more.

The introduction of disease to the native population had substantial impacts, with the deaths of 40 million people within a century.[298] Although that significant decline in the native population occurred after Cortés, his expedition unintentionally introduced the epidemic and affected the Mexica population during the conquest. A more significant factor in Cortés's success was native disunity: neighboring tribes intensely disliked the Mexica. Native peoples viewed themselves as "members of particular communities or city-states" and "very seldom as members of larger ethnic groups and certainly not as anything even approaching the category of 'Indians' or 'natives.'"[299] Cortés took advantage of native disunity and effectively utilized tribes hostile to the Mexica as military allies during the conquest. Finally, Spanish military tactics and weapons played an important role in the success of the expedition. Particularly, Spanish swords, made from steel, proved far superior to the obsidian weapons of the Mexica. Indeed, "a Spaniard could fight for hours and receive light flesh wounds and bruises while killing many natives."[300]

The conquistadors, as "armed entrepreneurs," did not desire the extermination of native peoples. Rather, they wanted subservient laborers for the land they hoped would bring wealth, comfort, and productive prosperity to them for years. Cortés, as governor of New Spain, established hospitals to care for native peoples as well as schools and printing presses for their education. Contrary to the myths of the secular historical attack, "the majority of natives subject to colonial rule continued to live in their own communities, speak their own languages, work their own fields, and be judged and ruled by their own elders."[301] As a result, the indigenous people of the Americas were not despoiled or left desolate by the conquest. In fact, native peoples proved resilient and adapted to the arrival of Europeans, "and many natives, especially elites, found opportunity in Conquest-era transition."[302]

There is no doubt that the Spanish conquistadors and subsequent colonization severely impacted the indigenous peoples of the New World, both negatively and positively. Negatively, the Spanish conquest of the Mexica resulted in a catastrophic death toll from violence and the unintended introduction of European diseases. Positively, Cortés's expedition ended the barbaric practice of human sacrifice in the Aztec Empire, and Spanish evangelization efforts, undertaken without much success until the appearance of Our Lady of Guadalupe a decade afterward, brought the light of Christ to a new area of the world.

Hernán Cortés was no saint, but neither should he be a lightning rod for all that modern-day secularists believe is wrong with the Church and Western civilization. Cortés was a man of his age and culture, who, at least in part, was motivated by a desire to see the gospel communicated to people enslaved in darkness. Catholics cannot justify all of his actions in the New World, but understanding the man in the historical context of his age is vital to defending his memory from the secular historical attack.

Marie Antoinette

> *She was the victim of a vicious, shrewdly sustained process of character assassination from the moment she set foot in France, a sinister, carefully orchestrated campaign of calumny, which tried in particular to destroy her moral reputation. An intellectual climate fanatically hostile to traditional monarchy, and sheer human jealously, exploited the xenophobic hatred of her as an Austrian and her own aloofness to make her the scapegoat for all French ills.*[303]

In the gallery of canceled Catholics, pride of place is given to Marie Antoinette (1755–1793), queen of France. There is perhaps no other Catholic in history who was maligned just as much during her life as she was after her death.

Marie's main crime was that she was not born in France. Despite her deep love for her adopted homeland, she was treated as a foreigner and reviled in the most grotesque manner in the Parisian media.

The myths, falsities, gossip, and calumny about this devoted Catholic woman continue centuries after her violent death at the hands of an illegal and demonic revolutionary movement. Erroneously portrayed in modern-day media, Marie Antoinette is still a (false) symbol of an aloof, uncaring, rich monarch who flippantly responded (allegedly) with a quip about cake when her subjects were starving in the streets. The secular historical attack, rooted in liberal and Marxist ideology, utilizes Marie Antoinette as the perfect example of the evil Catholic monarch and an illustration of why the Church and politics should be separated completely.

The myth of Marie and the use of her memory by enemies of the Church is deeply ingrained in the modern mind—such that it becomes nearly impossible to tell the real story of the famous queen of the French, who was a loving, faithful wife, mother, and daughter of the Church, and who brought to France one of the most recognizable "French" products in the world: the croissant.

The monarchy and the Church in France had been closely aligned since the baptism of Clovis in the late 400s. Powerful prelates played pivotal roles in the governance of France over the centuries. For example, Abbot Suger of St. Denis (c. 1081–1151), creator of French ("Gothic")-style architecture, served as regent during Louis VII's (r. 1137–1180) absence from the kingdom while participating in the Second Crusade (1147–1149). Perhaps the most (in-) famous example of the linkage between the Church and the French monarchy was the relocation of the papal residence from Rome to Avignon, in southern France, at the behest of King Philip IV (r. 1285–1314) in the fourteenth century—a move which kept the papacy in France for seventy years.

The reign of the "Sun King," Louis XIV (r. 1643–1715), marked a new development in the relationship between the

Church and the monarchy. Louis was not content with a close collaboration with the Church; instead, as part of his vision of an absolute monarchy, the king wanted to control the Church. Louis thought the Church in France should be subject to the king, but not in an English way, with the monarch as the supreme head of the Church.

Louis respected the papacy (to an extent) and desired doctrinal loyalty to Rome, but he believed that the Church in France should possess unique local powers that kept it semi-independent of the pope and more controllable by the monarch. This view became known as *Gallicanism*.

Louis adopted policies designed to isolate the Church in France from the pope, which culminated in the 1682 Gallican Articles, which decreed that the pope had no secular power in France. So he could not depose kings, nor were secular rulers required to obey him in temporal matters. The articles also posited the heresy of *conciliarism* by declaring the pope subject to ecumenical councils and, finally, demanded that the pope respect the ancient customs afforded the Church in France.

Pope Bl. Innocent XI (r. 1676–1689) condemned the Gallican Articles, but they shaped Louis's interaction with the Church throughout his reign. The close linkage between the monarchy and the Church in France led revolutionary elements to attack and destroy both vital institutions at the end of the eighteenth century.

Archduchess Maria Antonia Josefa Johanna was born on November 2, 1755 in the imperial palace of the Hofburg in Vienna as the fifteenth child (and last daughter) of the Holy Roman Emperor, Franz I (r. 1745–1765), and Empress Maria Theresa (r. 1740–1780). Every daughter of the imperial couple was given "Maria" as a first name, so the girls were usually known by their second names, hence the youngest daughter was called "Antonia" in the imperial household. The empress was exceedingly busy ruling the vast domain (a territory that comprised the modern-day nations of Austria, Hungary, the Czech Republic, Slovakia, half of Romania, a good portion of the Balkans, most of northern Italy, and parts of Germany), especially after her husband's death, when Antonia was nine years old, so, she spent little time with her children. Indeed, it was not uncommon for the empress to be absent from her children for as much as ten days.

Despite the absence of her mother, Antonia lived a charmed and comfortable life. She loved drawing, music, and dancing and learned to sing in French and Italian. As a young girl, Antonia met a young Wolfgang Amadeus Mozart when he came to the palace for a performance in 1767. Father Jacques de Vermond, the archduchess's first serious tutor, described the young Maria Antonia: "She has a most graceful figure; holds herself well; and if, as may be hoped, she grows a little taller, she will possess every good quality one could wish for in a great princess. Her heart and character are both excellent."[304] However, he was dismayed at her lack of education: the teenage Maria Antonia could not even write proper French or German, the result of negligence from her governess.

Maria Antonia knew from a young age that she was destined for a political marriage. The Hapsburg family motto was "Others make war, but thou, O happy Austria, makest marriages."[305] The empress wanted peace with France after years of warfare and proposed the marriage of Maria Antonia to Louis-Auguste, the dauphin of France. Maria Antonia was thirteen years old when the dauphin accepted the betrothal, and she left Austria on April 21, 1770, at the age of fifteen, never to see her homeland again.

Maria Antonia (known in France as Marie Antoinette) arrived in Strasbourg, a French border town, and was met by a French delegation that spoke to her in German. But the teenage archduchess replied, "Don't speak to me in German, *messieurs*, as from now on I only understand French."[306] She arrived in Compiègne on May 14, where she met King Louis XV and his grandson and her betrothed, Louis-Auguste. The dauphin was tall for his age, six feet by the age of sixteen, but was not handsome. He was overweight, ungainly, disheveled, shortsighted, inarticulate, and awkward. He liked to eat, hunt, and work on laborious and dirty projects, including blacksmithing.[307]

When the royal coaches made their way to Paris, they were forced to wait for some time due to an accident in the city from an overturned wagon that had killed a hundred and fifty people, who were trampled in the ensuing traffic jam. When news of the tragedy reached Marie, she cried for the victims and pledged along with Louis-Auguste to sacrifice a year's private spending money to aid the victims' families.[308]

The royal marriage occurred in 1771 and ultimately produced four children. In April 1778, a pregnant Marie Antoinette jested to the king, "I have come to complain, sire, about one of your subjects who has been rude enough to kick me in the belly."[309] A daughter, Marie-Thérèse Charlotte (1778–1851), was born later. A miscarriage followed the birth of Marie-Thérèse, but then a son, Louis Joseph (1781–1789), the new dauphin, was born. Another son, Louis-Charles (1785–1795) was born and would briefly reign as Louis XVII. Finally, another daughter, Marie Sophie, was born in 1786 but died eleven months later of tuberculosis.

Marie had been in France for five years before Louis-Auguste was crowned king (Louis XVI) in 1775, but she felt isolated in a strange and foreign land. As a young queen consort, Marie lived extravagantly. Versailles was the site of various entertainments, including races, hunting parties, masked balls, operas, and plays. Marie spent lavishly on jewels, especially diamonds, and clothes. She bought an average of one hundred and seventy new dresses annually and exceeded her clothing budget by 40,000 livres (around $600,000 today!).[310] The young queen also enjoyed gambling and once held a wagering party that lasted thirty-six hours. Her gambling habit proved problematic when she acquired a debt of 487,272 livres ($7.6 million today) by January 1777, which the king paid from his personal resources.[311]

The queen was not ill disciplined in all aspects of life. She practiced modesty in her style of clothes and did not take a lover. Moreover, unlike the king, Marie was moderate in eating and drinking. She rarely drank wine, and when she did, it was watered down. Her breakfast consisted of coffee and a croissant, the Austrian pastry she had brought to France, and she usually ate chicken (roasted or boiled) for dinner.[312] In contrast, the king's breakfast consisted of a whole chicken, four porkchops, ham, six baked eggs, and half a bottle of champagne.[313]

Marie's excessive expenditure of funds and the constant revelry at Versailles tainted her reputation among certain elements in French society. She was already disliked by most of the nobility due to her foreign-born status. Many French noblemen had fought against Austria in recent wars, and numerous noble families had lost relatives and neighbors in the fighting. Her immature and expensive cavorting at Versailles produced the derogatory nickname "Madame Deficit," and her Austrian origin earned the moniker *l'Autrichienne* ("the Austrian bitch") from members of the nobility. Her demise in 1793 was due in large part to the hostility of the nobility, as noted by her twentieth century biographer Stefan Zweig: "The axe of hatred which severed the queen's neck had been put into the executioner's hands by the delicate and bejeweled fingers of the aristocracy."[314]

In the 1780s, propaganda against Marie increased as printing presses throughout Paris spread lies about the queen. Salacious tales of sexual proclivities including orgies, lesbianism, and adultery were splashed across the pages of Parisian "newspapers" to the queen's detriment and the monarchy's reputation. Marie lamented the false reports and remarked that "calumny kills people better than anything, and it is by calumny that they will kill me."[315] The great irony is that during the period of intense and constant propaganda, the queen had lessened her gambling habit and decreased her clothing expenditures as motherhood produced a greater level of maturity.

Perhaps the most damning propaganda against Marie specifically and the monarchy in general was the "Affair of the Diamond Necklace" in 1785. Years before, the aged King Louis XV had ordered Charles August Böhmer, a Swiss jeweler, to make an elaborate and exceptionally expensive necklace, consisting of 647 diamonds of 2,800 carats, worth 1.6 million livres ($25 million today).[316] The old king died before the necklace was completed, which left the Swiss jeweler distraught (and in debt). Louis XVI offered to purchase the necklace for Marie to give as a future wedding gift to their daughter, but Antoinette refused and said the money should be used instead to construct a warship. Böhmer demanded that the queen buy the piece, or he would commit suicide. Marie did not give in to the jeweler's hysterics and suggested he break the necklace into smaller pieces in order to expedite its sale.

At this stage, the saga turned bizarre, with the introduction of a "cast of characters" who "seemed perfect symbols of a regime worm-eaten with corruption."[317] The archbishop of Strasbourg, Cardinal Louis de Rohan, a gullible man desirous of the queen's attention and favoritism, thrust himself into the story by offering to buy the necklace. The cardinal told Böhmer that the queen now wanted the piece and that he had been sent to acquire it for her. De Rohan had been convinced by Jeanne de La Motte, a charlatan, who hired an actress to portray the queen in an elaborate nighttime skit, where Marie supposedly told the cardinal she wanted the necklace. Additionally, de La Motte hired a forger to craft a letter from the queen to de Rohan about the necklace. Both duplicitous actions persuaded the cardinal that Marie needed him to acquire the precious piece.

Ultimately, Böhmer gave the necklace to de La Motte, acting on behalf of the cardinal, who then fled to England and sold it. When the jeweler came to Versailles to demand payment, the plot was discovered, and de Rohan was publicly arrested as he processed to the Royal Chapel to celebrate Mass. King Louis XVI was irate and ordered the cardinal imprisoned in the Bastille. Eventually, the duped cleric was tried by the Paris *Parlement* but, to the surprise of Louis and Marie, found not guilty and acquitted.

The public, kept abreast of the affair by press reports during the trial, blamed the queen for the entire episode. Opponents of Marie Antoinette used the "Affair of the Diamond Necklace" to transform public opinion against her so that she was seen by the people of France, both nobles and commoners alike, not as the beloved queen but as the "Austrian whore" who was concerned only about riches and ostentatious pieces of jewelry. Not only was the sordid affair a stain on Marie's reputation, but it seriously damaged the legitimacy of the monarchy and the Church in popular opinion, as one councilor of the Paris *Parlement* remarked that the situation was a "nice little smear of dirt on both crown and crozier."[318]

Propaganda directed against the queen during her lifetime manifested into later myths about her concern for the French people suffering during the height of the financial crisis in the 1780s. The secular historical attack continues to posit the myth that Marie, when told about the plight of her French subjects, callously remarked, "Let them eat cake." The phrase itself is poorly translated from the French, which includes the word *brioche* rather than *gâteau* (cake). *Brioche* was a pastry made with flour enriched with eggs and butter and thus more expensive than ordinary bread.[319]

But the difference between *brioche* and bread must be seen for the distraction that it is. The infamous quote remains fixed in the modern mind about Marie Antoinette and King Louis XVI despite the fact the queen never uttered it. The insensitive remark was never attributed to her during her lifetime or the French Revolution. Post-Revolution secular historians used the false quote to portray a corrupt, evil, and morally decadent monarchy linked with the Church to preclude a return of the crown.

The phrase first appears in Jean-Jacques Rousseau's *Confessions*, which was published in 1769, a year before Marie ever set foot in France. It is possible that the quote originated with Maria Theresa of Spain (1638–1683), the first wife of Louis XIV, who died seventy-two years *before* Marie Antoinette was born!

The truth is that the queen was very concerned with the health and well-being of her adopted subjects and established soup kitchens in Paris to feed the hungry during the difficult financial times in France. But the propaganda against the queen created a negative environment toward the monarchy so that when the kingdom was beset by severe financial problems in the late 1780s, people turned against Louis and Marie and viewed the Church and its wealth as a means to end the national suffering.

By 1789, the Catholic Church in France appeared on firm ground. It was structured into 139 dioceses, with 40,000 parishes staffed by 128,000 priests and women religious, and it owned ten percent of the land in France.[320] The country was overwhelmingly Catholic, with a small population of Protestants and Jews. France was one of the most powerful nations in the world. Its longtime rival, England, had an impressive navy but had just suffered a shocking loss in the American War of Independence (1775–1783), thanks in part to French military assistance to the colonies. For the most part, the kingdom appeared stable. Few would have predicted the end of both the monarchy and the Church in France by the end of the century.

Louis XVI was neither a tyrant nor an inspiring leader. He was a good man devoted to his people and the Church, but he was plagued with indecisiveness. He loved his people. He ceased government control of the grain trade, which reduced the price of bread; made the courts more just; abolished torture of accused prisoners; and ended the custom that required peasants to work two weeks a year without pay on public roads.

Louis's indecisiveness and the growing antagonism of an increasingly powerful and wealthy nobility led to the destruction of the monarchy. France in the 1780s was in severe financial straits, caused, in part, by its participation in the American war against England. Half the royal budget was spent servicing interest on loans, so Charles-Alexandre de Calonne, the royal finance minister, proposed a plan in 1786 to tax the nobility and clergy to increase royal revenue. The plan was not popular and caused significant disagreement. Instead, Louis cut royal expenditures. Nearly one hundred and seventy-five royal courtiers lost their positions at court. The grand falconer was fired, wolfhounds were sold, and six hundred members of the royal guard were released from duty. Additionally, the king auctioned several royal chateaus and abolished numerous royal household posts.[321]

Although cutting royal costs was a good decision, it was not enough to solve the financial crisis. Many argued for the confiscation of the wealth and property of the Church to stem the financial hemorrhage.

Revolutionary elements in French society increasingly viewed the dire financial situation as an opportunity to attack and, perhaps, destroy the monarchy and Church at the same time. Recognizing that the radical situation required a radical solution, Louis XVI abolished the Paris *Parlement* and called a meeting of the Estates-General for May 1, 1789. This deliberative body, comprising representatives from the Church (First Estate), the nobility (Second Estate), and the lower classes (Third Estate), had not met since 1614. The king hoped the assembled deputies would find a solution to the kingdom's financial crisis.

The meeting of the Estates-General did not proceed as the king envisioned. Bickering erupted over the manner of counting votes (by head or estate), which led to a prolonged stalemate. Frustrated with the situation, the Third Estate, with some members of the First Estate, declared themselves a "National Assembly" and announced their intention to proceed without the other two groups. Reacting to this unusual creation, royal officials locked the National Assembly out of the regular meeting hall at Versailles, so, the body occupied the royal indoor tennis court, where they vowed not to disperse until the writing of a new constitution. In early July, the king allowed the other estates to join the assembly, which renamed itself the National Constituent Assembly and proceeded with the task of developing the new governing document.

Fearful that the nobility would dissolve the Third Estate, revolutionary elements in Paris stormed the Bastille, a royal prison, on July 14, 1789. The Bastille, already scheduled for demolition by the king due to its high maintenance costs, contained only seven prisoners. The Parisian mob killed the commander and stuck his head on a pike.

The summer of 1789 was a time of crisis not only in France, but also for the royal family. Five weeks before the storming of the Bastille, Louis's and Marie's heir, Louis Joseph, died before his seventh birthday. Marie Antoinette grieved his death to the point that the anguish, and stress from the national situation, turned the thirty-four-year-old queen's hair white. Additional heartache and stress visited Marie when, a few months later, the royal family was forcibly removed from Versailles and placed effectively under "house arrest" in the Tuileries Palace in Paris.

Meanwhile, three groups had formed in the National Assembly: the "patriots," who wanted a new France free from the monarchy and the Church; the "monarchists," who desired an English type of constitutional monarchy; and the "traditionalists," who supported the *ancien régime* and wanted no changes to France's governing structure. These groups vied for power in the National Constituent Assembly, which forced the king to swear a public oath in July 1790 to "use all the powers delegated to me by the state's constitutional law to maintain the constitution decreed by the National Assembly."[322]

The new government moved against the Church. Church lands had already been confiscated in November 1789, and then, on July 12, 1790, the revolutionary government passed the Civil Constitution of the Clergy, which officially separated the Church in France from Rome. The government assumed control of the Church, as the people elected their bishops, diocesan boundaries were redrawn to match civil jurisdictions, parishes were closed, and clergy were considered employees of the state. As such, the clergy were required to take an oath of fidelity to the government, a scene similar to Henry VIII's England. However, unlike in England, the vast majority of French bishops (ninety-six percent) refused the oath, which

Pope Pius VI (r. 1775–1799) had condemned.[323] The creation of a national Church in France established a difficult situation for Catholics, who faced the choice between state-sanctioned clergy and "non-juring" priests.

Marie remained steadfast in her faith during this difficult and stressful time. She received the sacraments only from non-juring priests but officially participated in public liturgies from oath-taking clergy, without reception of the Eucharist.[324]

By the fall of 1790, Louis and Marie recognized the need to leave Paris for their safety, which proved extremely difficult, but the Knights of Malta provided funds to the royal family to establish a "shadow" government outside Paris. So, in the summer of 1791, the royal family, under disguise, sneaked out of Paris and made their way to the frontier, where loyalist forces waited for them. Unfortunately, Louis and Marie were discovered just short of their goal and were arrested and forcibly returned to Paris. Then, in the fall of 1791, the National Assembly was disbanded and replaced with the Legislative Assembly, formed to implement the newly created constitution (without Church participation), but this body proved extremely ineffective, which allowed violent and radical elements to exert influence.

On August 10, 1792, the final nightmare for the royal family began as an armed mob descended on the Tuileries and took Louis and Marie and their children into custody, after a heroic but futile stand by six hundred Swiss Guards. The king and queen were separated from each other and their children. Marie was imprisoned and later transferred to the Conciergerie, where she was provided two meals a day, including a lunch of soup, a plate of vegetables, and dessert along with a dinner of similar food but less in portions.

A month after the royal family's arrest, the monarchy was officially abolished, and the Reign of Terror began, when extreme revolutionaries went on a killing spree, which resulted in the deaths of more than 1,300 people, including several hundred non-juring bishops and priests.

The next year witnessed the height of the terror, which began with the execution of King Louis XVI in January. The king ascended the execution platform, was strapped to the guillotine, and shouted, "Frenchmen, I die innocent. May my blood strengthen the happiness of the Fr—" His head was held aloft to cries of "*Vive la Nation!*"[325]

With the death of the king, the destruction of the Church followed. The revolutionaries embarked on a de-Christianization campaign to rid France of its Catholic culture and history. The Gregorian calendar was changed to a "calendar of reason," with new names for the months and a new ten-day week, in order to abolish Sunday as the day of worship. The calendar now comprised ten months of three weeks, with every tenth day as a period of rest. New Year's Day was established as September 22 to honor the date in 1792 when the monarchy was officially overthrown. Churches were confiscated and turned into "temples of reason," and a prostitute was crowned "Goddess of Reason" in Notre Dame cathedral.

In an attempt to halt the destruction of the Church, a Catholic uprising began in the Vendée region (southwest France) in March 1793. The troops from the Vendée, under the command of Jacques Cathelineau, marched into battle under the banner of the Sacred Heart of Jesus. Sadly, at the Battle of Nantes in July, Cathelineau was killed by a well-placed sniper shot, which halted the movement. The failure of the uprising resulted in severe measures by the government, which engaged in the genocide of the Catholic people of the Vendée, killing hundreds of thousands.[326]

Almost ten months passed after the execution of the king, and during that time, people clamored for the trial of the queen. Parisian newspaper articles stirred emotions with words such as "the widow of [Louis] must be judged. Do Marie Antoinette's crimes, the crimes of a blasphemous woman driven by a demon, have to become even blacker before she can be condemned? She must pay with her filthy blood."[327] Charges including wasteful expenditures from the national treasury, collaboration with an enemy of France (Austria), opposition to the Revolution, and sexually abusing her son were levied against her. At her trial, the public prosecutor introduced this last charge by saying,

> Finally, the widow [of Louis], although immoral in every possible way, is so thoroughly perverted and so accustomed to every enormity that, regardless of her duty as a mother and of the laws of nature, she did not shrink from indulging with her own son Louis-Charles, as the latter attests, in indecencies of which the mere mention arouses a shudder of horrors.[328]

The false accusation was the last piece of spiteful propaganda attached to the foreign-born archduchess, brought to a strange land as a teenager, who, despite hateful and hurtful venom from her adopted people, deeply loved her subjects and France.

Marie was convicted on all counts on October 16, 1793, and, despite hope of deportation and exile, sentenced to death. The queen wrote a final letter to her sister illustrating her deep faith and love for Christ and the Church:

> I die in the Catholic, apostolic, and Roman religion, in the faith of my father in which I was brought up and which I have always professed. I sincerely beseech God to pardon me for all the sins I have committed since I was born and I trust that in his goodness he will hear my last petitions, and especially those I have made for many years that, of his mercy and goodness, he will receive my soul. I ask pardon of every one of my acquaintance. . . . I forgive all my enemies any harm they may have done me.[329]

Marie desired to receive the sacraments but told her sister that if a state-sanctioned priest came to her cell, she "will have nothing to say to him and will treat him as a total stranger."[330] Providentially, a non-juring priest ministered to her, and she went to confession and received the Eucharist.

The execution of Marie was a humiliating affair. Forced into an open cart from her cell in the Conciergerie, she was paraded before a crowd of 30,000 people with shouts of "there goes the Austrian! Death to the Austrian!" for an hour to the Place de la Révolution (now the Place de la Concorde), where she was guillotined.[331]

It is difficult to find a more perfect example of the Catholic scapegoat than Marie Antoinette, as "to the memory of no other woman, and few of either sex, has the verdict of her time and of history been so unjustly and vindictively destructive."[332]

Pope Bl. Pius IX

It is not as a petty Italian prince that Pio Nono will stand to be judged by history. He will have to be considered in his role as the most important opponent of the extravagant claims, political and ideological, of the nineteenth-century progressives, as the most obstinate and influential of those who denied the infallibility of progress, the moral authority of majorities, and the omnipotence of the State.[333]

Another Catholic target of the secular historical attack is the saintly pope who holds the longest reign of any pontiff except St. Peter.

Pope Bl. Pius IX's (r. 1846–1878) pontificate witnessed intense political and social turmoil. At his death, the papacy had radically changed. The pope's temporal possessions, known officially as the Patrimony of St. Peter and colloquially as the Papal States, were violently confiscated by anti-Catholic and anti-papal forces bent on Italian unification, and the princedom of the pontiffs, which had existed from the grant of Pepin the Short (718–768) in 754, ceased to exist in the late nineteenth century.

Pius IX was viciously attacked throughout most of his pontificate for his political policies; for his theological writings; for the pronouncement of papal infallibility at the First Vatican Council; and for a unique case, which became an international *cause célèbre*, involving the 1858 "kidnapping" of a Jewish boy from Bologna named Edgardo Mortara.

The criticism of Pius IX continued into the year 2000, when his beatification drew near. At this point, the memory of that Jewish boy, co-opted by an international pressure campaign, returned to the fore. As one example, a Jewish-American organization purchased a full-page ad in the *Washington Post* exhorting Pope St. John Paul II (r. 1978-2005) not to beatify the "kidnapper pope."[334]

The furor over Pius IX's beatification was also stoked, in part, by the 1998 book *The Kidnapping of Edgardo Mortara* by the American historian David I. Kertzer. Kertzer, a specialist in Italian history, has made a career out of writing critical and highly sensational books against Popes Pius IX, Pius XI, and Pius XII. Kertzer's book on the Mortara case focused heavily on the sensational aspects of the early years of Edgardo's life and limited discussion of the boy's later years, which tell a very different tale.

Despite the intense public pressure, John Paul II, on September 3, 2000, beatified Pius IX. Anti-clerical organizations in Italy listed Pius IX's beatification as one of the worst "Catholic infamies" and referred to the saintly man as a "criminal pope" who grabbed children from their families.[335]

The slander and calumny against Pius IX continued after his beatification. Sergio Minerbi, the former Israeli ambassador to Belgium, in a 2005 *Il Giornale* article, seriously misrepresented the Mortara case by writing that the boy "was kidnapped from his family in Bologna and baptized so as to make him become a priest."[336] Twenty years after his sensational book on the Mortara case, David Kertzer continued his assault on Pius IX with a critical book, *The Pope Who Would Be King*, on his political policies. Kertzer painted the pope as a power-hungry monarch who selfishly fought to maintain control of his Italian territory, which he (allegedly) ruled as a theocracy.

In Kertzer's view, Pius IX and the Church were the enemies of the modern secular principles of democracy, religious freedom, free speech, and the separation of Church and State. Kertzer maintains that Pius IX was more than critical of these principles; he argues the pope actually condemned and declared them as "incompatible with Christianity."[337] Additionally, Kertzer wrote that after the pope's return from exile in Naples, the Jewish people in Rome

> found themselves again confined to lives of poverty in the ghetto, objects of scorn and abuse. Worst of all, they lived in fear that their children might be taken from them, for should any Christian think to baptize a Jewish child, under the laws of the Church, that child had to be removed from his Jewish family to be raised a Catholic.[338]

The former Catholic seminarian and British author John Cornwell added to the chorus of critics of Pius IX, writing in his 2004 book *The Pope in Winter* (a critical work about Pope John Paul II) that "today, in any civil society, [Pius IX] would have faced a jail sentence for child molestation and kidnap."[339]

The Mortara case (discussed in more detail later in this section) is a complex and unique situation that occupies only a small portion of the multifaceted pontificate of Pius IX. However, it forms the basis for much of the secular historical attack against a pope who reigned during one of the most politically and socially turbulent times in history. Ultimately, the secular historical attack cancels Pius IX because he refused to bow to the revolutionary mob who desired the eradication of the Church and its influence in the world. His unwavering fidelity to Christ and his Church placed him in the crosshairs of enemies bent on remaking the world in their own image and likeness and who rejected the eternal truths of the Catholic faith. Portrayed as a relic of past papal despotic hegemony, Pius IX is used by the secular historical attack to maintain the false narrative that the Church desires total control over humanity.

By the 1700s, Italy had been the center of fighting and political turmoil for centuries. Various European powers jockeyed to control the northern and southern areas of the Italian peninsula. The pope had controlled most of central Italy from the eighth century onward, which secular rulers desired to control, forcing the Roman pontiff to raise armies to regain lost territory. Pope Julius II (r. 1503–1513), for example, known as the "Warrior Pope," launched and led military expeditions to restore conquered papal lands.

Criticism of papal governance in the Papal States increased in the mid-nineteenth century amid a growing clamor for Italian unification. By that time, the Patrimony of St. Peter was under attack from secular, atheistic, revolutionary forces who dreamed of creating an Italian Republic akin to the French, who had murdered their king and queen in a spasm of violence in the previous century.

The region of Piedmont in northern Italy was the epicenter of the Italian unification movement. The Piedmontese nobleman Massimo d'Azeglio criticized papal governance in the Papal States because of a confused legal system, a lack of financial transparency, high customs taxes, and a proliferation of papal legates, along with an economic backwardness expressed in a lack of railways, banks, and agricultural and scientific associations.[340]

Many European nations had established democratic, republican, and constitutional monarchies by 1850, and there were several groups in Italy that pursued those political goals. They recognized that the papacy and the Papal States were the central obstacles to their dream of a united Italian nation under a constitutional monarchy, so they exerted maximum effort to limit papal influence in politics and conquer the Papal States.

Pius IX's understanding of politics and religion differed greatly from the secularists of the day. He envisioned a close linkage between religion and politics. He viewed the Patrimony of St. Peter as the temporal guarantee of the pope's spiritual authority. Papal territory guaranteed the independence of the papacy in spiritual matters, as secular rulers could not directly threaten the pope's safety and pressure him to compromise on doctrine for political reasons. And so the full fury of atheistic, socialist, anti-Catholic, and anti-papal anger was unleashed on the jovial, unpretentious man from central Italy who occupied the See of Peter. A papacy that began with great fanfare ended with calumny, slander, and imprisonment.

Giovanni Mastai-Feretti was born in central Italy in 1792, a few months before violent revolutionaries initiated the demonic Reign of Terror in France. Although the bloodshed that began that year was far to the north, its events would haunt and taint Italian politics for the next century.

Recognized for his intellectual gifts, the young Giovanni was sent to Rome to study. He eventually entered the seminary and was ordained a priest in 1819. Pope Pius VII (r.

1800–1823) sent him to South America for a few years as an auditor to the apostolic delegate. In 1827, he was consecrated bishop of Spoleto in central Italy. Five years later, Pope Gregory XVI (r. 1831–1846) transferred Giovanni to the diocese of Imola in the Romagna, a piece of papal territory consisting of the cities of Ferrara, Bologna, Imola, Ravenna, Forli, and Rimini.

Bishop Mastai-Feretti was beloved by his people for his frequent acts of charity and piety. He organized retreats, encouraged prayer before the Blessed Sacrament, and was known for his great devotion to the Blessed Mother. The bishop was also greatly concerned about morality and exhorted his flock to refrain from sexual immorality, swearing, and blasphemy.

Political tensions were high in the Romagna during Giovanni's episcopacy. Revolts and frequent violence led to full prisons and exiles. The Carbonari, a secret society dedicated to attacking the Church and the papacy, was active in fomenting violence and revolution during this time. The group embraced French Enlightenment ideals such as rationalism and revolutionary utopianism and utilized Freemasonic principles in their tactics. Their influence grew steadily, and they became a source of friction for Gregory XVI and Bishop Mastai-Feretti.

When Pope Gregory XVI died in early June 1846, fifty cardinals gathered to elect his successor. They chose the fifty-five-year-old Giovanni Mastai-Feretti, the youngest pope in centuries, who took the name Pius to honor Pius VII, who had been imprisoned in France by Napoleon and, like Giovanni, was bishop of Imola before his pontificate.

Pope Pius IX, known as "Pio Nono," was an affable man who enjoyed tobacco and had an active sense of humor that was much on display with visitors to Rome. Once an Anglican clergyman in the city asked the pope for a blessing, so Pio Nono used the prayer in Latin for the blessing of incense as it is placed on the hot charcoal in the thurible: "May you be blessed by him in whose honor you are to be burned."[341] Another visitor, a nun, presented a picture of the pontiff—Pius IX himself—for the pope to sign. He wrote, "Fear not, for it is I."[342]

Unlike his predecessor, Pio Nono embraced many aspects of the modern world in the beginning of his pontificate. He enacted serious reforms in the Papal States by establishing a commission to bring railways to the territory. Additional infrastructure improvements included gas street lighting in Rome. He created an agricultural institute to assist farmers with more productive crops and passed tariff reforms to lower customs dues. Pio Nono desired friendly relations with the Jewish people in the Papal States, so he excused the obligation of Jews to listen to a Catholic homily every week and provided access to papal charities.[343]

The pope also reformed the criminal code and ordered a regular inspection of prison conditions and even visited the jails. Within a month of his election, he granted a large-scale amnesty on July 17, 1846, releasing more than a thousand prisoners and welcoming home those who had been exiled for various, mostly political, crimes. He also showed greater openness to a reform in papal governance when he established a free press on March 15, 1847, with newspaper articles subject to a review of five censors (four were laymen). This action produced a proliferation of periodicals in Rome so that by 1848, there were more than a hundred newspapers in the Eternal City.

These actions increased Pius' popularity throughout Italy. Many believed that the young pope would champion Italian unification and lead the new nation as president. Wherever he traveled, there were shouts of "Viva Pio Nono!", and much expectation was placed on his pontificate.

At the beginning of 1848, the pope stood at the crossroads to revolution and tradition, and many did not know which path he would choose. Events in the new year clearly chose the path for him . . . and led to much suffering for the saintly and jovial Pio Nono.

In the span of a year, barely at the middle of the nineteenth century, the old conservative political order, which had kept the peace in Europe for the thirty years since the close of the Napoleonic Wars, came crumbling down in a spam of violent political revolutions by working-class militants and middle-class progressives. Revolutions erupted in Paris, Milan, Venice, Naples, Palermo, Vienna, Prague, Budapest, Kraków, and Berlin. The authoritarian governments of the old European order were toppled and replaced by new liberal, constitutional governments centered on national identity and unification.

The new political order was not homogenous, but rather sharply divided between moderates, who desired parliamentary-style governments with limited voting rights among the populace, and democrats, who desired unlimited voting rights. Both groups also desired social reform and struggled once in power to deal with the widespread poverty created by national economies outpaced by growing urban populations.[344]

By the spring of 1848, Pio Nono was forced to address the growing Italian revolutionary movement known as the *Risorgimento* ("rising again"). Although focused on the larger goal of Italian national unification, political radicals in Italy were guided by fierce anti-Catholic, anti-papal, and anti-clerical principles. They demanded the confiscation of papal territory and a significantly reduced role for the Church in a new Italy. In April 1848, Pio Nono issued an allocution against the *Risorgimento,* which caused a change in perception of the previously popular pope. Declaring his opposition to the national unification movement, the pope crushed the hopes of many in Italy. The allocution, rooted in Pio Nono's understanding of the necessity of independent temporal territorial authority to guarantee the spiritual authority of the Roman pontiff, put the pope securely in the revolutionaries' crosshairs.

By the end of 1848, riots erupted in Rome, culminating in the death of Count Pellegrino Rossi, the pope's prime minister and personal friend. In a gruesome scene that deeply affected Pio Nono, an Italian revolutionary slashed Rossi's throat in public. Emboldened by Rossi's murder, a large group of revolutionaries, 6,000 strong, marched on the Quirinal Palace, the seat of papal governance in the city, demanding "democratic" reforms. The radicals insisted that Pio Nono call a constitutional assembly and support the proclamation of Italian nationality, the separation of papal temporal and spiritual powers, and authority for the new "democratic" government to declare war.[345]

The pope refused their demands, which produced a volley of gunshots into the palace. The shooting killed Bishop Palma, the pope's secretary. Foreign ambassadors from France, Spain, Bavaria, Portugal, Russia, Holland, Brazil, Belgium, and Prussia had sought shelter in the Quirinal, so Pius IX said to them, "I protest before you all against the force which is being used toward me; and I wish to say that, do what they will, I do not consent."[346]

To prevent further bloodshed, the pope agreed to the formation of a cabinet with representatives from the revolutionaries but consented only to a discussion of their four demands. The next day, the rebels disbanded the Swiss Guards and replaced them with a revolutionary Civic Guard that would "protect" the pope. Pio Nono was a prisoner inside the Quirinal Palace and recognized that his safety was not guaranteed. So the pope hatched an escape plan. On the evening of November 24, in dramatic fashion that included a disguise, a secret passage, a locked door, and tense moments waiting for a key while kneeling in prayer, the pope finally took flight and boarded a ship to Naples, where he remained for two years.

The next morning, when the revolutionaries discovered the pope missing, anti-Catholic demonstrations—including desecration of the Blessed Sacrament—flared up in Rome. A military junta was established in the city, which published a decree on December 29, 1848 calling for a Roman Constituent Assembly, comprising two hundred elected members, to meet in the new year for the formation of an Italian constitution. In February 1849, the Constituent Assembly voted (120 to 10, with 12 abstentions) to end the temporal power of the pope with the creation of a Republic of Rome. That news prompted the exiled pontiff to request international military aid from the Catholic powers of Europe (France, Austria, Spain, Naples) to restore papal governance.

Several months later, in the summer of 1849, French troops marched into the city and reclaimed it for the pope. A joyous and relieved Pio Nono said,

> The re-establishment of the papal authority is manifestly a work of Providence, and I am not a little proud that France should have been made its instrument. Upon the re-establishment of this authority rests the guarantee of the peace of the whole of Europe: it is a task which is equally both social and political.[347]

French troops would stay in Rome (excepting a brief return to France) to guarantee the pope's safety for the next twenty years. Pio Nono returned to a secured Rome on April 12, 1850 and chose to live on Vatican Hill rather than in the Quirinal Palace. He was grateful for the restoration of papal authority and his return to Rome, but if the pope thought these actions would bring peace, he was sorely mistaken.

About a year after Pio Nono's return, a boy was born to a Jewish family in Bologna, which was a legation of the Papal States. The boy was the ninth of ultimately twelve children of Salomone Levi Mortara and his wife, Marianna Padovani. The daughters from the Mortara family received an education and eventually married. One of the sons became an army officer, and several others became businessmen, but Edgardo, the boy born in 1851, became a household name in Europe and much of the world and a symbol of the supposed evils of papal governance specifically and the Church generally.

Contrary to the law at the time, the Mortaras hired a Catholic maidservant to assist with household chores. The law forbade Jewish families in the Papal States from hiring Catholics—not because of discrimination or antisemitism, but to safeguard Jewish parents from Catholics baptizing their children. Baptism, as the Catholic government of the time recognized, would confer certain rights on the new Catholic and obligations on his non-Catholic parents, which the government was prepared to protect and enforce.

When Edgardo was a year old, he contracted a serious illness and was, according to doctors, at the point of death. Anna Morisi, the Mortaras' hired Catholic help, decided to secretly baptize Edgardo to save his soul. Church law forbade the baptizing of children, especially from Jewish families, without parental consent except in two specific cases: if the child was abandoned or at the point of certain death. Absent those specific situations, a Catholic who baptized a Jewish child without parental consent faced severe legal penalties. The law also stipulated that Jewish children validly and licitly baptized must receive a Catholic education until the age of maturity, when the child was free to self-determine faith.

This law was not unique to the Papal States. In Catholic Austria, for example, the law stipulated that Jewish children baptized against parental consent should be "separated from the parents at once and raised as a Christian by honest persons" and educated at the expense of the baptizer. After the child learned a profession, he was free to choose his faith.[348]

These laws were found not only in Catholic nations, either. In Great Britain, the law provided for the separation of children from "unbelieving" parents who were not raising their children as Anglicans. The state sent these children to boarding schools run by the Church of England.[349]

Anna Morisi kept the baptism of little Edgardo a secret for five years until the same situation occurred with another Mortara child. In that case, Anna refrained from baptizing the infant, who died. When Anna finally told her secret to the religious authorities, the Church launched an investigation, which lasted eight months, to verify her story and the family situation.

After the investigation, the Church approached the parents with news of Edgardo's baptism and the legal requirement to raise him Catholic. The parents refused a Catholic education, as required by the law, for Edgardo, and were supported in their resistance by the Freemasons. The situation required papal intervention, so Pio Nono decided in June 1858 to remove the child from his home and raise him in a Catholic boarding school. The pope offered to pay for Edgardo's education in Bologna so his family could visit often, but when the family and the Freemasons made the situation public and stiffened their opposition, the pope feared for Edgardo's safety and moved him to Rome. Giacomo Cardinal Antonelli, Pius IX's Secretary of State, personally assured the Mortaras that Edgardo would be free to choose his faith when he turned seventeen. The Papal Gendarmerie Corps took the child on June 24, 1858.

Despite the tense and emotional event, Edgardo, writing in the third person, recalled later that

> in the most searing moment of the tragic and sorrowful separation from his parents, he did not complain or cry

> or put up the least resistance. Although he shed tears and called for his mother after he was taken from the house, just a few kind words were enough to calm him down completely. He did not cry anymore or ask about his family.[350]

Edgardo also recalled that he never once asked to return to his family. For a period of time, his parents visited him at the school daily for nearly two months, and they begged and bribed him with promised gifts to return home, yet he refused to do so. Edgardo insisted, "I am a Christian. If you want me to come with you, there is only one way: be converted, too."[351]

Pio Nono viewed Edgardo as a son, treated him as such, and looked after him. Upon reaching maturity, Edgardo chose to remain in the Faith, writing later, "The result for the child was complete and absolute detachment from his parents and family and a strong, lasting adherence to the maternal bosom of the Catholic Church, which had adopted him through the great Pope Pius IX."[352]

Edgardo proved a brilliant student and a gifted linguist. He learned German, Spanish, French, Latin, Greek, Hebrew, English, and Basque. He felt called to the religious life of his adopted faith and entered the Order of the Canons of the Holy Redeemer of the Lateran, making his simple profession at the age of sixteen and taking the religious name Pio Maria. He was later ordained a priest.

Edgardo wrote a memoir of his life, which presented his view of his unique and complicated upbringing. The work was published in 1893 and titled *The Mortara Child and Pius IX: The Autobiographical Account of the "Mortara Case" Written by the Protagonist, Reverend Father Pio Maria Mortara, CRL.*

The Edgardo Mortara case became a sensational story the world over and was used by enemies of the papacy and the Church to undermine papal authority and governance.

Anti-papal Italian nationalists used the case to argue for the confiscation of the Papal States, as Mortara wrote in his memoir:

> The antipapists . . . unanimously demanded reforms, or rather, the radical and final suppression of the temporal power of the popes. With Pius IX, they shouted, the temporal power had perpetrated the most despotic and barbaric act ever seen by mankind. He had taken an innocent child away from his parents, abandoning them to the deepest sorrow and plunging an unhappy family forever into the most pathetic poverty.[353]

On the contrary, although one would be hard pressed to dispute the Mortara parents' sorrow at losing custody of their son, it is worth correcting the record by noting that the Mortara family did not become destitute. Instead, they became enriched by donations from anti-papal and Jewish organizations throughout the world. Enemies of the Church "spewed their vengeance and their gall in bitter diatribes, atrocious invectives, and sacrilegious calumnies" in the cafés, theaters, and press to sensationalize the story and keep constant pressure on Pius to release the boy.[354] The story became so widespread that even President James Buchanan of the United States protested the removal of Edgardo from his family through diplomatic channels and urged the pope to return him.

Pio Nono steadfastly refused to acquiesce to the clamor of the mob, viewing the situation from an eternal perspective:

> The great and the lowly have done everything possible. Resorting to all sorts of expedients and tricks, to the press and diplomacy, all the governments of the Old and the New World united and conspired to take away from me, from Christ, and from his Church, the soul of this child. . . .

> I do not feel sorry, though, for what I have done on his behalf, to save a soul that cost the blood of God. On the contrary, I ratify and confirm everything. Protesting against these vain efforts, I declare to everyone that not even all the bayonets of the world will force me to hand this child over to the clutches of the revolution and the devil.[355]

The story of Edgardo Mortara became such a *cause célèbre* that when anti-papal forces finally conquered Rome in 1870, Fr. Mortara was forced to flee in fear for his life. The revolutionary forces wanted to return Edgardo, even against his will, to his family as a symbol of the final and total victory over the pope and the Church. Edgardo successfully escaped to Austria, where he spent a few years, and then relocated to France and then Spain.

The Mortara case is a classic example of enemies of the Church co-opting an emotional situation for their own benefit and sensationalizing and propagating half-truths to the detriment of the Faith. Few critics of the Church then or now have read the words of Edgardo and reflected on his viewpoint and conclusions about the major event of his life. He viewed Anna Morisi, the Catholic maidservant who secretly baptized him, "as his mother in the supernatural order" and was grateful for her sacramental action.[356] Concerning Pius IX, Edgardo wrote that "he neither stole nor kidnapped a child from his parents, as the anti-Catholic press repeated tirelessly," and he believed wholeheartedly that "there will come a day . . . once they have stopped listening to the calumnies . . . of the dregs of humanity," when

> posterity will accept the poor arguments of the Mortara child, so as to tie them into scented garlands of immortal flowers that will adorn and decorate the altar on which

> the Catholic world will greet, with enthusiastic acclamations, PIUS IX, THE SAINT.[357]

The separated child found love and truth in his adopted home and prayed fervently for the conversion of his family and the Jewish people.

In order to understand the prudential judgment of Pio Nono in this difficult and heart-wrenching case, we must recognize the complex religious and historical context that underlies his actions. The pope was neither an anti-Semite nor a tyrant; rather, he sincerely desired the salvation of all out of love for Christ and the Church. He may have acted in a manner unthinkable in the modern world, but we must understand that he also acted in accordance with that desire.

Following the Mortara affair, Pius IX's pontificate continued in controversy. He believed the time opportune to restore the Catholic hierarchy in England, which had been effectively removed since the reign of Queen Elizabeth I in the late sixteenth century. However, when the pope announced the restoration on September 30, 1850, Parliament expressed its great displeasure, and anti-Catholic processions, including the burning of the pope and cardinals in effigy, took place in the Protestant kingdom. Political predicaments in Italy also plagued the pontiff, as the Kingdom of Italy under King Victor Emmanuel was declared in 1861. The kingdom comprised all of Italy except for Venice, which was under Austrian control, and Rome and its environs.

Pio Nono recognized the need to raise an army to defend the remaining papal territory from Giuseppe Garibaldi's (1807-1882) revolutionary Red Shirts, since the small contingent of French troops in Rome was positioned only to maintain basic law and order in the city and safeguard the pope. The Papal Army was staffed with French officers and 10,000 volunteers from several European countries. However, several nations soon forbade the participation of their citizens in the Papal Army, which limited its size. Eventually, the French troops in Rome left Italy in 1866 by order of Napoleon III, although they returned the next year to assist the Papal Army and the Zouaves, a unit of independent Catholic soldiers from throughout the world, in the fight again Garibaldi's forces. Their defense was successful, but it staved off the ultimate demise of the Papal States by only a few years.

The last half of Pio Nono's pontificate was, perhaps, the most volatile, with the issuance of a controversial appendix to an encyclical, the calling of an ecumenical council and the promulgation of a divisive doctrine, and the conquering of the Papal States.

Pius IX promulgated the encyclical *Quanta Cura* in 1864, primarily to announce a Jubilee Year in 1865. The main narrative of the document condemned many modern political, religious, and social philosophies and ideologies, but in measured terms. Issued by itself, the document would not, more than likely, have engendered the debate that ensued, but it was accompanied by an appendix known as the *Syllabus of Errors*.

The *Syllabus*, along with the Mortara affair and the proclamation of papal infallibility from the First Vatican Council, makes for one of the main battering rams in the secular historical attack against Pope Bl. Pius IX. It condemns most of what secular modernity holds sacred and inviolable.

The *Syllabus* comprises eighty previously condemned propositions. So the document does not constitute anything new, but rather compiled already rejected ideologies and notions such as pantheism, naturalism, absolute rationalism, indifferentism, socialism, communism, and errors concerning the liberalism of the day. Whereas the secular world believed in the "wholesome" notions of liberty, equality, and fraternity, the Church's experience with these Enlightened secular "values" was more akin to atheism, theft, and murder: "After all that had happened in France and in Europe, it was really quite impossible that the Church should regard the popular freedom demanded by the advanced liberals as anything other than the unleashing of popular passion."[358]

The condemned proposition that facilitated (and still does) the largest outcry and misunderstanding is found in article 80: "The Roman pontiff can and should reconcile himself with and accommodate himself to progress, liberalism, and modern civilization." But critics then and now have failed to recognize that this condemned proposition is a direct quote from the March 18, 1861 allocution *Iamdudum Cernimus*, which concerned the situation in Italy only, especially in Piedmont, with its aggressive anti-papal seizure of territory, a focus on unification, and radical education laws. Although dedicated to the situation in Italy, which Italians understood implicitly, this article (it did not help that it was the last one and seemed to summarize all the previous articles) was interpreted by non-Italians as condemning every cherished political, religious, and social ideal of the secular modernists.[359]

Initially, there was little reaction to *Quanta Cura*, since it was a technical theological document addressed to the bishops, but then enemies of the papacy and the Church publicized it to create a firestorm of criticism and misinformation. The backlash proved problematic for bishops around the world, as it put them on the defensive in their home countries.

Criticism and misinterpretation of the *Syllabus* remains in the modern world, by "Catholics" and secularists alike. They fail to view the document in its particular historical context and instead make grandiose (and false) statements that Pio Nono dogmatically proclaimed that "no Catholic . . . could believe in freedom of speech, freedom of the press, or freedom of religion. Catholics had to believe the pope must rule over a state of his own."[360]

Although the *Syllabus* could have been presented better or explained in greater detail at its promulgation, the fact remains that its contents illustrate a proper reaction from the Church to Enlightened secular religious, political, and social ideologies. Modernity views the French Revolution and the creation of nineteenth-century "democratic" governments as events that fostered freedom, equality, and tolerance. The Church, however, viewed those events with abject horror, as it suffered persecution and martyrdom by the revolutionary forces. Popes Pius VI, Pius VII, and Pius IX suffered exile, imprisonment, violence, and the loss of a thousand-year-old territory at the bloody hands of progress and liberalism. The *Syllabus* may have been misunderstood by the world, but it was comprehensible to the Church and to Pio Nono.

A few years after the publication of the *Syllabus*, Pius IX convoked the First Vatican Council, which is, perhaps, his greatest lasting contribution to the Church. It too was highly criticized and misunderstood.

Recognizing that the world had significantly changed since the last ecumenical council had met three hundred years ago at Trent, Pio Nono called the bishops to assemble in Rome in December 1869. He envisioned the council restating the Catholic faith in areas where it had been attacked, especially concerning faith and reason; discussing the relationship between Church and State; and issuing a doctrinal statement on the Church.

The First Vatican Council was the first meeting with bishops from every inhabited continent and the first attended by bishops from the United States of America. Six hundred bishops attended from every country except Russia, where the government refused to allow its Catholic bishops to leave the country. The council fathers met for seven months and produced two documents before events forced an unintended adjournment. The first document, *Dei Filius*, was a statement on faith, reason, and revelation. It reaffirmed and defined Catholic teaching concerning God-given objective truth and the rational ability to know that truth. Additionally, the document explicated that the existence of God is knowable from reason, that man is instructed by divine revelation through Sacred Scripture, and that faith and reason are complementary. The council fathers wanted to restate the main teachings most attacked by the "post-Protestant rationalists and pantheists of the eighteenth and nineteenth centuries."[361]

The second document, *Pastor Aeternus*, generated significant angst and misunderstanding and produced a schism as well as a culture war.

Although Pius IX wanted the First Vatican Council to generate a holistic doctrinal statement on the Church, the council fathers had time only to write, debate, and vote on a document focused on the role of the papacy and the extraordinary charism of papal infallibility. This led to charges (then and now) that Pope Pius IX forced the council to create a document that solidified his power and authority, akin to a king demanding that Parliament pass favorable legislation. That critique fails to acknowledge that a larger and comprehensive ecclesial document had been planned and inappropriately characterizes Pius IX as a despot bent on consolidating and enhancing his spiritual power.

Pastor Aeternus teaches that St. Peter received true primacy of jurisdiction from Christ and that his successors, the bishops of Rome, also enjoy this privilege. Therefore, the Roman pontiff has full and supreme power of jurisdiction over the universal Church.

Although not originally on the conciliar agenda, the topic of papal infallibility was added to the document. *Pastor Aeternus* identifies the conditions under which the pope can teach infallibly:

- ❖ The pope must utilize his role as the universal teacher of the Church (and not simply as the bishop of Rome).
- ❖ He must exercise the full weight of his supreme apostolic authority.
- ❖ The teaching must be a personal act that is free from coercion and not the ratification of conciliar documents.
- ❖ The pope must intend to define the teaching infallibly and to proclaim that it must be definitively held by the faithful.
- ❖ The teaching must be promulgated and concern a matter of faith or morals.

There was great deliberation concerning this doctrine, as some bishops, especially those from German territories, Austria, and France, believed that it was a power play by the Roman Curia to consolidate papal power and centralize Church governance.

Other bishops were not doctrinally opposed to *Pastor Aeternus* but believed that its definition and pronouncement were inopportune. This group, led by Felix-Antoine Dupanloup, bishop of Orléans, comprised a number of European bishops and two thirds of the American hierarchy. Bishops in countries with a majority-Protestant population believed that the pronouncement would hinder their catechetical efforts. Others believed that Catholics would not fully understand the doctrine and elevate the pope to an inappropriate status that would antagonize many European governments.

The vote occurred on July 13, 1870 amid a raging thunderstorm. The document received 533 votes for and only two against.

The conciliar fathers wanted to complete the document with sections on the role of bishops, priests, religious, and the laity, but then France declared war on Prussia, and the 8,000 French troops guarding Rome, the pope, and the assembled bishops left the city. With their safety in doubt, Pio Nono had no choice but to suspend the council . . . which remained suspended until Pope John XXIII officially ended it in 1960 in preparation for the Second Vatican Council.

The vacuum left by the departure of the French troops from Rome provided the perfect opportunity for King Victor Emmanuel II to enter the city with his army on September 20, 1870, effectively ending the thousand-year-old Papal States. The Zouaves, who had faithfully defended papal territory and Pius IX, were disbanded the next day amid shouts of "Long Live Pius IX, Pontiff and King!"[362]

The next month, a plebiscite was held to determine the government of Rome and the Papal States. The vote was overwhelmingly in favor of annexation by and unification with the Kingdom of Italy.

Officially dethroned and robbed of the Petrine Patrimony, Pio Nono declared himself a "prisoner of the Vatican." For the remaining eight years of his pontificate, he never left Vatican Hill, and he refused to give the previously annual *Urbi et Orbi* ("to the city and the world") blessing.

The Italian government later passed the Law of Guarantees to regulate the unique political situation with Pius IX. The law invested the pope with the attributes of a sovereign so that he was declared sacred and immune from arrest and imprisonment. The pope was allowed to have diplomatic relations with other governments, a personal guard, a postal service, and exclusive use but not ownership of the Vatican, the Lateran, and Castel Gandolfo. The Italian government laid no claim to nominate bishops or control the Church and promised an annual payment to the papacy of 3.2 million *lire* as compensation for confiscating the Papal States. When the first payment arrived, a perturbed Pius IX said,

> I need money badly, but you, what do you bring me? A part of what you stole from me? Never will I accept it from you by way of reimbursement, and you will obtain no signature that might seem to imply an acquiescence in or a resignation to the spoliation.[363]

The diplomatic standoff, which became known as the "Roman Question," between the Italian government and the papacy continued beyond Pius IX through the pontificates of Leo XIII (r. 1878-1903), St. Pius X (r. 1903-1914), and Benedict XV (r. 1914-1922). During the pontificate of Pius XI (r. 1922-1939), the "Roman Question" was answered in 1929 with the creation of Vatican City-State, a sovereign nation of 108 acres in the heart of Rome, in the Lateran Treaty with Benito Mussolini's fascist government.

The remaining years of Pio Nono's pontificate were spent dealing with a precarious persecution of the Church in the newly united nation of Germany. The Prussian Army achieved victory in the Franco-Prussian War, which produced, through the actions of Otto von Bismarck (1815-1898), a new united German Empire under Prussian leadership. Previously, German territory consisted of a collection of thirty-five states, with Protestant Prussia as the dominant state in the north and Catholic Bavaria dominant in the south. The Prussian king Wilhelm I became emperor (kaiser) of a federation of twenty-five states that Bismarck desired to fully unite in a shared culture and religion.

The Church posed an obstacle to Bismarck's dream, especially in the populous Catholic regions of Bavaria and the Rhineland. As a means to lessen the influence of the Church in the new German Empire, Bismarck embarked on a *Kulturkampf*, or "culture war," and used the First Vatican Council document *Pastor Aeternus* as an excuse to attack the Church. Bismarck viewed the document as establishing the pope as a despotic and authoritative foreign ruler. *Pastor Aeternus*, according to Bismarck, created an infallible pope with unlimited spiritual and temporal power, who could nullify German law.

Believing that the pope should have no power over Germans, Bismarck initiated a series of anti-Catholic laws and persecutory measures to isolate the Church in Germany from Rome. A "Pulpit Law" was passed in 1871 that established severe penalties for any cleric who criticized the government from the pulpit. The next few years witnessed several anti-Catholic laws that forbade religious instruction in schools, refused legal recognition of Catholic marriages celebrated in the parish, and expelled the Jesuits from the German Empire. Additionally, Bismarck attacked the episcopacy to sever the bishops' relationship with the pope, as bishops were accused of being foreign enemy agents and expelled from the empire. The state demanded secular approval of ecclesial appointments and engaged in a harassment campaign of arrests, imprisonments, seizure of Church lands and schools, and closure of monasteries. German Catholics non-violently resisted these measures and formed their own political party, the Center Party, which won seats in the Reichstag in the 1874 national elections.

Nearing the end of his pontificate, Pius IX issued the encyclical *Quod Nunquam* about the situation in the German Empire and declared Bismarck's anti-Catholic laws invalid. The tense situation continued after Pio Nono went to his eternal reward, but an accommodation was reached between Bismarck and Pope Leo XIII, which finally ended the *Kulturkampf.*

Pope Bl. Pius IX died on February 7, 1878, after a nearly thirty-two-year reign as the bishop of Rome. Even after death, the hatred against the pope who stood against the progressive, "liberal," revolutionary elements of the day manifested itself when his body was moved to the Church of St. Lawrence Outside the Walls. Three years had elapsed, and Pope Leo XIII believed that the transfer was opportune, but a mob formed along the nighttime procession and hurled mud at the coffin. In the next century the church was hit with an American bomb in July 1943 during the Second World War that caused extensive damage.

The jovial and saintly pope was beatified during the Great Jubilee of the Year 2000 by Pope John Paul II, who recalled Pio Nono's "unconditional fidelity to the immutable deposit of revealed truth" during a long pontificate in which "he had much to suffer in fulfilling his mission of service to the gospel." In the final analysis, the Polish Pope recognized that Pio Nono "was much loved, but also hated and slandered. However, it was precisely in these conflicts *that the light of his virtues shone most brightly.*"[364]

Chapter 4

"Catholic" History

The Church is experiencing the dark night of the soul. The Church, which ought to be a place of light, has become a dwelling place of darkness. In the name of so-called intellectual positions, theologians amuse themselves by deconstructing dogmas and emptying morality of its profound meaning. The Church is suffering; she is trampled on, and her enemies are within. Trying to win popularity with the media at the expense of the truth amounts to doing the work of Judas.[365]

—Robert Cardinal Sarah

The insidious internal "Catholic" historical attack is, perhaps, the most grievous form of assault because it accepts and propagates the false historical narrative embraced by enemies of the Church, and it does so motivated either by a desire to change Catholic teaching or to criticize and weaken papal leadership and authority. "Catholic" attackers feign orthodoxy when, in reality, they embrace heterodoxy, they seek to remake the Church in their own image and likeness, and they desire to either change or abrogate doctrine.

The Church and the world faced a significant crisis at the mid-point of the twentieth century. The beginning of the century witnessed a Europe full of promise descending into a seemingly unstoppable barbaric display of violence, so abhorrent that it nearly defied description. The death toll was catastrophic: fifteen to twenty million people lost their lives. One nation, defeated on the battlefield and humiliated off it, embraced a totalitarian regime that spewed a venomous racial ideology that classified and viewed people as sub-human. Another bloody total war erupted that consumed the world and led to the deaths of more than fifty million people—and unlike in the First World War, most of those killed were non-combatants.[366]

These two global wars radically changed the world—not just physically, but also mentally and emotionally. Skepticism was the ultimate fruit of the so-called Enlightenment philosophy of the seventeenth and eighteenth centuries, and it germinated into a widespread mentality after the horrors of World War I and World War II.

Additionally, groups and governments utilized the power of propaganda to shape opinions and mold behavior. Lies and half-truths constantly propagated are easily believed, with the burden of refutation placed on the truth rather than on the propaganda. The totalitarian governments that plunged the world into the vicious conflict utilized propaganda effectively to control their people and maintain their power.

It is no surprise that just a few years after the Second World War, one of the greatest commentaries on the power and insidiousness of propaganda was illustrated in the work *1984* by George Orwell. Orwell imagined a future in which people are held subservient to the state through a constant feeding of propaganda about their country and the world. The state maintains its control through the dissemination of selective information, which it also modifies so that it is nearly impossible to discover the truth. "The Party" demands and ensures conformity by the language of Newspeak, in which words are manipulated and lose their traditional meaning. The book is a commentary on the evil of totalitarian political regimes, but it also illustrates the power of propaganda and its effect on people, who no longer know, discern, or care for the truth.

The Church recognized that the broken world after two nasty wars was in desperate need of Christ and his salvific message. So Angelo Roncalli, the newly elected Pope John XXIII (r. 1958-1963), called an ecumenical council. The wars had produced skepticism, a loss of faith and belief, and an exaltation of science to an idolatrous level. Society embraced

> a time in which the fundamental act of the human person, more conscious now of himself and of his liberty, tends to pronounce in favor of his own absolute autonomy, in emancipation from every transcendent law; a time in which secularism seems the legitimate consequence of modern thought and the highest wisdom in the temporal ordering of society; a time, moreover, in which the soul of man has plumbed the depths of irrationality and desolation.[367]

In this situation, the Second Vatican Council was convoked, amid much promise and hope. Pope St. John XXIII believed the world situation presented a unique opportunity for the Church to present its teachings anew to the modern world. He charged the conciliar fathers with the task of ecclesial renewal so that the Church could help modern man form a lasting relationship with Christ and his mystical body. The pope encouraged the bishops to focus on a return to the ancient sources of the Faith by emphasizing Sacred Scripture and the writings of the Church Fathers.

John XXIII desired the defense and advancement of the truth by way of a new presentation of the Faith, more comprehensible to modern man. The pope believed that the best approach was to demonstrate the validity of the Church's teachings rather than condemn anti-Christian ideologies and teachings. The council, it was hoped, would combat the evil ideologies that had produced the wars and would focus the Church on the fundamental task of evangelization and catechesis so that modern man would come to know and love Christ and live in the truth.

The Second Vatican Council opened on October 11, 1962 and concluded its first session at the end of the year. Before the second session opened, in the fall of the following year, Pope John XXIII died. The cardinals elected Giovanni Battista Montini, the archbishop of Milan, who had spent considerable time before that in the Secretariat of State, who took the papal name Paul VI (r. 1963-1978).

Paul VI initiated several Church reforms, fostered ecumenical relations, and traveled the world to spread the gospel message. Concerning the council, the newly elected pope continued its work but revised its governing statutes, expanded membership on its commissions, allowed greater debate, and invited the laity to participate as non-voting auditors.

The council met in three additional sessions, from 1963 to 1965, and produced sixteen documents. The final major constitution, *Gaudium et Spes* (the Pastoral Constitution on the Church in the Modern World), was a unique document in which "the council yearns to explain to everyone how it conceives of the presence and activity of the Church in the world today."[368] In this document, the conciliar fathers presented an excellent summary of the "situation of the world," recognizing the time as a "new stage of history" with significant cultural and social transformation, full of dichotomies. The world had plentiful resources and wealth, yet there were profound poverty, hunger, and illiteracy. The world's people exhibited a sense of unity through communications and modern means of travel, yet conflict continued. A general belief in the regulation of population growth and a desire to manipulate the gift of human sexuality pervaded many regions of the world, along with the discarding of traditional values and customs and the abandonment of religion. Summarizing this situation, the conciliar fathers commented, "the modern world shows itself at once powerful and weak; capable of the noblest deeds or the foulest; before it lies the path to freedom or to slavery."[369]

Gaudium et Spes stressed the dignity and worth of every human person and also highlighted the many offenses against that dignity prevalent in the modern world. Emphasizing "some problems of special urgency," the bishops reaffirmed the Church's teaching on marriage and family and the gift of human sexuality and called for Christians to evangelize the culture.

Gaudium et Spes called for the Church to have an active role in the modern world. A concern for human dignity and the propagation of the truth, it insisted, should motivate every member of the faithful to engage the modern world in a spirit of peace and love in imitation of Christ. Modern governments and society should allow for the public expression of the Faith and not regulate it to the private sphere. Catholics were called to live a unity of faith and life in an integrated way so that what they believed and practiced privately would imbue public attitudes and actions. The bishops emphasized the error of Catholics who chose to separate their faith from their public life: "This split between the faith which many profess and their daily lives deserves to be counted among the more serious errors of our age."[370]

The hope and promise of the council, expressed in *Gaudium et Spes* and its other documents, was at its height when Paul VI closed it in 1965, but the optimistic pope remarked just a few years later that something evil had crept into the Church.

Almost seven years after closing the Second Vatican Council, and on the Solemnity of Saints Peter and Paul in 1972, Pope

Paul VI issued, in his homily, a dire warning to the faithful. He said, "There was the belief that after the council there would be a day of sunshine for the history of the Church. Instead, it is the arrival of a day of clouds, of tempest, of darkness, of research, of uncertainty."[371] He reflected that there was something "preternatural" that had infected the world, which led to the conflict in the Church and the world despite the hope and promise of the council.

Paul VI recognized that the problem was not the council itself or the conciliar documents, but rather the use (or better, misuse) of those teachings by "Catholics" who desired a change in Church teaching and practice. Instead of embracing Christ and his Church, humanity had embraced secularism and selfishness.

The pope may have uttered these words due to the reception of his encyclical on transmitting human life, *Humanae Vitae*, which he promulgated three years after the council. The document was Paul VI's seventh encyclical in the sixth year of his pontificate, and, although he reigned for another ten years, it was also his last.

Humanae Vitae is perhaps the most contentious, well known, yet least understood papal intervention in Church history. Promulgated at the height of the "Sexual Revolution" in the Western world, *Humanae Vitae* reiterated the constant teaching of the Church on the duty of married men and women to transmit human life by exercising responsible parenthood, in keeping with respect for the unitive and procreative purposes of the marital act.

Before the encyclical's promulgation, when the world had only rumors to work with, false media reports and propaganda by certain "Catholic" groups and theologians created an expectation that the Church's timeless teaching on the inadmissibility of contraception would be overturned. When the pope reiterated Church teaching, these "Catholics" went on the offensive, criticizing the pope's decision, expressing outrage, and encouraging disobedience to the teaching. What followed in the remaining decades of the twentieth century was confusion and disunity in some regions of the Church. "Catholics" who disagreed with *Humanae Vitae*, and other teachings, hijacked the documents of the Second Vatican Council, claiming that their innovations, changes, and disobedience to Rome were in conformity with the "spirit of the council."

Ultimately, a unique situation occurred in the Church, which now contained a large group of baptized non-believers, who identified as "Catholic" but who did not believe or act in accordance with that identification. Most baptized non-believers did not agitate in any meaningful way to change the Church, but there were vocal groups and individuals who did. Although the cultural issues of the late twentieth century assisted in the creation of this situation, the foundation had been laid earlier in the century, as post-Enlightened secular ideologies seeped into the collective consciousness of most Western nations. None other than Fr. Edgardo Mortara put his finger on the problem, writing:

> These Catholics are more or less imbued or saturated with the dismal doctrines and tendencies of modern naturalism . . . the product and natural result of religious sentimentalism, which reduces everything to impressions and which can be summarized in the famous but most unfortunate maxim: "All that I like is good; all that I detest and dislike is bad."[372]

One aspect of this modern situation concerns an acceptance by many "Catholics" of the false narratives of Church history crafted by Protestants and secularists. In the minds of the baptized non-believers, this "Catholic" historical attack is a passive acceptance and regurgitation of historical myths and false narratives. However, in the hands of "Catholics" who purposefully advocate for doctrinal change, the "Catholic" historical attack becomes an aggressive attack against the Church generally and the papacy specifically.

Although the "Catholic" historical attack against the papacy has involved numerous time periods in Church history, the critical offensive has focused mostly on the pontificates of Pope Pius XII (r. 1939–1958) and Pope Benedict XVI (r. 2005–2013). Both men have been canceled by those desiring changes to the Church's teachings.

The wartime pontificate of Pius XII has been maligned by a cacophony of malcontents ranging from atheists, secularists, and communists to liberal "Catholics." Accused of being "Hitler's Pope" in a book by a former "Catholic" seminarian, the attacks on Pius XII range from ally of Hitler to rabid anti-Semite to dispassionate observer who should have done more to stop the Holocaust.

These "Catholics" also attack Pope Benedict XVI. Those criticisms began when Joseph Ratzinger was the prefect for the Congregation of the Doctrine of the Faith, and they continued into his pontificate. This peaceful, brilliant, and devoted man was slandered in the media as the "Panzer-Kardinal" bent on "rolling back" the "spirit of Vatican II" throughout the Church. The "Catholic" attack against Benedict XVI—portrayed as an archaic inquisitor general, zealously focused on uprooting and punishing dissident theologians—was motivated also by a desire to modify Church teaching by questioning papal authority and changing perceptions of the papacy among the general Catholic populace.

Pope Pius XII

> *The liberal bestselling attacks on the pope and the Catholic Church are really an intra-Catholic argument about the direction of the Church today. The Holocaust is simply the biggest club available for liberal Catholics to use against traditional Catholics in their attempt to bash the papacy and thereby smash traditional Catholic teaching—especially on issues relating to sexuality, including abortion, contraception, celibacy and the role of women in the Church.*[373]

Eugenio Pacelli was born into a family dedicated to serving the Church. His grandfather, Marcantonio, was a canon lawyer and adviser to Pope Pius IX, served as undersecretary of the interior in the Papal States and helped establish the Vatican newspaper *L'Osservatore Romano*. His father, Filippo, was also a canon lawyer and an adviser to Popes Pius IX and Leo XIII. His older brother, Francesco, another canon lawyer, served Pius XI and assisted Secretary of State Cardinal Gasparri. So it was unsurprising when Eugenio, a brilliant student and pious young man, entered the seminary at age eighteen.

Eugenio was known as a gifted linguist who was fluent in Latin, Greek, English, French, Spanish, German, Portuguese, and Aramaic. Ordained a priest on Easter Sunday in April 1899, Pacelli served a brief tour as a parish priest before earning doctorates in theology and canon and civil law. He later entered the Vatican diplomat training program.

When the First World War erupted in August 1914, Pope Benedict XV (r. 1914–1922) assigned the young diplomat to the Prisoners' Works Office, a new organization created by the pope and charged with maintaining a registry of POWs, facilitating communication with families, and arranging prisoner exchanges with the combatant nations.

Pacelli's time as a young diplomat during war was influential in his later life as Roman pontiff. He witnessed the actions of Pope Benedict XV, who had to navigate a difficult diplomatic situation among the European powers. It is nearly impossible to adequately comprehend the wartime actions of Pacelli as Pius XII without understanding the actions of Benedict XV during the First World War.

Giacomo Paolo Giovanni Battista della Chiesa was elected supreme pontiff, taking the name Benedict XV, on September 2, 1914, a little over a month after the start of the First World War. A trained diplomat from Genoa, who served as undersecretary of state for Popes Leo XIII and Pius X, della Chiesa was created cardinal only three months before his papal election. Faced with a major war among the European nations, Benedict recognized the need for delicate diplomacy. So he abided by three principles during the war: perfect neutrality, extension of charity to all victims of the war, and exhortations for peace at every opportunity.

Benedict XV pursued neutrality because it allowed the Church to remain free from political disputes, even though this position angered both sides. Perfect neutrality freed the Church from potential political control and propaganda value from the belligerents and allowed ecclesial organizations freedom in exercising charity for the suffering. Neutrality also offered the opportunity for the pope to exhort the combatants to moral conduct and to lodge public and private protests when that did not occur, especially when the Germans deported Belgians and French citizens in occupied territory to Germany as laborers and when chemical warfare was introduced on the battlefield.

The pope was especially worried about the impact of the war on families, so he created a new office in the Vatican to facilitate communication between prisoners of war and their families and aided prisoner exchanges, especially for wounded soldiers and fathers of three or more children. Additionally, Benedict XV gave money generously from the Vatican treasury to alleviate suffering throughout the war. The pope called for peace and urged nations to reduce their armaments, respect freedom of the seas, and settle disputes through international arbitration.

After the war ended, on the feast day of Saint Martin of Tours, November 11, 1918, the pope exhorted the victors to make peace without demanding reparations from Germany. Unfortunately, the Allies did not heed that advice.

Benedict XV acknowledged the sufferings of the Jewish people throughout history and issued a condemnation of antisemitism in 1916. He also supported the 1917 Balfour Declaration, which called for the creation of a Jewish homeland in Palestine, and met with Jewish supporters of the declaration.

Benedict's wartime actions and his support of the Jewish people made a considerable impression on Eugenio Pacelli as a young diplomat, and those impressions would influence his later pontifical actions during another brutal, all-encompassing world war.

Before the end of World War I, Pacelli was assigned as the papal nuncio to Bavaria in 1917, and in 1920, he was appointed ambassador for all Germany. His diplomatic mission was to negotiate concordats with Bavaria and establish relations with the other states of post-war Germany. During his time, Pacelli witnessed the rise of Adolf Hitler and the National Socialist German Workers' (Nazi) Party and criticized their policies and ideology in forty public speeches between 1918 and 1929.[374]

Ambrogio Damiano Achille Ratti was elected pope on February 6, 1922, taking the name Pius XI (r. 1922-1939).

A shrewd diplomat and scholar, Pius XI focused papal policy on reaching concordats with the nations of Europe. These agreements provided legal protection of Catholics and the Church and provided a basis for the Holy See to lodge diplomatic complaints against any violations. Agreements with Latvia (1922), Bavaria (1924), Poland (1925), and Romania (1929) were negotiated before Eugenio Pacelli's appointment as secretary of state.

Another major diplomatic negotiation that occurred before Pacelli's recall to Rome was the finalization of the "Roman Question" that had plagued relations between the pope and the nation of Italy since the end of Pope Bl. Pius IX's pontificate. The fascist government of Benito Mussolini was keen to regularize the relationship between the pope and Italy, so the Lateran Treaty was signed on June 7, 1929. It created the Vatican City-State and recognized the Roman pontiff as a sovereign head of state. The Catholic faith was designated the sole and official religion in Italy, Catholic education was made compulsory in all schools, holy days were made state holidays, and the Church officially recognized the united nation of Italy and agreed to divorce itself from active political participation.

Pope Pius XI created Pacelli cardinal on December 16 of that year and recalled him to Rome on February 7, 1930. The new cardinal was appointed secretary of state to replace Pietro Cardinal Gasparri, who had held the post since 1914, and worked tirelessly to accomplish the goals of Pope Pius XI.

With the diplomatic situation in Italy stabilized, Pius XI shifted focus to the rising totalitarian government in Germany. When Hitler and the Nazis came to power in 1933, the Church finalized a concordat with the new regime. Pacelli had worked diligently on the concordat with Germany before Hitler's party took control of the Reichstag, but it now became imperative to finalize the agreement. Pacelli hoped, but did not believe, that the concordat would protect the Church from Nazi persecution, but at the least, it would establish a legal basis for protest of Nazi abuses against Catholics.

Pius XI wanted to ensure that the Nazis would allow independent Catholic organizations, freedom for Catholic schools, free ecclesial communication with Rome, and government recognition of baptized Jews as Christians. In return, the Nazis demanded that the Church cease all political activity in Germany.

Any hope that the Nazis might actually honor the dictates of the concordat was shattered within five days of its signature, when the German government announced a new sterilization law and a change in marriage law that now allowed divorce for non-belief in Nazi teachings. The Nazis focused their ideological indoctrination on German youth and created the Hitler Youth program. The Catholic Youth League was an obstacle to their "education" plan, so the Nazis decreed in 1935 that only Hitler Youth groups could play organized sports, wear uniforms, and march in parades. Additionally, Hitler Youth meetings were purposefully held on Sunday mornings, forcing Catholic young people to choose between going to Mass and going to the meetings. The following year, all pretenses were finally dropped, and the government outlawed all youth groups except the Hitler Youth.

Throughout his tenure as secretary of state, Pacelli continued to warn the world about the Nazis and their malevolent ideology. Days after Hitler used the Enabling Act of 1933 to become dictator, Pacelli ordered the nuncio to Germany "to intervene with the government of the Reich on behalf of the Jews and point out all the dangers involved in an anti-Semitic policy."[375] At an address at Lourdes in April 1935, Pacelli told a group of 125,000 people that the Nazis were "possessed by the superstition of race and blood."[376] In 1936, he traveled to the United States, where he praised Jewish contributions to the nation, denounced antisemitism, and met with the American Jewish Congress.

The Nazis' violations of the concordat and their persecution of Catholics and the Church in Germany prompted Pope Pius XI to promulgate the only encyclical originally written in German, *Mit Brennender Sorge* ("With Burning Sorrow"), in 1937. Although the Church strove diligently to uphold the concordat, the pope criticized the German government, who "emasculated the terms of the treaty, distorted their meaning, and eventually considered its more or less official violation as a normal policy" (5). Pius attacked the core ideals of National Socialism in the document, particularly its racist policies.[377] Although issued under the pope's name and authority, the encyclical was drafted by Pacelli.

The Nazis were incensed after reading the encyclical and banned its publication and dissemination in Germany. In retaliation, the Germans arrested more than a thousand priests and deported more than three hundred to the concentration camp at Dachau, which provided a terrifying lesson to the Vatican that public condemnations of Nazi ideology and policies would result in increased persecution.

Pius XI was not intimidated by the German government and continued to demonstrate his displeasure with Nazi ideology. When Hitler visited Mussolini in Rome in May 1938, Pius XI left the city, and *L'Osservatore Romano* published a front-page article condemning Nazi racial teachings. Later that year, when Jewish businesses were destroyed throughout Germany in the *Kristallnacht*, Pius XI spoke out against the attacks. The incident also generated concerted efforts by Pacelli and the German bishops to acquire visas for Jewish people to emigrate from Germany to safer countries.

In the summer of 1938, Italy adopted the "Manifesto of the Race," a series of anti-Jewish racial laws similar to the Nazi Nuremberg racial laws, which, among other measures, prohibited attendance of Jewish students and employment of Jewish professors in schools and universities. In response, Pacelli appointed twenty-three Jewish scholars to positions in the Gregorian Pontifical Academy of Science and the Vatican Library.[378] Later that year, Pius XI said to a group of Belgian pilgrims visiting Rome that "antisemitism is unacceptable. Spiritually we are all Semites."[379]

Pius XI's actions against Nazi and fascist ideology laid the foundation for the continued activities of the Church under his successor. The courageous pope died on February 11, 1939, months before the world was once again plunged into a devastating and brutal war.

The cardinals in conclave took the shortest amount of time (one day) in three hundred years to elect the successor of Pope Pius XI. Given the world situation, it was an easy selection. Their choice was a veteran diplomat who had extensive experience in dealing with the powerful totalitarian regimes in Italy and Germany. Eugenio Cardinal Pacelli, the first Roman-born pope in two centuries, was elected pope on his birthday, March 2, 1939, and took the name Pius XII (r. 1939–1958).

German reaction to the news was not favorable. As one Berlin newspaper opined, "the election of Cardinal Pacelli is not accepted with favor in Germany because he was always opposed to Nazism."[380] The new pope's coronation occurred ten days later, when every European nation, except Germany, sent diplomatic representation to the ceremony.

Pius XII knew that war clouds loomed on the horizon and urged all nations to work toward peace. However, the German war machine was in full gear, and when the units of the *Wehrmacht* invaded Poland on September 1, 1939, one of the bloodiest conflicts in human history was unleashed. Indeed, "World War II exhausted superlatives," as an average of 27,000 people, mostly civilians, died per day through the six years of fighting.[381] The invasion of Poland witnessed severe persecution of the Church. Priests were shot, arrested, imprisoned, and sent to various concentration camps along with millions of Jewish people and others the Nazis deemed undesirable.

A few months after the war's outbreak, Pope Pius XII promulgated his first encyclical, *Summi Pontificatus*. He attacked Nazi and fascist ideology in the document by highlighting the two errors then affecting the world: the forgetfulness of the law of human solidarity and charity and the rise of the totalitarian state. The pope explained that the main problems with a totalitarian form of government are its emphasis on the state over the individual and the adoration of the state and its leader to the level of idolatry. The Germans were not pleased with the encyclical: Heinrich Müller, chief of the Gestapo, wrote, "This encyclical is directed exclusively against Germany, both in ideology and in regard to the German-Polish dispute. How dangerous it is for our foreign relations as well as our domestic affairs is beyond dispute."[382] The Nazis were so concerned about the document's influence that they even changed the text of the pope's plea concerning Poland to falsely indicate that Pius XII was sending a message to German soldiers and extolling the glory of the German nation![383]

Faced with the daunting task of ministering to a multinational flock engaged in and suffering from a terrible war, Pius XII followed the wartime policies of Pope Benedict XV during the world conflict earlier in the century: diplomatic neutrality (i.e., declining to officially align with any belligerent nation), charity to those affected by the war, and pleas for peace at every opportunity. Although his chief priority was to Catholics and the Church, Pope Pius XII and his Secretariat of State worked diligently to help all victims, especially the Jewish people.

The Roman pontiffs have been among the staunchest defenders of the Jewish people throughout Church history. The city of Rome has contained a sizable population of Jewish people since the Roman Empire, despite their banishment in 139 B.C. and again during the reigns of Tiberius and Claudius. In the late sixth and early seventh centuries, Pope St. Gregory the Great (r. 590–604) began the papal tradition of protecting Rome's Jewish people from harm when he forbade their forcible conversion and demanded toleration of Jewish worship and their freedom from violence. Throughout the medieval and Renaissance periods, the Jewish people were expelled from most of the major areas of Europe but found protection in Rome and the Papal States. Indeed, Popes Calixtus II (r. 1119–1124) and Innocent III (r. 1198–1216) condemned violence against the Jewish people, especially forced baptisms. When the "great pestilence" (later known as the Black Death) killed millions in mid-fourteenth-century Europe, some people blamed the Jews for the illness. This led to pogroms in southern France and Spain, where hundreds of Jewish people were killed. Appalled at the blame and violence inflicted on the Jewish people, Pope Clement VI (r. 1342–1352) promulgated a bull on July 4, 1348, excommunicating anyone who harassed Jews because of the plague. The pope discredited the belief that the Jewish people caused the plague by pointing out that they suffered and died from it as well. Clement VI exhorted bishops and priests throughout Christendom to shelter and protect the Jewish people from violence. In the fifteenth century, Pope Martin V (r. 1417–1431) issued multiple bulls declaring protection for the Jewish people.

Whereas secular rulers in the medieval and Renaissance periods, and later in the twentieth century, harassed the Jewish people, the papacy maintained a consistent policy of protection, as noted by Cecil Roth (1939-1964), the chair of Jewish history at Oxford University:

> Of all the dynasties in Europe, the papacy not only refused to persecute the Jews . . . but through the ages popes were protectors of Jews. . . . The truth is that the popes and the Catholic Church from the earliest days of the Church were never responsible for physical persecution of Jews and only Rome, among the capitals of the world, is free from having been a place of Jewish tragedy. For this we Jews must have gratitude.[384]

Pope Pius XII continued the long tradition of papal protection of the Jewish people during the Second World War. He sent top-secret orders to the nuncio in Poland to assist the Jewish people against harassment from the occupying Germans, and he instructed Angelo Roncalli, the nuncio in Turkey (and the future Pope John XXIII), to "prepare thousands of baptismal certificates to give the Jews which will allow them passage through Turkey to the Holy Land."[385]

Although the papal desire to assist the Jewish people was strong, the reality was that "from a juridical and diplomatic point of view . . . the Holy See was only authorized to intervene on behalf of Catholics around the world."[386] As the war progressed, the Germans and Italians classified Jewish people into two groups: practicing Jews, who were identified for deportation, and converts to the Christian faith. Those who hoped that conversion to the Faith would spare them suffering and death were sadly mistaken, as the Germans refined that distinction based on the timing of a conversion and whether it occurred long before, just before, or after the start of the war. The Nazis and fascists even harassed Christians of Jewish lineage, people who never practiced Judaism but came from extended families who did.[387]

These policies made it difficult for the Church to intervene as effectively as the pope wished. Protestations and requests for special actions were frequently rebuffed, especially when the Christian/Jewish individual lived in German-occupied Poland. Pius XII placed responsibility for special requests from baptized Jews and non-Catholics in the hands of a cabinet of diplomats led by Secretary of State Luigi Cardinal Maglione and included Msgr. Giovanni Battista Montini, the future Pope Paul VI. Recently released documents from the Vatican Archives illustrated the diligent, time-consuming, and often heart-wrenching work these men undertook in the heart of the Vatican to help the many people who wrote to Pius XII throughout Europe during the war. Success was difficult and working with representatives from the German and Italian governments frustrating, but this group tried to assist all those who pleaded for papal intervention.

The pope's stance on perfect neutrality was an asset in helping those suffering from the war, but it did not mean that the warring nations refrained from trying to influence the Holy See to support their war effort. The Allied and the Axis powers throughout the war pressured Pius XII to make statements in support of their policies and actions. It was a delicate diplomatic game, and Rome had to be careful to not fall into traps that could undermine "their ability to communicate with, and influence, all sides, even if that country shared their values. Furthermore, it had to avoid compromising its networks and the courageous individuals engaged in life-saving operations."[388]

Faced with an unprecedented and nearly impossible situation, Pius XII and the Church attempted to balance a number of priorities throughout the war while maintaining neutrality to help the greatest number of people. Despite these efforts, Pius's wartime actions have come under scrutiny in the modern world and in the "Catholic" historical attack. Modern accusations against Pius XII's actions and inactions for the suffering Jewish people during the war fall into the categories of not speaking out enough against the barbaric treatment toward the Jews; not doing enough to stop the evil Final Solution of the Nazis; and being an anti-Semite, which explains the previous two categories.

The historical record is clear that Pius XII spoke out publicly and privately against Nazi treatment of all peoples during the war. In March 1940, the pope met with Joachim von Ribbentrop, the Nazi foreign minister, and complained about reports of German atrocities he had received from bishops and nuncios throughout Europe. Von Ribbentrop called the charges "Allied propaganda" and proceeded to chastise the pope for siding with the Allies. The *New York Times* reported on the fruitless meeting by writing that "in the burning words he spoke to Herr Ribbentrop, [Pius XII] came to the defense of Jews in Poland and Germany."[389]

Pius XII continued to protest publicly and privately, especially in broadcasts on Vatican Radio. The *New York Times*' editorial board praised the pope's Christmas address in 1941: "The voice of Pius XII is a lonely voice in the silence and darkness enveloping Europe. . . . He is about the only ruler left on the continent of Europe who dares to raise his voice at all. The pope put himself squarely against Hitlerism."[390]

Pius XII knew the diplomatic tightrope walk required for public protests. He understood that strong public condemnations could make a bad situation worse. He shared this concern with the cardinals in an address on June 2, 1943:

> Every word we address to the competent authority on this subject, and all our public utterances, have to be carefully weighed and measured by us in the interests of the victims themselves, lest, contrary to our intentions, we make their situation worse and harder to bear.[391]

There was ample reason for the pope's caution: when the Dutch bishops publicly denounced Nazi mistreatment of Jews in 1942, the Germans retaliated by increasing the number of Jewish deportations, including Jewish people who had converted to the Catholic faith. Holland witnessed the largest percentage of Jewish people deported during the war—79 percent of the total Jewish population![392]

Bishops in Nazi-occupied territory as well as Jewish leaders cautioned Pius XII against making forceful public protests. Msgr. Domenico Tardini, secretary for extraordinary ecclesiastical affairs and a member of the Pope's Cabinet established to help those suffering from the war, explained the reasons for the multifaceted concern with vehement public papal protests in a letter to Adam Stefan Cardinal Sapieha, the archbishop of Kraków:

> In fact, given the actual circumstances, a public condemnation by the Holy See would be exploited for political reasons by one of the parts in this conflict. Moreover, the German government, feeling attacked, would without doubt do two things: it would tighten the screws even more on the persecution of Catholicism in Poland, and would impede in all ways any contact between the Holy See and the Polish episcopacy. And also, it would obstruct that charitable work, that today both the episcopacy and the Holy See can achieve—even if in this present moment in a reduced form. Therefore, a public declaration by the Holy See would be distorted in itself and exploited for governmental and further persecution.[393]

Despite the difficulties and the risks, Pius XII and his cabinet continued efforts to assist Jewish people in German-occupied territories as best as possible throughout the war. The recently released documents from the Vatican Archives contain a collection known as the "Ebrei Files," which document nearly three thousand requests for intervention and assistance from mostly Christians of Jewish lineage caught in a legal and bureaucratic nightmare in German-occupied territories or in sympathetic Nazi nations.[394] Practicing Jewish people also wrote to the pope requesting assistance as a last-gasp measure; sadly, many of these pleas arrived too late for the "Pope's Cabinet" to help.

Pius XII could offer more immediate help in Italy. After Mussolini's overthrow in the summer of 1943 and the German conquest of Italy, the Nazis arrested 12,000 Jews in Rome for deportation to concentration camps. When news reached the Vatican, Pius XII directed Secretary of State Maglione to tell the German ambassador, Ernst von Weizsäcker, that a public papal denouncement of the arrests and planned deportation was forthcoming unless the operation ceased immediately. That message eventually reached SS Reichsführer Heinrich Himmler, who ordered a cessation of the deportation operations.[395]

After the war, individual Jews and many Jewish organizations expressed profound gratitude to Pius XII for his heroic activity and the actions of many Catholics who helped Jewish people escape the clutches of the Nazis. Isaac Zolli, the chief rabbi of Rome during the war, converted to the Catholic faith and took the baptismal name Eugenio, in part due to the witness of the pope and Catholics during the war. Zolli considered Pius XII a great friend to the Jewish people and remarked, "No hero in all history was more heroic than Pope Pius and his readiness to defend the children of God."[396] The World Jewish Congress, the American Jewish Committee, the Jewish

Theological Society of America, the Jewish Assistance Committee, the United Jewish Appeal, and the Union of Italian Jewish Communities, among others, all gave their thanks to Pope Pius XII and the Church for their actions on behalf of the Jewish people during the war. Indeed, the Jewish historian Pinchas E. Lapide estimated that the actions of Pope Pius XII and the Catholic Church during the Second World War resulted in the rescue of 860,000 Jewish people from the Nazis, representing 37 percent of those who survived the war.[397]

With the recognition Pius XII and the Church received after the war by those directly affected by it, it is difficult to comprehend the vitriol leveled against the pope and the Church in the modern era by, in part the "Catholic" historical attack. The myths and false narratives of Pius XII's wartime actions are created and used by enemies of the Church, especially former Catholics and "Catholics" who desire changes in the Church's moral and doctrinal teachings.

The notion that the pope was silent during the war and provided implicit acceptance of the Final Solution entered the modern mind nearly twenty years after the end of the Second World War, in large part because of the play *The Deputy*, written by former Hitler Youth member Rolf Hochhuth, which was later turned into the motion picture *Amen* (2002). In *The Deputy*, the same actor plays Pius XII and the fictional Baron Rutta, a character who serves as an advocate for the policies of the Third Reich. Since the same actor plays both characters, the audience is guided toward viewing Pius XII as a Nazi collaborator.

The plot centers on the actions of Fr. Riccardo Fontana, a fictional naïve young Jesuit who trades passports with a Jewish man to help him escape the Nazis. Fontana is arrested instead and sent to a concentration camp, where he is eventually shot. Throughout the play, Fontana complains loudly and frequently about Pope Pius XII. In one scene, he shouts,

"His voice? Where is his voice? Doing nothing is as bad as taking part. . . . God can forgive a hangman for such work, but not a priest, not the pope!"[398]

The play was performed internationally and had a three-hundred-performance run on Broadway, which led to the reception of the 1964 Best Producer (Dramatic) Tony Award for Herman Shumlin. It tarnished Pius XII's reputation, as it gave the audience the impression that he was a money-grubbing hypocrite and a passive and disinterested coward who should have been more vocal during the war.

When asked about the play at the end of his 1964 international trip to Jordan and Israel, Pope Paul VI, who was a member of the Pope's Cabinet, established to assist people harassed by the Nazis, emphatically stated,

> History, not the artificial manipulation of the facts and their preconceived interpretation as operated in *The Deputy*, will claim the truth about Pius XII's action during the last war against the criminal excesses of the Nazi regime, and will demonstrate how vigilant, assiduous, selfless, and courageous it was, in the real context of the facts and conditions of those years.[399]

Sadly, Paul VI's faith in history has proved overly optimistic, as the succeeding sixty years has witnessed a proliferation of anti-Pius XII publications.

The "Catholic" historical attack against Pope Pius XII and the Church began in earnest with the publications of former Catholic seminarian John Cornwall's 1999 book *Hitler's Pope.* Cornwall opined that Pius XII did not speak out against Nazi treatment of the Jewish people during the war because he was an anti-Semite and used a letter then-nuncio Pacelli wrote in 1919 to Rome reporting on political unrest in Munich caused by the militant pro-Soviet German Communist Party, which contained many secular Jewish members. Pacelli's letter was six pages long, but Cornwall (mis)translated and used only two paragraphs of the document to "prove" Pacelli's antisemitism.[400] Several years later, Cornwall published another book, *Constantine's Sword: The Church and the Jews—A History* (2001), in which he claimed that the Church has always taught antisemitism and hatred of the Jewish people because of Jesus' crucifixion and death.

The "Catholic" historical attack on Pius XII does not rely solely on the works of former Catholic scholars; it also embraces non-Catholic scholars with an animus against Pius and the Church. Daniel Jonah Goldhagen's 2002 book *A Moral Reckoning: The Role of the Catholic Church in the Holocaust and its Unfulfilled Duty of Repair* repeats Cornwall's claim that the Church has always preached antisemitism, which, ultimately, produced the Nazis' Final Solution. Additionally, periodicals, such as the *New York Times*, which during the war praised Pius XII, now joined in the chorus of slander and libel against the pope and the Church.

Any hope that the decision by Pope Francis in March 2020 to open fully the archives of the Vatican from the Second World War would lead to a final refutation of the false claims against Pius XII were crushed with the publication of David I. Kertzer's 2022 book *The Pope at War: The Secret History of Pius XII, Mussolini, and Hitler.* Kertzer opined that the newly released Vatican documents illustrated that the pope was "intimidated" by Hitler and Mussolini and was therefore unwilling to confront them about the treatment of the Jewish people. Additionally, Kertzer faulted the pope for (seemingly) caring more about the "institutional Church's" position, power, and authority than about people during the horrors of the war. Although he acknowledged the pope's difficult situation during the war years, Kertzer's final analysis is that

> as a moral leader, Pius XII must be judged a failure. He had no love for Hitler, but he was intimidated by him, as he was by Italy's dictator as well. At a time of great uncertainty, Pius XII clung firmly to his determination to do nothing to antagonize either man. In fulfilling this aim, the pope was remarkably successful.[401]

So, despite access to the most critical documents of Pius XII's pontificate, which had been inaccessible for sixty years, Kertzer's conclusion is the same as those who have written before him without access to those documents: the pope did not do enough. It is a conclusion rooted in bias and animus against the papacy and the Church and embraced by the proponents of the "Catholic" historical attack.

Although the Second World War dominated Pius XII's pontificate, he continued to shepherd the Church for years after that cataclysmic event. He wrote forty encyclicals, including *Mystici Corporis Christi* (1943) on the Church as the mystical body of Christ; *Divino Afflante Spiritu* (1943) on biblical scholarship; and *Humani Generis* (1950), which discussed Darwinism and evolution. Perhaps his most enduring legacy to the Church was the proclamation in 1950 of the dogma of the Assumption of the Most Blessed Mary.

In the history of the papacy, it is difficult to find a pope who experienced a more challenging set of circumstances during his reign than Pius XII. He truly showed a deep love of Christ, the Church, and all peoples throughout one of the most perilous and heart-wrenching times. It is a travesty of charity and justice that this venerable man's words, actions, and decisions are manipulated by enemies of the Church to use him as a scapegoat when he should be recognized as a true hero of God and a saint.

Pope Benedict XVI

The election of Ratzinger was greeted with grief and horror by those heretical theologians and cafeteria Catholics whose heresies and backsliding equivocations had been condemned by the new pope during his many years as prefect of the Congregation for the Doctrine of the Faith. As usual, these wolves in sheep's clothing howled in unison with the wolves in the secular media, uniting themselves with the avowed enemies of the Church in their hatred of the hero of orthodoxy who had forced them into retreat during his years as John Paul II's faithful and fearless servant.[402]

Although the historical attack against the Church tries to cancel the memory of many popes, there is one man, Joseph Ratzinger, who was maligned as such both before and during his papacy. From a secular and "Catholic" historical attack perspective, Ratzinger was one of the most polarizing figures in the Church's recent history, despite the reality that he was a humble, brilliant, and devoted man of the Church.

Ratzinger was canceled by those who hated his defense of the Faith and his articulation of an authentic interpretation of the documents of the Second Vatican Council because he stood in the way of their misuse of the council to further their agenda. He was vilified by the "Catholic" historical attack because of his embrace of traditional liturgy and its expanded use but also criticized by "Catholic" commentators who were shocked not only by his abdication, but also by the pontificate of his successor. These critics blame Ratzinger for the perceived problems of his successor's pontificate because without Benedict's abdication, they believe, Jorge Bergoglio would not be pope.

Contradictions followed Benedict XVI throughout his public life because secular and "Catholic" detractors found it difficult to define him within their boxes. Before his papal election, when he was the faithful servant of Pope John Paul II, he was contradictorily described as "an aggressive German of lordly air, an ascetic who carries the cross like a sword," "an earthy Bavarian of friendly visage who lives unpretentiously in a modest dwelling in the vicinity of the Vatican," and, "an ironclad cardinal [*Panzer-Kardinal*] who has never laid aside the splendid robes and golden pectoral cross of a prince of the Roman Church."[403] The real Joseph Ratzinger was, like all canceled Catholics, more than the false descriptions and slanderous labels. He was a dedicated man of the Church, a brilliant theologian and thinker, and a faithful servant of Christ.

Joseph Ratzinger was born on Holy Saturday, April 16, 1927, in Marktl am Inn in Upper Bavaria, near the Austrian border. His hometown is ten miles from the Marian shrine in Altötting and only eighteen miles from the Austrian town of Braunau an Inn, the birthplace of Adolf Hitler, a man whose politics greatly impacted the Ratzinger family.

Joseph was the youngest of three children born to Mary and Joseph Ratzinger. During the Second World War, Joseph was conscripted into the German Army, at the age of sixteen, and spent a year as an antiaircraft battery observer.

The Ratzinger family was devoted to the Catholic faith, and both Joseph and his brother Georg entered the seminary in Munich. Joseph studied philosophy and theology from 1946 to 1951 at the University of Munich and at Freising. Joseph and Georg were ordained together on June 29, 1951. Joseph continued his studies and received a doctorate in theology with a dissertation on Saint Augustine and became a teacher at Freising in 1957 and later at Bonn. He also served as a lecturer in dogmatic theology at the German universities of

Münster (1963–1966), Tübingen (1966–1969), and Regensburg (1969–1977).

During his years as a professor, Ratzinger published many essays and books, including *Introduction to Christianity* in 1968. The series of lectures, turned into a book, was translated into seventeen languages and established Ratzinger's reputation as an outstanding theologian. Influential members of the Church read the book, including Pope Paul VI, who appointed the young theologian to the International Theological Commission in 1969.

Before *Introduction to Christianity*'s publication, Ratzinger served as a theological adviser to Josef Cardinal Frings of Cologne at the Second Vatican Council. He attended all four sessions of the council and played an instrumental role in drafting several of the conciliar documents. As throughout his professional life, Ratzinger proved a contradiction, as he was viewed at the time of the council as a liberal reformer and "progressive," but that view was proved mistaken in the post-conciliar years.

Despite the protestation of many within the Church, Pope John XXIII (r. 1958–1963), less than three months after his election, announced the calling of the Second Vatican Council. The pope believed that the Church was in need of renewal and reform to successfully engage the modern world, rooted in the errors of the "Enlightenment" and modernism. Ratzinger agreed with the papal decision, and after the council, he published a book on his reflections as a participant. He opposed those in the Church who grumbled at the pope's decision, and he highlighted the internal and external areas that required focused ecclesial attention. Ratzinger identified these areas as encompassing the renewal of the liturgy and greater lay participation; reform of the Roman Curia; relations with non-Catholic Christians; interactions between the

Church and new nation-states; the role of faith and science in the modern world; and the teachings of the Church *vis-à-vis* the modern industrial world, including new moral problems associated with new technologies.[404]

Ratzinger also understood the centrality of Christ in the renewal and reform of the Church. The conciliar efforts could not be divorced from that centrality, since "the measure of the renewal is Christ . . . and if renewal seeks to think through and to speak the gospel of Christ in a way understandable to contemporary man . . . then the objective is precisely that Christ may become understood."[405]

The hope and promise of the council at its conclusion was not realized throughout the Church in the subsequent years, as various groups, especially in the Western world, misused the conciliar documents to further their own agenda, which Ratzinger fought vigorously. In a 1985 interview-turned-book, Ratzinger, then a cardinal, stated, "the council wanted to mark the transition from a protective to a missionary attitude. Many forget that for the council the counter-concept to 'conservative' is not 'progressive' but 'missionary.'"[406]

Ratzinger's participation at the Second Vatican Council and his theological writings enhanced his reputation and led to his appointment as archbishop of Munich on March 24, 1977. Three months later, Pope Paul VI created him cardinal. Less than a year later, Ratzinger participated in his first conclave to elect the successor to Paul VI. That year, 1978, was the year of three popes, which saw the pontificate of Paul VI end; the election of John Paul I, who died barely a month after his election; and then the selection of the fifty-eight-year-old cardinal-archbishop of Kraków, Karol Wojtyła, who took the name John Paul II.

It was the pontificate of John Paul II that elevated Cardinal Ratzinger to greater responsibility, recognition, and criticism.

On November 25, 1981, John Paul II appointed Ratzinger as the prefect of the Congregation for the Doctrine of Faith (CDF), the curial office in charge of maintaining doctrinal orthodoxy in the Church. He served in this office for more than twenty years, gaining a public reputation, through the media, as the "Panzer Cardinal" and "God's Rottweiler." Privately, however, he was known as an intelligent, charitable, and brilliant theologian who loved the Church and desired to ensure the bold and authentic proclamation of the gospel truth. Despite media portrayals as "right-wing" and engaging in a crackdown on "left-wing" theologians and ecclesial dissidents, for Joseph Ratzinger, the "political concepts of right and left are ultimately meaningless because life is not about left and right but right and wrong."[407]

During his tenure at the CDF, Ratzinger also served as the president of the Biblical Commission, the Pontifical International Theological Commission, and the Commission for Drafting the *Catechism of the Catholic Church*, which was a six-year effort to produce the first universal catechism for the Church since the sixteenth century. Although Cardinal Ratzinger served faithfully, he desired to return to Germany to research and write. But John Paul II denied his resignation requests, believing that the Church required the services of this intellectual giant and faithful defender.

Ratzinger hoped that his longed-for dream of retirement was close at hand when the pope he faithfully served for twenty-four years died in April 2005. As dean of the College of Cardinals, Ratzinger preached the homily at the Mass before the conclave. He highlighted the dangers of the modern world, where "having a clear faith based on the Creed of the Church is often labeled as fundamentalism." Whereas the secular world extols personal freedom and independence, it actually produces "a dictatorship of relativism that does not recognize anything as definitive and whose ultimate goal consists solely of one's own ego and desires." The Christian understands that the "measure of true humanism" is found not in self, but in "the Son of God, the true man," and possessing a mature faith means a deep friendship with Jesus, which provides the "criterion by which to distinguish the true from the false."[408] It may have been a surprise to the humble theologian that the cardinals elected him as the successor to John Paul II, but he accepted their decision, and he chose the name Benedict XVI.

At one of his Wednesday General Audiences, Pope Benedict XVI reflected on the reason for choosing his papal name. It was to honor the memory of Benedict XV, the champion of peace during the First World War, and to recall the significance of St. Benedict of Nursia (480–543) in shaping Europe. The pope desired to highlight the life of the humble monk who lived during a dark time of great political and social chaos, but who established a place of light at Monte Cassino. He wrote a Rule to govern life at the monastery, which became the foundational document for Western monasticism. Benedict's monastic life flourished and spread throughout Europe, and his monks became missionaries of light and order in a dark and chaotic time. Their focus on prayer and work provided stability, and their efforts in the scriptorium ensured that documents of antiquity were preserved. Benedict, the new pope insisted, had "changed the face of Europe . . . inspiring a new spiritual and cultural unity, that of the Christian faith shared by the peoples of the Continent. This is how the reality we call 'Europe' came into being."[409]

Benedict XVI knew that the Church in Europe was suffering from a serious identity crisis, so he utilized his Wednesday General Audiences to recall the lives and deeds of the great men and women in Church history, beginning the discussion with St. Peter on May 17, 2006 and ending with the Little Flower, St. Thérèse of Lisieux, on April 6, 2011. Remembering Church history was a vital component of Benedict's pontificate, as was exhortation to virtue, especially the three theological virtues of faith, hope, and love. These virtues formed the foundation for the three encyclicals of Benedict's pontificate, *Deus Caritas Est* (December 25, 2005), *Spe Salvi* (November 30, 2007), and *Caritas in Veritate* (June 29, 2009). The theological virtues are gifts from God that help Christians live in relationship with the Trinity. The pope desired Christians to re-dedicate their lives to God and specifically to embrace Christ-centered lives, which he believed possible with a cultivation of faith, hope, and love.

Ever the teacher and theologian, Benedict XVI continued to write books during his pontificate and published a trinity of works, called *Jesus of Nazareth*, on the life and mission of Christ: *From the Baptism in the Jordan to the Transfiguration* (September 15, 2008), *Holy Week: From the Entrance into Jerusalem to the Resurrection* (March 20, 2011), and *The Infancy Narratives* (November 21, 2012). The pope also promoted the work of the New Evangelization begun during the reign of Pope John Paul II by establishing the Pontifical Council for Promoting the New Evangelization. The new curial office was charged with the mission to bring the gospel back to areas of the world previously evangelized but now having forgotten or rejected the message of Jesus through the spread of anti-Christian ideology, especially secularization.

Early in his pontificate, Benedict XVI became the scapegoat for a spasm of violence that erupted in some areas of the Muslim world when he gave an academic speech at the University of Regensburg during his apostolic visit to Bavaria. In his address, the pope quoted the Eastern emperor Manuel II Palaeologus (r. 1391–1425) in a dialogue with a Muslim on the difference between the Islamic and Christian faiths. The question between the two men concerned the use of violence in religion and its unreasonableness. The emperor retorted to his Muslim opponent: "Show me just what Muhammad brought that was new, and there you will find things only evil and inhuman, such as his command to spread by the sword the faith he preached."[410] The media misrepresented the pope's address and fanned the flames of fanaticism, resulting in rioting in some Muslim countries, attacks on Christians and the killing of a priest in Iraq, and the killing of a religious sister in Somalia. Benedict's intended use of the quote was to posit the academic thesis that true peace is possible only if faith and reason are in unity. However, the modern world rejected that discussion and, instead, proved the point with attacks on the pope, calling him "undiplomatic," "insensitive," and "un-ecumenical." Sadly, the lecture, which was one of the most important intellectual statements in recent memory, was grossly misunderstood and misused to the detriment of the pope and the Church.

Proponents of the "Catholic" historical attack criticized Benedict XVI for his July 7, 2007, *motu proprio* called *Summorum Pontificum*, which allowed for wider use of the Roman missal that preceded the liturgical reforms following the Second Vatican Council. Benedict XVI had great devotion to the Church's liturgy and desired that the faithful enter more deeply into the sacred mysteries. Before his papacy, Ratzinger wrote *The Spirit of the Liturgy* (2000) as "an aid to the understanding of the Faith and to the right way to give the Faith its central form of expression in the liturgy."[411] Ratzinger believed that an authentic liturgical movement would assist the Church "toward the right way of celebrating the liturgy, inwardly and outwardly" and hoped his book might contribute to a renewal as called for by the Second

Vatican Council.[412] Some quarters of the Church applauded his *motu proprio*, but others were angry and used the document to cancel the pontiff and the Church as old-fashioned, conservative, and out of touch with modernity.

Benedict XVI shocked the Church and the world at the Consistory on February 11, 2013, when he told the assembled cardinals, "After having repeatedly examined my conscience before God, I have come to the certainty that my strengths, due to an advanced age, are no longer suited to an adequate exercise of the Petrine ministry." Benedict believed that his age and health had led to an inability to "adequately fulfill the ministry entrusted to me" and stated that "with full freedom I declare that I renounce the ministry of the bishop of Rome, successor of St. Peter."[413] The pope specified that his abdication was effective at 8:00 P.M. on February 28, at which time the process to elect a new supreme pontiff could commence. Benedict chose the date to announce his abdication because it was halfway between Christmas and Easter and afforded the cardinals enough time to have a successor in place by Easter Sunday.

Although the faithful were stunned when the news was released, Benedict, in hindsight, had provided clues concerning his future decision. On April 28, 2009, he visited the tomb of Pope St. Celestine V at the Basilica of Collemaggio in the town of L'Aquila, in a region that had been ravaged by a devastating earthquake. During the visit, Benedict told a group of volunteers, first responders, and military personnel that he had placed his papal pallium from his inauguration on the tomb of the thirteenth-century pope, who had abdicated the papacy after only five months in office. Several months later, he authorized the Apostolic Penitentiary to grant a special plenary indulgence to those who visited and prayed at the tomb of this saintly pope during the Year of St. Celestine V

(August 28, 2009–August 29, 2010), which was instituted to honor the 800th anniversary of the pope's birth. The next year, in 2010, Benedict visited the Cathedral of Sulmona, where he addressed a group of young people and encouraged them to further their devotion to Celestine. Benedict reflected on the need of the modern world to rediscover what Celestine knew and lived deeply—that is, "the ability to listen to God in external and above all internal silence. St. Peter Celestine was first and foremost this: a man of listening, of inner silence, a man of prayer, a man of God."[414]

Although Benedict's resignation shocked the world at the time, papal abdication had occurred several times before him.

- The first papal abdication occurred in the third century, when Pope St. Pontian (r. 230–235) resigned the papacy before his exile to the salt mines of Sardinia by the Roman authorities.

- The eleventh century witnessed the bizarre case of Pope Benedict IX (r. 1032–1045, 1045, 1047–1048), the only man to reign three separate times as pope. Papal elections, heavily influenced by local Italian noble families, were farcical events, and the papacy itself was embroiled in a game of power politics. When Pope John XIX (r. 1024–1032) died, his nephew was elected pope, taking the name Benedict IX. The young man's lifestyle was ill suited to the clerical state, and, restless with papal duties, he abdicated the throne, allegedly to marry his cousin. Gregory VI (r. 1045–1046) was elected, but the former pope soon tired of his non-papal life and returned to Rome, demanding re-instatement as supreme pontiff. Accused of simony, Gregory VI abdicated the papacy, and Clement II (r. 1046–1047) was elected as successor, but upon his death, Benedict IX managed to return to the papacy.

- In the thirteenth century, Pope Celestine V (r. 1294) reigned for a brief five months before his abdication. The simple hermit-turned-supreme pontiff quickly realized his inadequacy for the demands of the office and resigned.
- Finally, the last pope to abdicate before Benedict XVI was Gregory XII (r. 1406–1415), who, in a final effort to heal the Great Western Schism, recognized the validity of the Council of Constance and then abdicated the papacy to make way for a new pope whom all Christendom would recognize (Martin V, r. 1417–1431).

Reaction to Pope Benedict XVI's abdication at the time mostly centered on shock and sadness. Some critics believed that Benedict was betraying tradition and the memory of Pope John Paul II, who died in office despite serious health issues, which greatly limited his exercise of the Petrine ministry in his last years.

Regardless of the criticism, Benedict XVI abdicated on February 28, 2013. He remained in Rome, kept his papal name, adopted the title "Pope Emeritus," and wore the customary papal white cassock but no longer exercised the authority of the Petrine office. He promised "unconditional reverence and obedience" to the future pontiff, who was elected on March 13, 2013, taking the name Francis.

As the years have progressed since his abdication and eventual death in 2022, the memory of Pope Benedict XVI has been attacked by some Catholics, who blame him for their disagreements with Pope Francis. In their minds, the problems associated with the current papacy could never have existed, because if Benedict had not abdicated, then Francis would never have been elected.

Proponents of this reasoning resort to the "Catholic" historical attack from an internal perspective rather than the common external attack seen with most canceled Catholic historical persons. However, the attack is unsustainable—after all, Benedict offered his full support to Francis, and there is no reason to believe that someone substantially different from or "better than" Francis would have been elected had Benedict stayed in office. There is not even any guarantee that Benedict, subjecting himself to the intense stress and pressure of the papacy, would have lived long past 2013, and thus Francis might have been elected anyway! So this attack is nothing more than an effort to cancel a humble, faithful, and dedicated son of the Church for the perceived problems of a successor.

The reasoning is infantile. And the denigration of Benedict XVI, one of the most gifted theologians of the past century, is no less shameful than the Enlightenment, secular, and Protestant historical attacks against Catholics of the past.

Conclusion

The anti-Catholic tradition could not be kept alive, would die of exhaustion without a continual supply of fable.[415]

—St. John Henry Newman

Nearly a century ago, the Catholic author, historian, and politician Hilaire Belloc (1870-1953) wrote an intriguing examination of the Church and the modern world in his 1929 book *Survivals and New Arrivals*. Belloc was gravely concerned that the English Catholics of his time were not aware fully of the anti-Catholic situation in their homeland. He wanted his fellow Catholics to recognize "that the air we breathe is anti-Catholic; that the history we are taught, the moral ideas behind the legal system we obey, the restrictions imposed on us, the political conceptions embodied in every public act, the general attitude toward foreign countries" were the product of a Protestant perspective embodied in the English nation.[416]

Belloc believed that an assessment of the enemies of the Church was warranted so that defenders of the Faith could mount a proper Catholic defense in the future. He stressed that Catholics should investigate which opponents at the time were in a weakened state, which ones were in full potency, and what new adversaries would arise. He categorized these attacks into *survivals*, the *main opposition*, and *new arrivals*.

Belloc defined *survivals* as the old forms of attack that were weakening and not sustainable into the future—among them "the historical attack," which sought to discredit the Catholic faith through disproving from history certain claims of the Church. Critics utilizing this attack accomplished that goal by two methods: "proving" not that a doctrine, teaching, practice, or tradition of the Church was false, but rather that it formed no part of the original Apostolic Church (e.g., the role and authority of the papacy), and proving that some claim or custom was false (e.g., the presence of one relic of the same saint in different locations). This second approach focused on disproving traditions and legends associated with the Faith, which would, the critics hoped, lessen acceptance of the truths of the Church.

Belloc noticed that the Church remained on the defensive for centuries concerning the historical attack. It took several centuries of sustained Protestant attacks against the history of the Church for its defenders to effectively launch a counter, but, as Belloc noted, serious Catholic and non-Catholic scholars had joined the fray and mounted a bold defense of the Church's history. This fact convinced Belloc that the "historical attack" was a "survival" and that the future would reveal the disappearance of critics utilizing this form of assault against the Church.

Sadly, Belloc's prediction proved incorrect, as modern-day historians with an animus against the Church pursued a relentless campaign of canceling historical Catholics. This attack is widespread and pernicious due to the arrival of the internet and modern means of communication, especially social media, which allow anyone with an opinion on any subject to proclaim it boldly, broadly, and boastfully. Enemies of the

Church have greatly multiplied in the modern world and are effectively utilizing the historical attack in its Enlightenment, secular, Protestant, and "Catholic" forms to cancel individual Catholics of the past to discredit the Church and weaken its influence in society. Pope Francis lamented this situation in his "Letter on the Renewal of the Study of Church History" (November 21, 2024) when he wrote, "Nowadays we are flooded with 'memories,' often false, artificial, and even mendacious," and "a tendency to dismiss the memory of the past or to invent one suited to the requirements of dominant ideologies."

Amid the historical attacks against the Church and her past members, Catholics today are oftentimes bewildered and unsure how to respond. Catholics are susceptible to two erroneous responses to these anti-Catholic historical criticisms: an unflinching and uncritical triumphalism that highlights the good and ignores the bad of Church history and the "ostrich" approach of ignoring the controversy at best and implicitly accepting the false historical narrative at worst.

The Catholic defender of Church history must fight these extreme positions and seek the historical truth through knowledge; understanding the context of historical events; and recognizing that people in the past were men and women endowed with free will, which was sometimes exercised virtuously and sometimes not. Defense of Catholic personages and historical events from the cancel culture of the present does not indicate complete acceptance of past persons or actions, but instead seeks authentic understanding so that controversial persons and events can be explained (but not necessarily justified).

The authentic story of the Templars, Pope Innocent III, the Spanish inquisitors, Constantine, Mary Tudor, Guy Fawkes, Columbus and the conquistadors, Marie Antoinette, Popes

Pius IX, Pius XII, and Benedict XVI (and others) must be taught and learned boldly, unequivocally, truthfully, and from a Catholic perspective, so that the Church they loved, served, and sometimes died for can fight the forces of evil and darkness and restore all things in Christ.

About the Author

Steve Weidenkopf teaches at the Christendom College Graduate School of Theology, Virginia. He is the author of *Light from Darkness: Nine Times the Catholic Church Was in Turmoil—and Came Out Stronger Than Before* (2021); *The Church and the Middle Ages: 1000–1378* (2020); *Timeless: A History of the Catholic Church* (2019); *The Real Story of Catholic History: Answering Twenty Centuries of Anti-Catholic Myths* (2017); and *The Glory of the Crusades* (2014) and a contributor to *Religion and World Civilizations: How Faith Shaped Societies from Antiquity to the Present* (2023) and *The Palgrave Handbook of Religion and State*, volume II (2023).

Steve is the creator and co-author of *Epic: A Journey Through Church History* and the author of the Early Church adult faith formation studies. He is a member of the Society for the Study of the Crusades and the Latin East, an international academic group dedicated to the field of crusading history. He is also a Knight of the Equestrian Order of the Holy Sepulchre of Jerusalem. Steve and his wife live in Virginia and are blessed with six children and two grandchildren.

Endnotes

1 Susan Doran and Thomas S. Freeman, eds., *The Myth of Elizabeth* (New York: Palgrave Macmillian, 2003), 2–3.

2 See Donal Dorr, "The Scapegoat," *The Furrow* 62, no. 2 (February 2010), 92.

3 Tacitus, *Annals*, XV, 44, quoted in Jean Comby, *How to Read Church History: From the Beginnings to the Fifteenth Century*, vol. 1 (New York: Crossroad, 2001), 38.

4 See Ray Allen Billington, "Maria Monk and Her Influence," *Catholic Historical Review* 22, no. 3 (October 1936), 283.

5 According to the research of Ray Allen Billington in 1933, as cited in William S. Cossen, "Monk in the Middle: *The Awful Disclosures of the Hotel Dieu Nunnery* and the Making of Catholic Identity," *American Catholic Studies* 125, no. 1 (Spring 2014), 34.

6 Billington, "Maria Monk," 284.

7 Cossen, "Monk in the Middle," 28–29.

8 See Billington, "Maria Monk," 284.

9 See Cossen, "Monk in the Middle," 25.

10 Billington, "Maria Monk," 289.

11 See Lorraine Boissoneault, "How the 19th-Century Know Nothing Party Reshaped American Politics," *Smithsonian Magazine*, January 26, 2017.

12 Ibid.

13 Michael F. Holt, "The Politics of Impatience: The Origins of Know Nothingism," *Journal of American History* 60, no. 2 (September 1973): 324.

14 Christopher Shannon and Christopher O. Blum, *The Past as Pilgrimage: Narrative, Tradition, and the Renewal of Catholic History* (Front Royal, VA: Christendom Press, 2014), 39.

15 Robert Louis Wilken, *The First Thousand Years: A Global History of Christianity* (New Haven, CT: Yale University Press, 2012), 1.

16 See Warren H. Carroll, *The Founding of Christendom: A History of Christendom*, vol. 1 (Front Royal, VA: Christendom College Press, 1985), 11–12.

17 See Keith Windschuttle, *The Killing of History: How Literary Critics and Social Theorists are Murdering Our Past* (San Francisco: Encounter Books, 1996), 243–244.

18 Ibid., 2–8.

19 Ibid., 19.

20 John Paul II, *Memory and Identity: Conversations at the Dawn of a Millennium* (New York: Rizzoli, 2005), 10, 97.

21 Brennan Pursell, *History in His Hands: A Christian Narrative of the West* (New York: Crossroad, 2011), 192.

22 See Rodney Stark, *Bearing False Witness: Debunking Centuries of Anti-Catholic History* (West Conshohocken, PA: 2016), 91.

23 Ibid., 194.

24 See Michel-Rolph Trouillot, *Silencing the Past: Power and the Production of History* (Boston: Beacon Press, 1995), 74–82.

25 Martin P. Harney, *The Jesuits in History* (New York, 1941), 292, quoted in Warren H. Carroll and Anne Carroll, *The Revolution against Christendom: A History of Christendom*, vol. 5 (Front Royal, VA: Christendom Press, 2005), 83.

26 Marcus Bull, *Thinking Medieval: An Introduction to the Study of the Middle Ages* (New York: Palgrave Macmillan, 2005), 17.

27 Christopher Tyerman, *The Debate on the Crusades* (New York: Manchester University Press, 2011), 67.

28 Quoted in Jean Richard, *The Crusades, c. 1071–c. 1291*, trans. Jean Birrell (Cambridge: Cambridge University Press, 2001 [1996]), 475.

29 Ibid.

30 See Hannes Möhring, *Saladin: The Sultan and His Times, 1138–1193*, trans. David S. Bachrach, intro and preface Paul M. Cobb (Baltimore: Johns Hopkins University Press, 2005), 91–104.

31 Otto of Freising, *Chronica sive historia de duabus civitatibus*, ed. A. Hofmeister and W. Lammers, trans. A. Schmidt (Darmstadt, 1961), 514–515, quoted in Jonathan Phillips, *The Second Crusade: Extending the Frontiers of Christendom* (New Haven, CT: Yale University Press, 2007), 2.

32 Jonathan Riley-Smith, *Templars and Hospitallers as Professed Religious in the Holy Land* (Notre Dame: University of Notre Dame, 2010), 6.

33 Ibid., 61.

34 *Vitae paparum Avenionensium*, ed. Etienne Baluze and Guillaume Molat, 4 vols. (Paris, 1914–1927), 3.151, quoted in Riley-Smith, *Templars and Hospitallers*, 61.

35 Dan Jones, *The Templars: The Rise and Spectacular Fall of God's Holy Warriors* (New York: Penguin Books, 2017), 1.

36 Bernard of Clairvaux, *On the Praise of the New Knighthood*, chap. 4.

37 Ibid., chap. 2.

38 Malcolm Barber, *The New Knighthood: A History of the Order of the Temple* (Cambridge University Press, 1994), 61.

39 Isaac of L'Etoile, *Sermons*, ed. Anselme Hoste and Gaetano Raciti, 3 vols. (Paris, 1967–1987), 3.158–60, quoted in Riley-Smith, *Templars and Hospitallers*, 14.

40 See Barber, *The New Knighthood*, 230.

41 Ibid., 282–283.

42 See Helen J. Nicholson, *The Knights Templar* (Leeds: Arc Humanities Press, 2021), 2.

43 *Cartulaire general de l'Ordre du Temple 1119?–1150: Recueil des chartes et des bulles relatives à l'ordre du Temple*, ed. Marquis d'Albon (Paris, 1913), no. 207, 144, quoted in Barber, *The New Knighthood*, 55.

44 See Barber, *The New Knighthood*, 185.

45 Ibid.

46 Ibid., 182.

47 Ibid., 220.

48 Quoted in Jonathan Riley-Smith, *The Crusades: A History*, 2nd ed. (New Haven, CT: Yale University Press, 2005), 71.

49 Nicholson, *The Knights Templar*, 62.

50 The Würzburg annalist, quoted in *Chronicles of the Crusades: Nine Crusades and Two Hundred Years of Bitter Conflict for the Holy Land Brought to Life through the Words of Those Who Were Actually There*, ed. Elizabeth Hallam (New York: Weidenfeld and Nicolson, 1989), 147.

51 See Barber, *The New Knighthood*, 229.

52 The description of Nogaret is from Georges Digard, *Philippe le Bel et le Saint-Siège de 1285 à 1304* (Paris, 1936, quoted in Warren H. Carroll, *The Glory of Christendom* (Front Royal: Christendom Press, 1993), 334.

53 See Barber, *The New Knighthood*, 304.

54 Ibid., 318.

55 Jane Sayers, *Innocent III: A Leader of Europe, 1198–1216* (London: Longman, 1994), 193.

56 The term "theocratic doctrine" and its description is found in Brian Tierney, *The Crisis of Church and State 1050–1300* (Toronto: University of Toronto Press, 1988 [1964]), 127–128.

57 Henri Daniel-Rops, *Cathedral and Crusade*, trans. John Warrington (London: J. M. Dent and Sons, 1957), 138.

58 See *Readings in Church History*, vol. 1, *From Pentecost to the Protestant Revolt*, ed., Colman J. Barry, O.S.B. (Westminster, MD: Newman Press, 1960), 424.

59 See John C. Moore, *Pope Innocent III (1160/61–1216): To Root Up and to Plant* (Notre Dame: University of Notre Dame Press, 2009), 30.

60 Ibid., 48–49.

61 *Gesta Innocentii III*. PL 214:xvii, in David Gress-Wright, ed., "The '*Gesta Innocentii III*': Text, introduction and commentary." Bryn Mawr College dissertation, 1981, 1. Quoted in Moore, *Pope Innocent III*, 253.

62 The work survived in seven hundred manuscripts and fifty printed editions by the year 1700. See Moore, *Pope Innocent III*, 276.

63 See Brett Edward Whalen, *The Medieval Papacy* (New York: Palgrave Macmillan, 2014), 133.

64 Quoted in Moore, *Pope Innocent III*, 22.

65 Frederich Kempf, S.J., "Innocent III's Claim to Power," in James M. Powell, ed., *Innocent III: Vicar of Christ or Lord of the World?*, 2nd, expanded ed. (Washington, D.C.: Catholic University of America Press, 1994), 175.

66 Sayers, *Innocent III*, 91.

67 *Barnwell Chronicle of Coventry*, quoted and trans. Cheney, *Innocent III and England*, 333, quoted in Moore, *Pope Innocent III*, 215.

68 The quote is from Blessed Pope Urban II, quoted in C. Morris, *The Papal Monarchy: The Western Church from 1050 to 1250* (Oxford, 1991), 125. Quoted in Eamon Duffy, *Saints and Sinners: A History of the Popes* (New Haven, CT: Yale University Press, 2006), 128.

69 Joseph R. Strayer, *The Albigensian Crusades* (Ann Arbor: University of Michigan Press, 1992), 19.

70 Omer Englebert, *St. Francis of Assisi* (Chicago, 1965), 107–114, cited in Warren Carroll, *The Glory of Christendom: A History of Christendom*, vol. 3 (Front Royal, VA: Christendom College Press, 1993), 163.

71 See Moore, *Pope Innocent III*, 237–239.

72 Gary Dickson, *The Children's Crusade: Medieval History, Modern Mythistory* (New York: Palgrave Macmillan, 2010), 31.

73 Innocent III, *Solitae*, from A.J. Andrea, *The Medieval Record: Sources of Medieval History* (Boston, 1997), 9n4, quoted in Jonathan Phillips, *The Fourth Crusade and the Sack of Constantinople* (New York: Penguin Books, 2004), 5.

74 Christopher Tyerman, *God's War: A New History of the Crusades* (Cambridge, MA: Belknap Press, 2006), 480.

75 Quoted in Riley-Smith, *The Crusades*, 148–149.

76 L. and J. Riley-Smith, *The Crusades: Idea and Reality, 1095–1274* (London, 1981), 123–124, in Norman Housley, *Fighting for the Cross: Crusading to the Holy Land* (New Haven, CT: Yale University Press, 2008), 75.

77 Villehardouin, *Conquête de Constantinople*, sec. 83, I: 82–84, in Donald E. Queller and Thomas F. Madden, *The Fourth Crusade: The Conquest of Constantinople*, 2nd ed. (Philadelphia: University of Pennsylvania Press, 1997), 75.

78 Quoted in Queller and Madden, *The Fourth Crusade*, 102.

79 Ibid.

80 Innocent III letter to crusade leaders, in *Chronicles of the Crusades*, ed. Elizabeth Hallam (New York: Weidenfeld and Nicolson, 1989), 211.

81 Horace K. Mann, *The Lives of the Popes of the Middle Ages*, vol. 12 (London, 1925–1932), 266–267; Mary Purcell, *St. Anthony*

and His Times (Dublin, 1960), 26, quoted in Carroll, *The Glory of Christendom*, 158.

82 Moore, *Pope Innocent III*, 262.

83 Philip Wayne Powell, *Tree of Hate: Propaganda and Prejudices Affecting United States Relations with the Hispanic World* (Albuquerque, NM: University of New Mexico Press, 1971), 27.

84 Helen Rawlings, *The Spanish Inquisition* (Malden, MA: Blackwell Publishing, 2006), 1.

85 Henry Kamen, *The Spanish Inquisition: A Historical Revision* (New Haven: Yale University Press, 1997), 306.

86 William S. Maltby, *The Black Legend in England, The Development of Anti-Spanish Sentiment, 1558–1660* (Durham, NC: Duke University Press, 1971), 35, quoted in Rawlings, *The Spanish Inquisition*, 5.

87 See Gretchen Starr-LeBeau, *Seven Myths of the Spanish Inquisition* (Indianapolis: Hackett Publishing, 2023), xvii.

88 John Motley, *The Rise of the Dutch Republic* (London, 1912 [1855]), 165, quoted in Kamen, *The Spanish Inquisition*, 306–307.

89 See Starr-LeBeau, *Seven Myths of the Spanish Inquisition*, xvi.

90 Janus, *The Pope and the Council*, trans. unknown, 2nd ed. (London, Oxford, and Cambridge: Rivingtons, 1869), 235. Quoted in Starr-LeBeau, *Seven Myths of the Spanish Inquisition*, 5.

91 Montesquieu, fragment excluded from XXV.12 of *The Spirit of the Laws*. Quoted in Edward Peters, *Inquisition* (Berkeley: University of California Press, 1988), 176.

92 Starr-LeBeau, *Seven Myths of the Spanish Inquisition*, xix.

93 See Rawlings, *The Spanish Inquisition*, 145.

94 Llorente, *A Critical History of the Inquisition of Spain*, xvi-xvii (italics original). Quoted in Starr-LeBeau, *Seven Myths of the Spanish Inquisition*,106.

95 William Hickling Prescott, *History of the Reign of Ferdinand and Isabella the Catholic* (London: R. Bentley, 1854), 292. Quoted in Rawlings, *The Spanish Inquisition*, 7.

96 See Edward Peters, *Torture,* expanded ed. (Philadelphia: University of Pennsylvania Press, 1985), 41.

97 See Lu Ann Homza, ed. and trans., *The Spanish Inquisition, 1478-1614: An Anthology of Sources* (Indianapolis: Hackett Publishing Company, 2006), xiii.

98 See Rawlings, *The Spanish Inquisition*, 174.

99 See Starr-LeBeau, *Seven Myths of the Spanish Inquisition*, 32-33.

100 Ibid., 28-29.

101 Ibid., 31.

102 William Thomas Walsh, *Characters of the Inquisition* (Rockford, IL: Tan Books and Publishers, Inc., 1987 [1940]), 149.

103 See Kamen, *The Spanish Inquisition: A Historical Revision*, 280.

104 See Rawlings, *The Spanish Inquisition*, 14-15.

105 Ibid., 102.

106 See Jean-Pierre Dedieu, "'Christianization' in New Castile: Catechism, Communion, Mass, and Confirmation in the Toledo Archbishopric, 1540–1650," in *Culture and Control in Counter-Reformation Spain*, ed. A.J. Cruz and M.E. Perry (Minneapolis: University of Minnesota Press, 1991), 15, quoted in Rawlings, *The Spanish Inquisition*, 115–116.

107 See Rawlings, *The Spanish Inquisition*, 25.

108 See Starr-LeBeau, *Seven Myths of the Spanish Inquisition*, 17.

109 Ibid., 26.

110 See Starr-LeBeau, *Seven Myths of the Spanish Inquisition*, 77.

111 Ibid., 76.

112 See Walsh, *Characters of the Inquisition*, 131.

113 Ibid., 133.

114 Ibid., 168.

115 Quoted in Walsh, *Characters of the Inquisition*, 180.

116 See Starr-LeBeau, *Seven Myths of the Spanish Inquisition*, 70.

117 See Kamen, *The Spanish Inquisition: A Historical Revision*, 184; Walsh, *Characters of the Inquisition*, 163; Rawlings, *The Spanish Inquisition*, 33; and Starr-LeBeau, *Seven Myths of the Spanish Inquisition*, 117.

118 See Kamen, *The Spanish Inquisition: A Historical Revision*, 62.

119 Ibid., 195.

120 See Starr-LeBeau, *Seven Myths of the Spanish Inquisition*, 98.

121 See Rawlings, *The Spanish Inquisition*, 35.

122 See Starr-LeBeau, *Seven Myths of the Spanish Inquisition*, 121.

123 See Homza, *The Spanish Inquisition, 1478–1614: An Anthology of Sources*, xxvii.

124 See Starr-LeBeau, *Seven Myths of the Spanish Inquisition*, 124.

125 Ibid.

126 See Homza, *The Spanish Inquisition, 1478-1614*, xxvii.

127 See Rodney Stark, *Bearing False Witness*, 118.

128 See Kamen, *The Spanish Inquisition: A Historical Revision*, 60.

129 Jaime Contreras and Gustave Henningsen, "Forty-Four Thousand Cases of the Spanish Inquisition (1540–1700): Analysis of a Historical Data Bank," in *The Inquisition in Early Modern Europe: Studies on Sources and Methods*, ed. Gustave Henningsen and John Tedeschi, 100–129 (DeKalb: Northern Illinois University Press, 1986), cited in Stark, *Bearing False Witness*, 122.

130 William J. Callahan, *Church, Politics and Society in Spain, 1750–1874* (Cambridge, MA: Harvard University Press, 1984, 33, quoted in Rawlings, *The Spanish Inquisition*, 136.

131 Starr-LeBeau, *Seven Myths of the Spanish Inquisition*, 107.

132 V.A.C. Gatrell, *The Hanging Tree: Execution and the English People, 1770–1868* (Oxford: Oxford University Press, 1994), 7, cited in Stark, *Bearing False Witness*, 122.

133 Windschuttle, *The Killing of History*, 165.

134 See Starr-LeBeau, *Seven Myths of the Spanish Inquisition*, 134.

135 Rawlings, *The Spanish Inquisition*, 2.

136 Leo XIII, *Saepenumero considerantes.*

137 Martin Luther, *An Appeal to the Christian Nobility of the German Nation: Three Treatises* (Philadelphia: Fortress Press, 1970), 23.

138 John Calvin, *Institutes of the Christian Religion*, i.13.29.

139 Heiko A. Oberman, trans. Eileen Walliser-Schwarzbart, *Luther: Man between God and the Devil* (New Haven CT: Yale University Press, 1989), 79.

140 See Hilaire Belloc, *The Great Heresies* (Rockford, IL: TAN Books, 1991 [1938]), 99–110.

141 Ibid., 110.

142 There were ten Renaissance popes stretching the pontificates of Nicholas V (r. 1447–1455) to Leo X (1513–1521).

143 John Vidmar, O.P., The *Catholic Church through the Ages: A History* (New York: Paulist Press, 2005), 183.

144 Jared Rubin, "Printing and Protestants: An Empirical Test of the Role of Printing in the Reformation," *Review of Economics and Statistics* 96, no. 2 (May 2014), 272.

145 Ibid.

146 Ibid.

147 G.K. Chesterton, *The Resurrection of Rome, CW* 21:349–350, quoted in G.K. Chesterton, *Lepanto*, ed. Dale Ahlquist (San Francisco: Ignatius Press, 2004), 85.

148 Peter J. Leithart, *Defending Constantine: The Twilight of an Empire and the Dawn of Christendom* (Downers Grove, IL: IVP Academic, 2010), 9.

149 See Mary Beard, *SPQR: A History of Ancient Rome* (New York: Liverlight Publishing, 2015), 530.

150 See Adrian Goldsworthy, *How Rome Fell: Death of a Superpower* (New Haven, CT: Yale University Press, 2009), 158, and David Potter, *Constantine the Emperor* (Oxford: Oxford University Press, 2013), 70.

151 David Potter, *Constantine the Emperor* (Oxford: Oxford University Press, 2013), 92.

152 See ibid., 92.

153 Leithart, *Defending Constantine*, 9–10. The Lutheran Gottfied Arnold (1666–1714) posited the belief that Constantine marked the division between the pure early Church and the post-Constantinian "Roman" Church.

154 Leithart, *Defending Constantine*, 176.

155 See Leithart, *Defending Constantine*, 253.

156 Ibid., 253–254, 310–311.

157 This was the phrase originally rendered on Roman coins. See Charles Matson Odahl, *Constantine and the Christian Empire* (London: Routledge, 2004), 318–319, cited in Leithart, *Defending Constantine*, 70. Other accounts indicate the phrase was *in hoc signo vinces* (in this sign, conquer).

158 Andreas Alfoldi, "The Helmet of Constantine with the Christian Monogram," *Journal of Roman Studies*, 22, no. 1 (1932), cited in Leithart, *Defending Constantine*, 69.

159 Potter, *Constantine the Emperor,* 3.

160 Alan Watson, *The Law of the Ancient Romans* (Dallas: Southern Methodist University, 1970), 11–12, cited in Leithart, *Defending Constantine*, 205.

161 More than half of his appointments to these positions were given to Christians. See Stark, *Bearing False Witness*, 57.

162 See Leithart, *Defending Constantine*, 216–217.

163 Ibid., 223–224.

164 Potter, *Constantine the Emperor,* 169.

165 Ibid., 269.

166 Ibid., 196.

167 Quoted in Philip Hughes, *A History of the Church*, vol. 2, *The Church and the World the Church Created* (London: Sheed and Ward, 1993 [1979]), 4.

168 See Potter, *Constantine the Emperor*, 149.

169 Quoted in Michael Grant, *Constantine the Great: The Man and His Times* (New York: Charles Scribner's Sons, 1993), 171–172.

170 Leithart, *Defending Constantine*, 83.

171 Ibid., 148.

172 Potter, *Constantine the Emperor*, 234.

173 See Stark, *Bearing False Witness*, 53.

174 Leithart, *Defending Constantine*, 232.

175 Linda Porter, *The First Queen of England: The Myth of "Bloody Mary"* (New York: St. Martin's Press, 2007), 418.

176 Anna Whitelock, *Mary Tudor: England's First Queen* (New York: Penguin Books, 2009), xvii.

177 Quoted in Whitelock, *Mary Tudor*, 336.

178 Ibid.

179 Ibid.

180 Ibid.

181 Miranda Twiss, *The Most Evil Men and Women in History* (London: Michael O'Mara, 2002), 85–87, cited in Whitelock, *Mary Tudor*, 336.

182 Porter, *The First Queen of England*, 10.

183 Ibid., 13–14.

184 Whitelock, *Mary Tudor*, 187–188.

185 See Porter, *The First Queen of England*, 132.

186 Ibid., 51.

187 Whitelock, *Mary Tudor*, 51.

188 Ibid., 53.

189 See Porter, *The First Queen of England*, 107.

190 Ibid., 122.

191 Quoted in Whitelock, *Mary Tudor*, 141.

192 Ibid., 164.

193 Ibid., 188.

194 Quoted in Porter, *The First Queen of England*, 178–179.

195 Traditionally, it was believed the boy king died from tuberculosis, but it is generally agreed now that the king died from a lung infection. See Porter, *The First Queen of England*, 187.

196 Porter, *The First Queen of England*, 218.

197 Ibid., 267.

198 See Porter, *The First Queen of England*, 230.

199 See Cesare V. Malfatti, ed., *The Accession, Coronation and Marriage of Mary Tudor* (Barcelona: C.V. Malfatti, 1956), 91, quoted in Porter, *The First Queen of England*, 230.

200 Porter, *The First Queen of England*, 270–271.

201 Ibid., 324.

202 Whitelock, *Mary Tudor*, 233.

203 See Eamon Duffy, *Fires of Faith: Catholic England under Mary Tudor* (New Haven and London: Yale University Press, 2009), 3–4.

204 Ibid., 117.

205 D.A. Bellenger and S. Fletcher, *Princes of the Church: A History of the English Cardinals* (Stroud: Suton, 2001), 81. Quoted in Diarmaid MacCulloch, *The Reformation: A History* (New York: Penguin Books, 2003), 282.

206 See Duffy, *Fires of Faith*, 23.

207 Quoted in Warren H. Carroll, *The Cleaving of Christendom: A History of Christendom*, vol. 4 (Front Royal, VA: Christendom Press, 2000), 249.

208 Porter, *The First Queen of England*, 357.

209 See Susan Doran and Thomas S. Freeman, eds., *Mary Tudor: Old and New Perspectives* (New York: Palgrave Macmillan, 2011), 78.

210 Ibid., 21, 31.

211 Ibid., 8, 35.

212 Ibid., 81.

213 Porter, *The First Queen of England*, 362.

214 Doran and Freeman, *Mary Tudor: Old and New Perspectives*, 90.

215 Quoted in Porter, *The First Queen of England*, 351.

216 See Duffy, *Fires of Faith*, 114.

217 Ibid., 128–130.

218 Ibid., 142.

219 See Porter, *The First Queen of England*, 401–402.

220 Ibid., 401.

221 Ibid., 406.

222 Ibid., 418.

223 Whitelock, *Mary Tudor*, 338.

224 Quoted in Allan Metcalf, *The Life of Guy: Guy Fawkes, the Gunpowder Plot, and the Unlikely History of an Indispensable Word* (New York: Oxford University Press, 2019), v.

225 Hilaire Belloc, *Characters of the Reformation: Historical Portraits of 23 Men and Women and Their Place in the Great Religious Revolution of the 16th Century* (Rockford, IL: TAN Books, 1992 [1936]), 102.

226 See Doran and Freeman, *The Myth of Elizabeth*, 16.

227 Ibid.

228 Carroll, *The Cleaving of Christendom*, 258.

229 Philip Hughes, *A Popular History of the Reformation* (New York: Image Books, 1960), 322.

230 See Alice Hogge, *God's Secret Agents: Queen Elizabeth's Forbidden Priests and the Hatching of the Gunpowder Plot* (New York: HarperCollins, 2005), 86.

231 Ibid., 17.

232 Carroll, *The Cleaving of Christendom*, 382.

233 See MacCulloch, *The Reformation: A History*, 392.

234 See Hogge, *God's Secret Agents*, 73.

235 See Nick Holland, *The Real Guy Fawkes* (South Yorkshire, UK: Pen and Sword Books, 2017), 78.

236 See Hogge, *God's Secret Agents*, 303.

237 Ibid., 304.

238 Ibid., 320.

239 Ibid., 321.

240 Ibid., 322.

241 See Holland, *The Real Guy Fawkes*, 35.

242 Quoted in Hogge, *God's Secret Agents*, 210.

243 Ibid., and Quoted in Holland, *The Real Guy Fawkes*, 38.

244 Quoted in Holland, *The Real Guy Fawkes*, 40.

245 See Holland, *The Real Guy Fawkes*, 41.

246 Father Francis Edward (ed.) *The Narrative of Oswald Tesimond Alias Greenway* (The Folio Society), 29. Quoted in Holland, *The Real Guy Fawkes*, 75-76.

247 Quoted in Hogge, *God's Secret Agents*, 328.

248 Ibid., 331.

249 See Holland, *The Real Guy Fawkes*, 124.

250 Quoted in Hogge, *God's Secret Agents*, 345.

251 Quoted in Holland, *The Real Guy Fawkes*, 173.

252 Ibid., 177.

253 Quoted in Metcalf, *The Life of Guy*, 68-69.

254 See Holland, *The Real Guy Fawkes*, 177.

255 Ibid., 192.

256 Holland, *The Real Guy Fawkes*, 203.

257 Quoted in Hogge, *God's Secret Agents*, 379.

258 Ibid., 380.

259 John Paul Davis, *Pity for the Guy* (Peter Owen, 2009), 236-237. Cited in Holland, *The Real Guy Fawkes*, 206.

260 This prohibition, along with the system of male primogeniture, was finally lifted in the Succession to the Crown Act in 2013, which came into force in 2015.

261 Quoted in Metcalf, *The Life of Guy*, 82.

262 Christopher Dawson, *The Formation of Christendom* (San Francisco: Ignatius Press, 2008 [1965]), 36.

263 Shannon and Blum, *The Past as Pilgrimage*, 27.

264 See Windschuttle, *The Killing of History*, 7-8.

265 Ibid., 16.

266 Ibid., 240–244.

267 John T. Noonan Jr., "Development in Moral Doctrine," *Theological Studies* 54 (December 1993): 675, quoted in Joel S. Panzer, *The Popes and Slavery* (New York: Alba House, 1996), 2.

268 See Roger Crowley, *Empires of the Sea: The Siege of Malta, the Battle of Lepanto, and the Contest for the Center of the World (New York: Random House, 2009), 73–74.*

269 Robert Royal, *Columbus and the Crisis of the West* (Manchester, NH: Sophia Institute Press, 2020), 23.

270 See Powell, *Tree of Hate*, 35.

271 Ibid., 16.

272 Ibid., 18.

273 Quoted in Royal, *Columbus and the Crisis of the West*, 41.

274 Dan Jones, *Crusaders: The Epic History of the Wars for the Holy Lands* (London: Viking, 2019), 364–365.

275 See Rodney Stark, *Bearing False Witness*, 1; Samuel Eliot Morison, *Admiral of the Ocean Sea: A Life of Christopher Columbus*, vol. 1 (Boston: Little, Brown, 1942), 87, 131–132, cited in Carol Delaney, *Columbus and the Quest for Jerusalem* (New York: Free Press, 2011), 60, 63.

276 Quoted in Delaney, *Columbus and the Quest for Jerusalem*, vii.

277 Near the end of his life, Columbus compiled a book, *Libro de las profecías* (*Book of Prophecies*), about the connection between the liberation of Jerusalem and the Second Coming.

278 Quoted in Henri Daniel-Rops, *The Catholic Reformation*, vol. 2, trans. John Warrington (New York: Image Books, 1964 [1955]), 27.

279 See Delaney, *Columbus and the Quest for Jerusalem*, 97.

280 Columbus, *Diario*, 281, quoted in Delaney, *Columbus and the Quest for Jerusalem*, 107.

281 Royal, *Columbus and the Crisis of the West*, 66.

282 Ibid., 76.

283 Ibid., 57.

284 Royal, *Columbus and the Crisis of the West*, 59; Restall, *Seven Myths of the Spanish Conquest*, 9.

285 See Restall, *Seven Myths of the Spanish Conquest*, 35–38.

286 Ibid., 33.

287 Ibid., 43.

288 Ibid., 12.

289 Ibid., 65.

290 Ibid., 129.

291 For example, Nicole Canún, "5 Most Brutal Conquistadors of the New World," Spanish Academy, March 21, 2022, https://

www.spanish.academy/blog/5-most-brutal-conquistadors-of-the-new-world/.

292 Bernal Díaz, *Chronicles*, as translated by Maurice Keatinge (New York, 1927), II, 529 and by Salvador de Madariaga in *Hernan Cortés, Conqueror of Mexico* (Chicago: Henry Regnery, 1955), 103–104, quoted in Carroll, *The Cleaving of Christendom*, 24.

293 Restall, *Seven Myths of the Spanish Conquest*, 19.

294 Ibid., 24, 49.

295 See Windschuttle, *The Killing of History*, 66.

296 Ibid., 67.

297 See Victor Davis Hanson, *Carnage and Culture: Landmark Battles in the Rise of Western Power* (New York: Anchor Books, 2001), 195.

298 See Restall, *Seven Myths of the Spanish Conquest*, 102.

299 Ibid., 141–142.

300 Ibid., 142–143.

301 Ibid., 73.

302 Ibid., 102.

303 Desmond Seward, *Marie Antoinette* (UK: Lume Books, 2022 [1981]), 2.

304 Ibid., 12.

305 Ibid., 11.

306 Ibid., 15.

307 Ibid., 16.

308 Ibid., 20.

309 Ibid., 60–61.

310 Ibid., 40. Modern-day valuation achieved by converting eighteenth-century French livres to English pounds (http://www.pierre-marteau.com/currency/converter/fra-eng.html) and then converting value of English pounds in 1775 to U.S. dollars in 2024. Eric W. Nye, "Pounds Sterling to Dollars: Historical

Conversion of Currency," accessed Tuesday, March 26, 2024, https://www.uwyo.edu/numimage/currency.htm.

311 Ibid.

312 The croissant originated in late seventeenth-century Vienna, when food was scare during the Ottoman Turks' siege of the city. Flour supplies were running low, so bakers ceased making full loaves of bread and instead made smaller pieces that they shaped in the form of a crescent to remind the inhabitants of the reason for their meager rations. These small pastries acquired the name *croissant* for their crescent shape and are usually associated with France, but their origin stems from the 1683 siege of Vienna and are rightfully considered Austrian. Legend has it that the French adopted the tasty pastry when Marie Antoinette, who was born in Vienna, brought the item with her to France. See Simon Millar, *Vienna 1683: Christian Europe Repels the Ottomans* (New York: Osprey Publishing, 2008), 63.

313 See Seward, *Marie Antoinette*, 56.

314 Ibid., 71.

315 Ibid., 125.

316 See Warren H. Carroll and Anne Carroll, *The Revolution against Christendom* (Front Royal, VA: Christendom Press, 2005), 116. Modern-day valuation achieved by converting eighteenth-century French livres to English pounds (http://www.pierre-marteau.com/currency/converter/fra-eng.html) and then converting value of English pounds in 1777 to U.S. dollars in 2024. Nye, "Pounds Sterling to Dollars."

317 Simon Schama, *Citizens: A Chronicle of the French Revolution* (New York: Alfred A. Knopf, 1989), 205.

318 Quoted in Seward, *Marie Antoinette*, 83.

319 David A. Bell, "Five Myths about the French Revolution," *Washington Post*, July 9, 2015, https://www.washingtonpost.com/opinions/5-myths-about-the-french-revolution/2015/07/09/6f27c6f0-25af-11e5-b72c-2b7d516e1e0e_story.html.

320 See Walter Cardinal Brandmüller, *Light & Shadows: Church History amid Faith, Fact and Legend*, trans. Michael J. Miller (San Francisco, CA: Ignatius Press, 2009), 190.

321 See Seward, *Marie Antoinette*, 92–93.

322 Quoted in Seward, *Marie Antoinette*, 137.

323 See Emmet Kennedy, *A Cultural History of the French Revolution* (New Haven, CT: Yale University Press, 1989), 151, cited in Stark, *Bearing False Witness*, 196.

324 See Seward, *Marie Antoinette*, 174.

325 Ibid., 203.

326 See Reynald Secher, *A French Genocide: The Vendée*, trans. George Holoch (Notre Dame, IN: University of Notre Dame Press, 2003 [1986]), 212.

327 Quoted in Seward, *Marie Antoinette*, 203.

328 Ibid., 225.

329 Ibid., 231.

330 Ibid.

331 Ibid., 234.

332 Carroll and Carroll, *The Revolution against Christendom*, 117.

333 E.E.Y. Hales, *Pio Nono: A Study in European Politics and Religion in the Nineteenth Century* (Fitzwilliam, NH: Loreto Publications, 2016 [1954]), xi.

334 See Vittorio Messori, trans. Michael J. Miller, *Kidnapped by the Vatican? The Unpublished Memoirs of Edgardo Mortara* (San Francisco: Ignatius Press, 2015 [2005]), 8–9.

335 Ibid., 8.

336 Quoted in Messori, *Kidnapped by the Vatican?*, 19.

337 David I. Kertzer, *The Pope Who Would Be King: The Exile of Pius IX and the Emergence of Modern Europe* (New York: Random House, 2019), 347.

338 Ibid., 338.

339 Quoted in Messori, *Kidnapped by the Vatican?*, 69.

340 See Hales, *Pio Nono*, 15.

341 Quoted in Duffy, *Saints and Sinners*, 293.

342 Ibid.

343 Hales, *Pio Nono*, 44.

344 See Mike Rapport, *1848: Year of Revolution* (New York: Basic Books, 2008), x.

345 Warren H. Carroll and Anne W. Carroll, *The Crisis of Christendom: A History of Christendom*, vol. 6 (Front Royal, VA: Christendom Press, 2013), 120.

346 Hales, *Pio Nono*, 80.

347 Ibid., 109.

348 See Messori, *Kidnapped by the Vatican?*, 43.

349 Ibid., 58.

350 Ibid., 104.

351 Ibid., 106.

352 Ibid., 107.

353 Ibid., 94.

354 The words are Edgardo Mortara's. See Messori, *Kidnapped by the Vatican?*, 96.

355 Messori, *Kidnapped by the Vatican?*, 91.

356 Ibid., 149.

357 Ibid., 175, emphasis in the original.

358 Hales, *Pio Nono*, 32.

359 Ibid., 260.

360 Kertzer, *The Pope Who Would Be King*, 340.

361 See Hales, *Pio Nono*, 300.

362 Ibid., 319

363 Ibid., 322.

364 John Paul II, Beatification Homily, September 3, 2000, emphasis in the original, https://www.vatican.va/content/john-paul-ii/en/homilies/2000/documents/hf_jp-ii_hom_20000903_beatification.html. Accessed on April 9, 2024.

365 Robert Cardinal Sarah with Nicholas Diat, *The Day Is Now Far Spent*, trans. Michael J. Miller (San Francisco: Ignatius Press, 2019), 11–14, 17.

366 See Victor Davis Hanson, *The Second World Wars: How the Global Conflict was Fought and Won* (New York: Basic Books, 2017), 38, 463.

367 Pope Paul VI, Address during the Last General Meeting of the Second Vatican Council, December 7, 1965, https://www.vatican.va/content/paul-vi/en/speeches/1965/documents/hf_p-vi_spe_19651207_epilogo-concilio.html.

368 *Gaudium et Spes*, 2.

369 Ibid., 9.

370 Ibid., 43.

371 Paul VI, Homily, June 29, 1972, https://www.vatican.va/content/paul-vi/it/homilies/1972/documents/hf_p-vi_hom_19720629.html.

372 Quoted in Messori, *Kidnapped by the Vatican?*, 171.

373 David G. Dalin, *The Myth of Hitler's Pope: How Pope Pius XII Rescued Jews from the Nazis* (Washington, D.C.: Regnery, 2005), 2.

374 Ibid., 63.

375 Margherita Marchione, *Did Pius Help the Jews?* (New York: Paulist Press, 2007), Kindle ed., location 600.

376 Ibid., location 692.

377 Ibid., 8.

378 See Gordon Thomas, *The Pope's Jews: The Vatican's Secret Plan to Save Jews from the Nazis* (New York: St. Martin's Press, 2012), 5.

379 Holy See: Commission for Religious Relations with the Jews, "We Remember: A Reflection on the Shoah," March 16, 1998, https://www.ewtn.com/catholicism/library/we-remember-a-reflection-on-the-shoah-2481.

380 Ronald J. Rychlak, *Hitler, the War, and the Pope* (Huntington, IN: Our Sunday Visitor, 2000), 110.

381 Hanson, *The Second World Wars*, 3, 380.

382 Quoted in Dalin, *The Myth of Hitler's Pope*, 73.

383 See Johan Ickx, *The Pope's Cabinet: Pius XII's Secret War for Saving Jews* (Manchester, NH: Sophia Institute Press, 2022), 163.

384 Quoted in Dalin, *The Myth of Hitler's Pope*, 19.

385 See Gordon Thomas, *The Pope's Jews*, 49.

386 Ickx, *The Pope's Cabinet*, 55.

387 Ibid., 56.

388 Ibid., 95.

389 Quoted in Dalin, *The Myth of Hitler's Pope*, 74.

390 "The Pope's Message," *New York Times*, December 25, 1941, quoted in Rychlak, *Hitler, the War, and the Pope*, 166.

391 Marchione, *Did Pius Help the Jews?*, locations 712, 717.

392 See Pinchas E. Lapide, *Three Popes and the Jews* (New York: Hawthorn Books, 1967), 202.

393 Ickx, *The Pope's Cabinet*, 276.

394 Ibid.

395 Of the 12,438 Roman Jews, 1,007 were arrested and sent to Auschwitz before the cessation order was received; of those 1,007, only 196 survived the war. See Thomas, *The Pope's Jews*, 230.

396 Quoted in Thomas, *The Pope's Jews*, 157.

397 Lapide, *Three Popes and the Jews*, 215.

398 Rolf Hochhuth, *The Deputy*, trans. Richard and Clara Winston (New York: Grove Press, 1964), 100, 155.

399 Quoted in Ickx, *The Pope's Cabinet*, 4.

400 See Dalin, *The Myth of Hitler's Pope*, 53.

401 Kertzer, *The Pope at War*, 480.

402 Joseph Pearce, *Benedict XVI: Defender of the Faith* (Gastonia, NC: TAN Books, 2021), 3.

403 Joseph Cardinal Ratzinger with Vittorio Messori, *The Ratzinger Report: An Exclusive Interview on the State of the Church,* trans. Salvator Attanasio and Graham Harrison (San Francisco: Ignatius Press, 1985), 9.

404 See Joseph Ratzinger, *Theological Highlights of Vatican II* (New York: Paulist Press, 1966), Kindle ed., location 937.

405 Ibid., preface.

406 Ratzinger and Messori, *The Ratzinger Report*, 13.

407 Pearce, *Benedict XVI*, 53.

408 Joseph Cardinal Ratzinger, Homily, April 18, 2005, https://www.vatican.va/gpII/documents/homily-pro-eligendo-pontifice_20050418_en.html.

409 Benedict XVI, Wednesday General Audience on St. Benedict of Norcia, April 9, 2008.

410 Benedict XVI, *Faith, Reason, and the University: Memories and Reflections*, no. 12, in James V. Schall, S.J., *The Regensburg Lecture* (South Bend, IN: St. Augustine's Press, 2007), 133.

411 Joseph Ratzinger, *The Spirit of the Liturgy* (San Francisco: Ignatius Press, 2000), 8.

412 Ibid.

413 Benedict XVI, *Declaratio*, February 11, 2013, https://www.vatican.va/content/benedict-xvi/en/speeches/2013/february/documents/hf_ben-xvi_spe_20130211_declaratio.html.

414 Benedict XVI, Meeting with Young People, Cathedral of Sulmona, July 4, 2010, http://www.vatican.va/holy_father/benedict_xvi/speeches/2010/july/documents/hf_ben-xvi_spe_20100704_giovani-sulmona_en.html.

415 John Henry Newman, *Lectures on the Present Position of Catholics in England* (London: Aeterna Press, 2015), 74.

416 Hilaire Belloc, *Survivals and New Arrivals: The Old and New Enemies of the Catholic Church* (Rockford, IL: TAN Books, 1992 [1929]), 21.